ENVIRONMENTAL RISK MODELLING IN BANKING

Environmental risk directly affects the financial stability of banks since they bear the financial consequences of the loss of liquidity of the entities to which they lend and of the financial penalties imposed resulting from the failure to comply with regulations and for actions taken that are harmful to the natural environment.

This book explores the impact of environmental risk on the banking sector and analyzes strategies to mitigate this risk with a special emphasis on the role of modelling. It argues that environmental risk modelling allows banks to estimate the patterns and consequences of environmental risk on their operations and to take measures within the context of asset and liability management to minimize the likelihood of losses. An important role here is played by the environmental risk modelling methodology as well as the software and mathematical and econometric models used. It examines banks' responses to macroprudential risk, particularly from the point of view of their adaptation strategies; the mechanisms of its spread; risk management and modelling; and sustainable business models. It introduces the basic concepts, definitions, and regulations concerning this type of risk within the context of its influence on the banking industry.

The book is primarily based on a quantitative and qualitative approach and proposes the delivery of a new methodology of environmental risk management and modelling in the banking sector. As such, it will appeal to researchers, scholars, and students of environmental economics, finance and banking, sociology, law, and political sciences.

Magdalena Zioło is Full Professor of Banking and Finance at the Faculty of Economics, Finance and Management, University of Szczecin, Poland.

Routledge International Studies in Money and Banking

Central Banks in Organizational Networks
Entangled Market Actors
Christoph F-D. Wu

Responsible Finance and Digitalization
Implications and Developments
Edited by Panu Kalmi, Tommi Auvinen and Marko Järvenpää

Digital Currencies and the New Global Financial System
Edited by Ranjan Aneja and Robert Dygas

Negative Interest Rates and Financial Stability
Lessons in Systemic Risk
Karol Rogowicz and Małgorzata Iwanicz-Drozdowska

Digital Finance and the Future of the Global Financial System
Disruption and Innovation in Financial Services
Edited by Lech Gąsiorkiewicz and Jan Monkiewicz

Sovereign Debt Sustainability
Multilateral Debt Treatment and the Credit Rating Impasse
Daniel Cash

Environmental Risk Modelling in Banking
Edited by Magdalena Ziolo

For more information about this series, please visit: www.routledge.com/Routledge-International-Studies-in-Money-and-Banking/book-series/SE0403

ENVIRONMENTAL RISK MODELLING IN BANKING

Edited by Magdalena Zioło

Routledge
Taylor & Francis Group
LONDON AND NEW YORK

Designed cover image: Getty Images/RomoloTavani

First published 2023
by Routledge
4 Park Square, Milton Park, Abingdon, Oxon OX14 4RN

and by Routledge
605 Third Avenue, New York, NY 10158

Routledge is an imprint of the Taylor & Francis Group, an informa business

British Library Cataloguing-in-Publication Data
A catalogue record for this book is available from the British Library

Library of Congress Cataloging-in-Publication Data
Names: Ziolo, Magdalena, 1976– editor.
Title: Environmental risk modelling in banking / edited by Magdalena Zioło.
Description: Abingdon, Oxon ; New York, NY : Routledge, 2023. | Series: Routledge international studies in money and banking | Includes bibliographical references and index.
Identifiers: LCCN 2022035085 (print) | LCCN 2022035086 (ebook) | ISBN 9781032315102 (hbk) | ISBN 9781032315119 (pbk) | ISBN 9781003310099 (ebk)
Subjects: LCSH: Banks and banking—Environmental aspects. | Environmental economics. | Risk management. | Sustainable development.
Classification: LCC HG1601 .E46 2023 (print) | LCC HG1601 (ebook) | DDC 332.1—dc23/eng/20220923
LC record available at https://lccn.loc.gov/2022035085
LC ebook record available at https://lccn.loc.gov/2022035086

ISBN: 978-1-032-31510-2 (hbk)
ISBN: 978-1-032-31511-9 (pbk)
ISBN: 978-1-003-31009-9 (ebk)

DOI: 10.4324/9781003310099

Typeset in Bembo
by Apex CoVantage, LLC

CONTENTS

ACKNOWLEDGEMENTS

The research results presented in the chapters 1–8 are elements of a research project financed by the National Science Center Poland (NCN) OPUS16 2018/31/B/HS4/00570; the research results presented in chapter 9 are an element of a research project financed by the National Science Center Poland (NCN) OPUS13 2017/25/B/HS4/02172.

I *would like* to *thank* the *reviewer Zbysław Dobrowolski, Dr.hab., Professor, Jagiellonian University,* for *valuable* and *constructive comments* and *suggestions*.

TABLES

FIGURES

CONTRIBUTORS

Iwona Bąk, PhD, is an Associate Professor at West Pomeranian University of Technology, Szczecin, Poland. She is an expert in the field of quantitative methods, specializing in analyses regarding the use of quantitative methods in economic research, with particular emphasis on international comparisons in the area of sustainable development, competitiveness of the national economy, and regional development, and experience in working with advanced statistical packages: STATISTICA, R program, and so on. She is author and coauthor of scientific articles published in scientific journals from the JCR list, also having practical experience in the implementation of projects carried out on behalf of public institutions.

Beata Zofia Filipiak is Professor at University of Szczecin, Poland. He is the head of the Department of Sustainable Finance and Capital Markets at the University of Szczecin as well as a member of the University Council of the University of Szczecin. Her research and teaching scope focus on finance, finance management in the public sector, and sustainability. She has extensive experience in financial institutions and financial markets. She was a scholarship holder of the Flemish government at the University of Antwerp in 1999 and has received scholarships from DAAD (2007–2008 and 2008–2009) and DPWS (2016–2018), Erasmus +. She is a member of the Financial Sciences Committee of PAS (the Polish Academy of Sciences) and an expert of the National Center for Research and Development (NCBR). She was an expert of the Polish Accreditation Commission and a board member of the Polish Association of Finance and Banking. She has been a licensed financial adviser since 1998. She was involved in 26 scientific projects regarding corporate financial strategies, financial strategies of LGUs, and sustainable development. She carries out research supported by the National Science Center, Poland, in the scope of financing sustainable development. She is the author and editor of numerous books, mostly about financial management and financing sustainable development.

Her research interests include sustainable finances, use of financial instruments ("green financial instruments") in creating sustainable development, ESG risk, financial strategies and their connection with business models, policy of public authorities toward sustainable development (instruments, decisions, effects).

Krzysztof Kluza, Dr.hab., is Associate Professor at Warsaw School of Economics (SGH), Poland. He was the Fulbright Scholar at Columbia University, New York City, and also a Scholar of the Foundation for Polish Science. His scientific interests focus on public finance, sustainable finance, local governments, corporate strategy, and change management areas. He has published over 80 peer-reviewed articles. He received the award "For merits for the development of the financial market for local government units" established by the Association of Polish Banks and the Forum of Modern Local Government. He has over 25 years of professional experience in the manufacturing and financial sector. Among others, he worked as the executive director of the State Development Bank in Poland, chief financial officer in a multinational industrial enterprise, and chief executive officer and general manager in a large high-tech industrial enterprise (over 1,500 employees).

Ewa Kulińska-Sadłocha, PhD, has a PhD in economics and finance. Her research and teaching scope focus on cost accounting, banking, and sustainability. She has over 20 years of teaching and organizational experience as a lecturer as well as extensive experience in business practice: banking, accounting, and controlling. She has received scholarships from the Osteuropa-Sonderprogramm (University of Zurich). She is author and coauthor of numerous scientific and popular scientific publications in the field of finance, controlling, sustainable development, and social market economy. She is also a member of the Polish Economic Society, Poznan Society of Friends of Sciences, and the editorial committee of the scientific journal *Bezpieczny Bank/Safe Bank*.

Maciej Oesterreich, PhD, is an Assistant Professor at the Department of Applied Mathematics in Economics at the West Pomeranian University of Technology in Szczecin and specializes in econometric modelling and forecasting as well as the application of quantitative methods in the analysis of socioeconomic phenomena. He is author and coauthor of over 40 scientific papers (articles, chapters of monographs) and a member of the Polish Statistical Society and the Polish Economic Society.

Anna Spoz, PhD, is Assistant Professor at the Department of Finance and Accountancy at the John Paul II Catholic University of Lublin, Poland. Her research and teaching scope focus on finance—particularly, corporate finance, accounting and tax, and sustainable finance. She is author and coauthor of numerous publications on finance, accounting, reporting, and management and a reviewer of international publications. She combines teaching and scholarly activities with work in the business.

Magdalena Zioło is Full Professor at the University of Szczecin, Poland. Her research and teaching scope focus on finance, banking, and sustainability. She has extensive experience in financial institutions. She has received scholarships from the Dekaban-Liddle Foundation (University of Glasgow, Scotland) and Impakt Asia Erasmus + (Ulan Bator, Mongolia). She is a member of the Polish Accreditation Commission, Financial Sciences Committee of PAS (the Polish Academy of Sciences), and Advisory Scientific Committee of the Financial Ombudsman and an expert of the National Centre for Research and Development, National Science Centre, National Agency for Academic Exchange, and Accreditation Agency of Curacao. She was a member of State Quality Council, Kosovo Accreditation Agency, and visiting professor of University of Prishtina (Kosovo). She is principal investigator in research projects funded by the National Science Center, Poland, in the field sustainable finance. She is the author and editor of numerous books, mostly about financing sustainable development.

1
INTRODUCTION

Magdalena Ziolo

Environmental risk in the banking sector is currently one of the most discussed risks because of the increasing impact of nonfinancial risk on business, society, and the economy (Global Risks Report, 2022). Environmental risk in the banking sector can be divided into direct and indirect impacts. Direct impacts are linked to physical risks, and they reflect, inter alia, physical damages in assets as a result of extraordinary weather events, such as floods, fires, and droughts (due to climate change). Indirect impacts refer to losses in operational activities that are caused by reputation risk (e.g., banks cooperate with the "dirty sector"), which has an impact on demand and can lead to a loss of customers, and default risk, which is related to the deteriorating liquidity of cooperating companies that are forced to cover climate risk–adaptation costs or that are affected by business and market risks due to climate risk and have lost customers or market shares because of restrictions to the production of certain products (e.g., European Union regulations (zero emissions by 2030), which state that, by 2030, there will only be electric cars on the streets and renewable energy, which means transformation costs and new business models for some sectors, such as the car industry). Environmental risk is incorporated into the decision-making process in financial institutions, and in financial reporting there are disclosure commitments so that every stakeholder has access to information about the "greening" process of financial institutions. This context puts pressure on the banking sector to become sustainable to be more competitive.

The role of banks as financial intermediaries means that the challenges posed by ESG factors, especially climate change for the financial system, require them to take adjustment measures. The scope of these activities includes the development and implementation of ESG risk management systems, methodologies, modelling and adjustment of the product and service offer in such a way so as to ensure the support and promotion of good practices in the field of sustainable development, and finally the implementation of a business model based on creating sustainable

DOI: 10.4324/9781003310099-1

value. Regulations also play an important role in protecting against environmental risk. Environmental risk management is carried out by including this risk in the decision-making process of financial institutions, which requires the development and implementation of an ESG risk management strategy. The development of such a strategy is preceded by an analysis during which the financial institution determines the level of expectations and integration of ESG factors in the decision-making process and the type of ESG risk to which the financial institution is exposed. Financial institutions distinguish processes by managing ESG factors and by identifying the sectors exposed to ESG risk with which they cooperate. As a result of these activities, decision-making processes are designed, and the importance of each of the factors (environmental, social, and managerial) for the institution is determined. For examples of ESG processes identified by Allianz, refer to Allianz (2019, p. 7) recommending (decision-making) processes, a list of countries exposed to ESG risk, guidelines and guides to good ESG management practices, ratings methodologies, risk modelling, climate stress tests, and scoring assessments or subjective and objective exemptions given in the policies of the institution's operation. Recommendation processes are of particular importance, as these processes involve financial decisions that are subject to ESG risk. An important element of ESG risk analysis and assessment is its measurement and modelling, most often with the use of aggregated risk measures or indices, scoring, and rating or the so-called risk metrics. One of the examples of metrics ensuring the comparability of data and their comprehensiveness is the MSCI ESG Metric. On a 0–10 scale, the MSCI ESG Metric measures the extent to which an entity is exposed to a specific ESG risk (MSCI ESG Metric, 2020). The higher the risk exposure, the greater the ESG risk. There are many models of ESG risk measurement using specialized software, and the quality and scope of data included in these models primarily depend on the institution using these models. It is also worth commenting on the ESG risk in the context of legal regulations and the impact of new technologies on the operations of financial institutions. This relationship is primarily visible in the context of the demand for electricity reported by financial institutions, which grows with the share of new technologies in the banking and financial sector (e.g., as a result of the development of direct service channels, the fintech market, and the digital currency market), the development of blockchain technology, and the collection and processing of large datasets or big data. Increased energy demand also affects the carbon footprint of financial institutions, adversely affecting the environment (resulting in greenhouse gas emissions and, consequently, an increase in climate risk). At the same time, new technologies in the banking and financial sector highlight the need for further spheres of regulation. The digital transformation and its impact on the banking and financial sector are related to, inter alia, actions and regulations recorded in documents such as Directive 2014/65/EU of the European Parliament of 15 May 2014 on markets in financial instruments; the Act on Trading in Financial Instruments; Consultation document on the EBA approach in the field of financial technologies (fintech) (Deloitte, 2021); PSD2 Directive (EU) 2015/2366 of the European Parliament and of the Council of 25

November 2015 on payment services in the internal market. There is, therefore, a direct link between the digital transformation of financial institutions and environmental risk and the increasing number of financial regulations.

The aim of the monograph is to discuss the impact of environmental risk on the banking sector and analyze strategies to mitigate this risk with a special emphasis on the role of environmental risk modelling. The impact of environmental risk on the financial sector is discussed using banks as an example. The response of banks to environmental risk is considered, particularly the banks' adaptation strategies, risk management and modelling, and sustainable business models. The monograph introduces the basic concepts, definitions, and regulations concerning environmental risk in the context of its impact on the banking sector. The category of environmental risk, the mechanisms of its spread, methods of mitigating this risk, and preventive and adaptive actions of banks as a response to environmental risk exposure are the focus of interest as well as the special role of environmental risk modelling. The mechanisms of environmental risk spread and its incorporation into the business models of financial institutions are discussed using banks as an example.

The book consists of eight chapters. Chapter 1 is the introduction. Chapter 2 discusses the impact of environmental risk on banks and indicates ways to mitigate this kind of risk. The main directions and spheres of environmental risk impact on the operational and strategic activity of banks are discussed. Environmental risk is discussed against nonfinancial risk as one of its components: component "E." This chapter focuses on the of environmental risk and the typology of these definitions, discussing the determinant of environmental risk and identifying the areas of activity of banks most exposed to this risk.

Chapter 3 presents regulations aimed at reducing and preventing environmental risk. Obligatory and optional regulations concerning environmental risk are discussed. Good practices, guidelines, recommendations, and legal provisions that support banks and other entities exposed to environmental risk in mitigating this risk are presented. In particular, the solutions adopted by the European Union are described, and international guidelines, particularly those adopted by the United Nations, are discussed. The chapter aims to address the restrictions that banking regulations have implemented toward environmental risk in the context of the integration of banking ESG to meld better with corporate ESG goals.

Chapter 4 discusses the quantitative methods used in environmental risk forecasting and its assessment. The chapter provides knowledge on the quantitative methods used in the environmental risk assessment process. In particular, attention is focused on econometric modelling, prediction models, and quantitative risk analysis tools (three point estimate, decision tree analysis, expected monetary value (EMV), Monte Carlo analysis, sensitivity analysis, fault tree analysis (FMEA), and value-at-risk). IT tools are also introduced, particularly software-supporting environmental risk analysis, databases, data engineering, and big data.

Chapter 5 discusses the role of decision support methods in environmental risk modelling. In particular, the decision-making dilemmas faced by banks in the context of environmental risk management are presented, and the possibilities offered by MCDA methods to solve decision-making problems are indicated in the context of assumptions for environmental risk modelling. Traditional and fuzzy approaches are presented.

Chapter 6 shows the possibility of using the network approach to analyze the spread of environmental risk and to track the effect of the infection of individual network units with this type of risk. In particular, the influences of the state, banks, and companies on the spread of environmental risk are shown, and the possibilities of controlling this process in the context of limiting its negative effects on network participants are discussed.

Chapter 7 discusses the impact of environmental risk on banks' business models. This chapter identifies the components of the business model on which this risk has the greatest impact and discusses the triple business model canvas in the context of its suitability to include nonfinancial factors, including environmental risk, in the analysis of business models. The archetypes of banks' business models analyzed thus far as well as the mechanism of building sustainable value in the bank's business model are presented.

Chapter 8 presents the impact of environmental risk on the financial standing of banks and the potential problems associated with this type of risk leading to default risk. Previous models of environmental impact are discussed, and, against the background of this analysis, environmental factors are considered as a new aspect of default risk.

The book is a source of knowledge on the environmental risk in the banking sector from the perspective of banks and companies and is dedicated to all those interested in information linked to this scope of interest—in particular, to the researchers and practitioners dealing with the aspects and problems of environmental risk from a financial risk perspective.

References

Allianz ESG Integration Framework. (2019). https://www.allianz.com/content/dam/onemarketing/azcom/Allianz_com/sustainability/documents/Allianz_ESG_Integration_Framework.pdf (accessed: 18.09.2022).

Deloitte. (2021). *FSOC Report on Climate-Related Financial Risks 2021*. www.2deloitte.com (accessed: 18.09.2022).

Global Risks Report. (2022). https://www.weforum.org/reports/global-risks-report-2022/ (accessed: 18.09.2022).

MSCI ESG Metric. (2020). https://www.msci.com/our-solutions/esg-investing/esg-ratings (accessed: 18.09.2022)

2

ENVIRONMENTAL RISK AS A CHALLENGE FOR THE BANKING SECTOR

Magdalena Zioło

2.1 Introduction

Risk has always been a factor that has influenced the stability and safety of the banking sector. The main banking risks include credit, interest rate, market, liquidity, country, and solvency risks (Johnson, 2008); however, according to reports on the risks (Global Risks Report, 2021; KPMG, 2021) and the increasing number of ESG regulations (176 reported for Europe in 2020, Drei et al., 2019), interest in the escalating importance of nonfinancial risk factors is increasing. Documents related to the EU Sustainable Finance Action Plan and the Central Bank (ECB, ECB2020) and guidelines and recommendations related to risk management (UNEP, 2019; Equator Principles, 2006; Wright and Rwabizambuga, 2006), inter alia, also emphasize the importance of this type of risk.

The influence of ESG factors is visible within the context of their impacts in both the economic and financial spheres. These impacts have multidimensional consequences: they determine the quality of life, safety, and functioning of societies as well as the costs incurred by market participants. The effects of climate change are particularly severe and are a cause for concern. Environmental risk directly affects the profitability of businesses, as financial institutions may decide to resign from providing services to a given sector that is defined as a "dirty business" due to the increased risk to their services, reputations, and credit. Environmental risk also affects the operational risks of financial institutions because it affects the value of receivables (e.g., loans granted to companies from the "dirty business" sector, which may potentially be at-risk loans due to the transformation costs that these companies must bear to adapt to ESG requirements). Moreover, the costs of sustainable adaptation have an impact on the financial standing of companies (Degryse et al., 2021). For banks, credit risk is increasing, as GHG-reduction policies generate costs for high-carbon sectors and companies. Price

DOI: 10.4324/9781003310099-2

volatility in carbon markets (CO_2, oil, gas, and coal) and climate-related goods leads to uncertainty in financial projections. Climate change and climate policy affect financial institutions (Fatica et al., 2019) by increasing the risks to their clients. Climatologists predict the intensification of changes in and occurrences of extreme weather events (storms and floods) (Bernstein et al., 2019; Breitenstein et al., 2021). At the same time, the cooperation of financial institutions with entities that violate environmental standards creates the risk of reputation loss. The role of banks as financial intermediaries means that the challenges posed by ESG factors, and especially climate change for the financial system, require that they make adjustments.

The main aim of this chapter is to discuss the impact of environmental risk on banks and indicate ways to mitigate this kind of risk. The chapter is organized as follows: Section 2.1 introduces the chapter; in Section 2.2 theoretical aspects and typology referring to environmental risk are presented. Section 2.3 discusses the role of central banking in the context of environmental sustainability. Section 2.4 concludes the chapter.

2.2 Environmental risk in banking

Environmental risk is one of the components of the nonfinancial risk factors that are referred to by the acronym ESG (environmental, social, and governance). The 2006 United Nations Principles for Responsible Investment (PRI) report, which consists of the Freshfield report and "Who Cares Wins," was the first to mention ESG issues. For the first time, ESG criteria had to be included in the financial evaluations of companies (Forbes, 2020). Environmental risk is also related to sustainability risk or climate-related risk. Sustainability risk is mentioned in Regulation (EU) 2019/2088 of the European Parliament and the Council of 27 November 2019 on sustainability-related disclosures in the financial services sector and is explained as: "an environmental, social or governance event or condition that, if it occurs, could cause a negative material impact on the value of the investment." Sustainability risk is divided into two categories (Table 2.1):

- Transition risk, the sources of which are legal (regulatory), technological, climate change, the aging of societies, changes in consumption patterns, exclusion, digitization, market changes that are initiated as adaptation activities to changes taking place in the environment, and so on, which have an impact on the business models of enterprises.
- Physical risk, which can be chronic and acute, and which is caused by extreme weather events due to climate change that, for example, may damage or destroy fixed assets or negatively affect the supply chains of enterprises.

The categorization of environmental risk and its relationship to financial risk is presented in Table 2.2, and the main causes and effects of environmental degradation are presented in Table 2.3.

TABLE 2.1 Definitions of physical and transition risk

Physical risk	*Transition risk*
Refers to the financial impact of a changing climate, including more frequent extreme weather events and gradual climate change as well as environmental degradation such as air, water, and soil pollution; water stress; biodiversity loss; and deforestation. Physical risk is, therefore, classified as "acute" if it results from extreme events such as droughts, floods, and storms and as "chronic" if it results from progressive shifts such as rising temperatures, sea level rise, water stress, biodiversity loss, land use change, habitat degradation, and resource scarcity.	Refers to an institution's financial loss that may result, directly or indirectly, from the process of adapting to a low-carbon and more environmentally sustainable economy. This may be due, for example, to the relatively sudden adoption of climate and environmental policies, technological advances, or changes in market sentiment and preferences.

Source: ECB (2020, November 2020), Guide on climate-related and environmental risks: Supervisory expectations relating to risk management and disclosure, p. 10.

TABLE 2.2 Linkages between environmental risk and financial risk

Environmental risk			
Physical risk		*Transition risk*	
Resource availability	Impact of physical damages	Technology	Policy
Business risk	Market risk	Credit risk	Legal risk
Financial risk			

Source: Own elaboration based on: Breitenstein, M., Nguyen, K., and Walther, T. (2021), Environmental Hazards and Risk Management in the Financial Sector: A Systematic Literature Review, *Journal of Economic Surveys* 35(2): 512–538.

TABLE 2.3 The main causes and effects of environmental degradation responsible for environmental risk

Causes	Overpopulation, deforestation, landfills, consumption behavior, waste production, lack of education, illegal dumping, agriculture pollution, littering, mining, plastic pollution, resource depletion
Effects	Acid rain, biodiversity loss, floods, landslides, soil erosion, endangerment of species, natural disasters, global warming, public health problems, loss of livelihood, famines, wars, spread of diseases, loss in tourism, economic effects
Climate-related risk	Physical—extreme weather, chronic weather patterns Transition—policy and regulation, technology, market sentiment
Environmental risk	Physical—water stress, resource scarcity, biodiversity loss, pollution, other Transition—policy and regulation, technology, market sentiment

Source: Thoreau, H. D. (2020), 36 Causes, Effects & Solutions for Environmental Degradation, ECB, https://environmental-conscience.com/causes-effects-solutions-for-environmental-degradation/ (accessed: 18.04.2022).

TABLE 2.4 Top five global risks in terms of impact

2016	*2018*	*2020*	*2022**
Climate action failure Weapon of mass destruction Water crises Involuntary migration Energy price shock	Weapon of mass destruction Extreme weather Natural disasters Climate action failure Water crises	Climate failure Weapon of mass destruction Biodiversity loss Extreme weather Water crises	Climate action failure Extreme weather Biodiversity loss Social cohesion erosion Livelihood crises Infectious diseases Human environmental damage Natural resource crises Debt crises Geoeconomic confrontation

Source: World Economic Forum Global Risks Perception Survey 2021–2022,[1] Global Risks Report 2022, 17th edition, p. 14; World Economic Forum, Global Risks Report 2020, 15th edition, p. 2.

* The most severe risks on a global scale over the next 10 years; climate change was mentioned the first time in 2011 and was at the second position in the risk ranking.

Climate-related and environmental risk has an impact on conventional banking risks, such as credit, market, and operational risks, among others. I present the links between the conventional banking risks and environmental and climate-related risk in Table 2.4.

According to Wild-River and Cunningham (1997), the leading environmental risks are as follows: site contamination, stormwater pollution, excess trade waste, and air pollution. Wildfires, floods, snowfall, temperature, and drought are the best examples of physical environment risks (USGCRP, 2017). For example, in 2020, multiple cities around the world experienced extreme temperatures that had not been seen for years, such as a record high of 42.7°C in Madrid, and a 72-year low of −19°C in Dallas, and regions such as the Arctic Circle had average summer temperatures that were 10°C and higher (Global Risks Report, 2022, p. 8).

In recent Global Risks Reports, researchers rank the environmental and climate-related risk as first in terms of impact strength (Table 2.4). In the 2021–2022 GRPS, researchers added an extra question on international risk-mitigation efforts. The respondents believed that the current state of the risk-mitigation efforts regarding "artificial intelligence," "space exploitation," "cross-border cyberattacks and misinformation," and "migration and refugees" fell short—that is, efforts had "not started" or were in "early development." Meanwhile, the respondents assessed the risk-mitigation efforts regarding "trade facilitation," "international crime," and "weapons of mass destruction" as "established" or "effective" (Global Risks Report, 2022).

According to the Deloitte Global Risk Management Survey, in 2021, the members of financial institutions worried about the following types of risks:

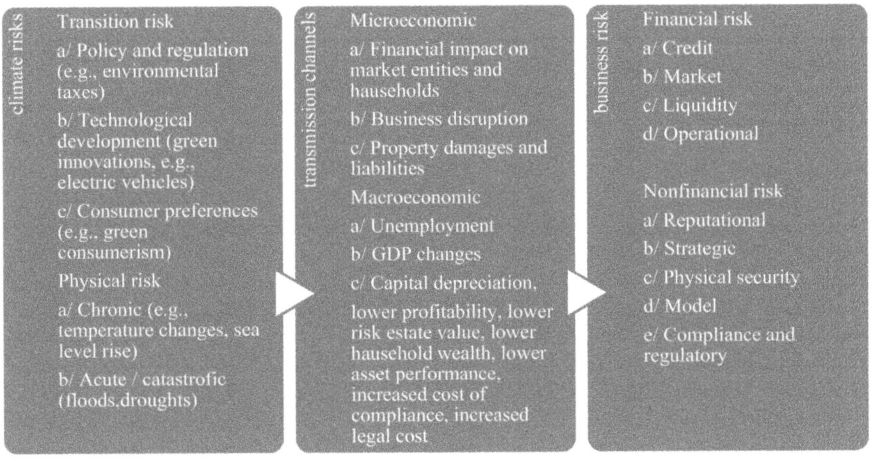

FIGURE 2.1 Relationship between climate-related, environmental risk and business risk in banking.

Source: Own elaboration based on: European Banking Authority (EBA) (2021), Report on Environmental, Social and Governance (ESG) Risks Management and Supervision, www.eba.europa.eu/eba-publishes-its-report-management-and-supervision-esg-risks-credit-institutions-and-investment (accessed: 20.04.2022); Martinez, R., Monaco, M., Goldblum, C., and Hales, D. (2021), Embedding Climate Risk into Banks' Credit Risk Management: Practical Considerations, Deloitte, https://www2.deloitte.com/xe/en/insights/industry/financial-services/climate-change-credit-risk-management.html (accessed: 20.04.2022).

ESG, cybersecurity, credit, regulatory/compliance, strategic, operational resilience, conduct and culture, and reputation (Onaran, 2021). One of the challenges that banks face is the identification of the possible effects and consequences of the impacts of environmental and climate-related risk, which is particularly difficult in the case of indirect impacts (i.e., mainly related to transition risk) (Martinez et al., 2021). In this case, banks should materialize the transition risk and define its impact on the behavior of market participants (e.g., the impact of carbon taxes or new plastic-packaging taxes on corporate decisions) or assess government policy and regulations in the field of transformation toward a green and sustainable economy and their impact on demand and the demand for sustainable financial products (e.g., loans for the thermal modernization of buildings or the purchase of electric cars). In Figure 2.1, after Deloitte (2021), examples of the materialization of climate-related and environmental risk and its translation into business risk are presented.

In the case of banking, environmental risk is often mentioned in the debate (Grippa et al., 2019) as well as dissatisfaction over the requirement that the banking sector adapt to changing environmental conditions; however, the banking sector does not consider the environmental risk to be as severe as the cybersecurity risk, although the ECB (2020) listed the climate risk among their four (as Priority 3, Table 2.5) priorities.

TABLE 2.5 SSM supervisory priorities for 2022–2024 in addressing vulnerabilities in banks

Priority 3	*Emerging risks are tackled*
Climate and environmental risk	Exposure to climate-related and environmental risk
Market risk and credit risk	Exposures to counterparty credit risk, especially toward nonbank financial institution
Operational risk	Deficiencies in IT outsourcing and cyber resilience

Source: ECB Banking Supervision (2020, pp. 9–10).

According to the Fitch rating report, rather than the environmental factor, "governance issues dominate: governance is by far the single most important ESG factor in ratings assigned by Fitch to banks" (Fitch, 2022). According to the Fitch ratings (2020), "the Environmental risk category is today the one area with a very limited credit impact on financial institutions. Emissions & Air Quality, together with energy management affect only leasing nonbank financial institution issuers while not impacting any entities in the other sub-factors" (Table 2.6).

Environmental risk has an impact on banking—particularly through its impact on the credit risk, which is because it has an impact on the financial standing of market entities (especially enterprises) that operate in environmentally sensitive sectors. These entities are obliged to comply with the regulations in the field of environmental protection and to adjust their activities to meet environmental requirements. Banks are exposed to environmental risk through its impact on the valuation (value) of assets that make up collaterals (green or brown); its impact on financial standing; and, in particular, its impact on the liquidity of entities that provide loans and the profitability of bank-financed investment projects. The transmission mechanisms and financial impacts of ESG risks on financial institutions are presented in Figure 2.2.

The impact of ESG factors applies not only to the general categories of assets, liabilities, and costs but also to the relationships between these factors and to parameters such as EBIT, EITDA, and OpEx. I present the impact of individual ESG factors on selected financial parameters in Figure 2.3. The impact of ESG factors on financial parameters is increasingly noticeable, which is due to, among other things, a number of adaptation measures that are mainly related to climate change that have forced companies to adapt their business models to the requirements of sustainability. An example may be the European Green Deal or Fit for 55 (i.e., documents that support the green transformation, which requires financing and the involvement of financial institutions, including banks). According to McKinsey (2019), ESG is related to cash flow in five crucial ways: (1) facilitation of top-line growth; (2) reduction in costs; (3) minimization of regulatory and legal interventions; (4) increase in employee productivity; and (5) optimization of investment and capital expenditures (Table 2.7).

TABLE 2.6 Impact of environmental risk on financial institutions

Factor	*Banks*	*NBFIs*	*Insurance, Non-life*	*Insurance, Life*
GHG Emissions and air quality	n.a.	Regulatory risks, emissions fines, or compliance costs related to owned equipment, which could impact asset demand, profitability, and so on.	n.a.	n.a.
Energy management	n.a.	Investments in or ownership of assets with below-average energy/ fuel efficiency, which could impact future valuation of these assets.	n.a.	n.a.
Water and wastewater management	n.a.	n.a.	n.a.	n.a.
Waste and hazardous materials management; ecological impacts	n.a.	n.a.	Underwriting/reserving exposed to asbestos/hazardous materials risks	n.a.
Exposure to environmental impacts	Impact of extreme weather events on assets and/ or operations and corresponding risk appetite and management; catastrophe risk; credit concentrations.		Underwriting/reserving exposed to environmental and natural catastrophe risks; impact of catastrophes on own operations or asset quality; credit concentrations	Impact of extreme weather events/natural catastrophes on operations or asset quality; credit concentrations

Source: ESG in Credit (2020), FitchRatings, p. 29, www.fitchratings.com/white-papers/esg-in-credit (accessed: 20.04.2022).

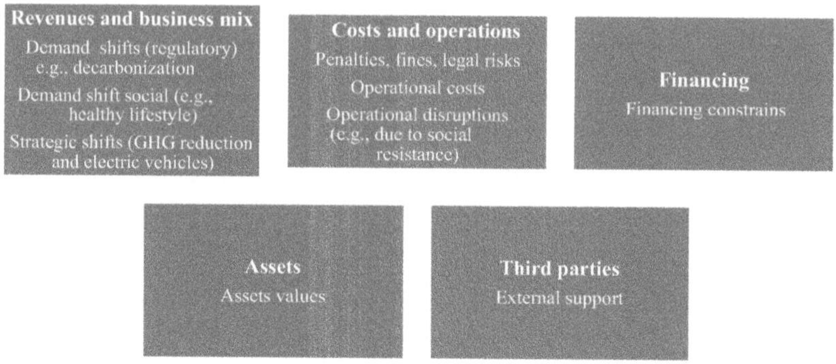

FIGURE 2.2 Transmission mechanisms of ESG risk on financial institutions.

Source: Own elaboration based on: ESG in Credit (2020), FitchRatings, p. 9, www.fitchratings.com/white-papers/esg-in-credit (accessed: 20.04.2022).

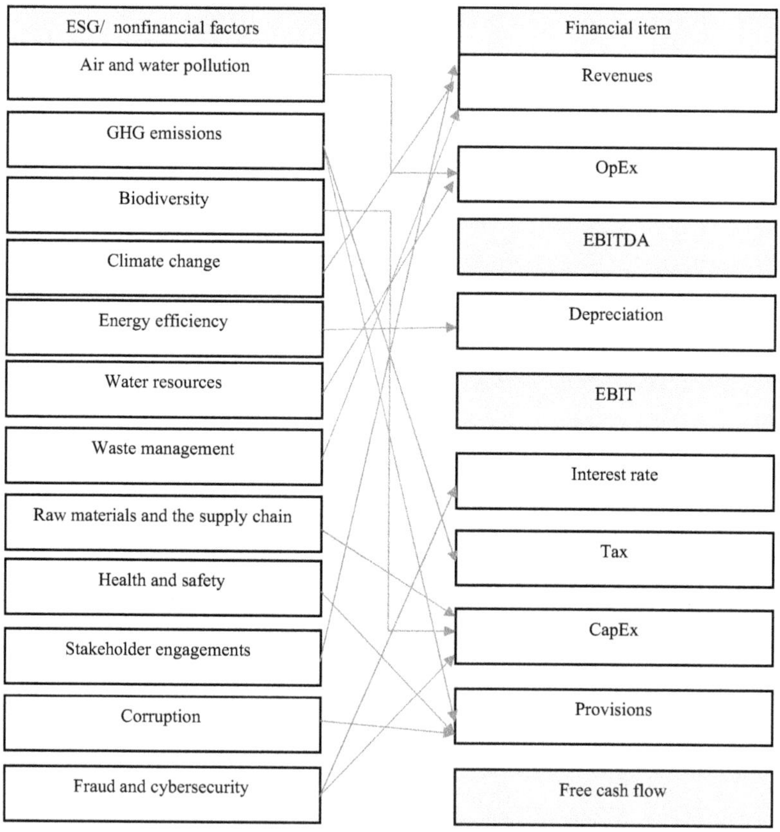

FIGURE 2.3 Impact of ESG on selected financial indicators.

Source: Own elaboration based on: B Capital Partners (2018), *Guidance Note Integrating ESG Factors into Financial Models for Infrastructure Investments*, WWF Switzerland, p. 11, http://awsassets.panda.org/downloads/wwf_guidance_note_infra_.pdf (accessed: 21.04.2022).

TABLE 2.7 Impact of ESG risk on cash flow and value creation

Links to cash flow and value creation	*Strong ESG proposition*	*Weak ESG proposition*
Top-line growth	Attract B2B and B2C customers with more sustainable products Achieve better access to resources	Lose customers (poor sustainability actions), loss of access to resources
Cost reductions	Lower energy consumption, reduce water intake	Generate unnecessary waste-related cost
Regulatory and legal interventions	Deregulation and greater strategic freedom Access to government support	Suffer restrictions, fines, penalties
Productivity uplift	Boost employee motivation, talent attraction	Lose talent, suffer "social stigma"
Investment and assets optimization	Better allocation of capital and enhance of investment returns, avoiding investment that may not pay off due sustainability reasons	Suffer stranded assets, fall behind competitors

Source: Own elaboration based on: McKinsey (2019), Five Ways That ESG Creates Value, *McKinsey Quarterly*, www.mckinsey.com/business-functions/strategy-and-corporate-finance/our-insights/five-ways-that-esg-creates-value (accessed: 24.04.2022).

According to KPMG (2021), sustainability is going to have a comprehensive impact on banks, which will affect entire value chains from both perspectives (strategic and operational). The actions recommended to banks to respond to sustainability requirements and regulations are as follows (KPMG, 2021):

- Inclusion of sustainability in the business strategy and organizational setup/governance;
- Adaptation of products and customer portfolios;
- Identification and typology of sustainable assets;
- Design and provision of sustainable financing to customers;
- Refinancing with sustainable instruments;
- Incorporation of ESG (risks) in pricing and risk management;
- Inclusion of ESG risks within the capital charge;
- Consideration to the ESG criteria in the distribution process (including MiFID);
- Reporting of ESG risks and their impacts to supervising authorities and stakeholders;
- ESG data management.

The European Banking Authority (EBA) proposes steps and recommendations in the scope of ESG disclosures in the final draft of the document titled: "Implementing Technical Standards (ITS) on Pillar 3 (P3) Disclosures on Environmental, Social and Governance (ESG)." The EBA accordingly divided the possible actions

TABLE 2.8 Quantitative disclosures

Type of risk/actions	*Template*	*Purpose*	*Transitional measures*
Transition risk	Credit quality of exposures by sectors, emissions, and residual maturity Loans collateralized by immovable property; energy efficiency of collateral Alignment metrics for the banking group Exposures in the banking book to the top 20 carbon-intensive firms in the world	Disclose assets that are most exposed to transition risk Disclose the energy efficiency of the bank's real estate portfolios Report scope 3 emissions by sector and relative to IEA's alignment metrics Report exposures to the top 20 most carbon-intensive firms	Disclosures of scope 3 emissions is required by 30 June 2024 Full disclosure required by 30 June 2022 Disclosure of alignment metrics by 30 June 2024 Full disclosure required by 30 June 2022
Physical risk	Exposures subject to physical risks	Disclose the assets most exposed to chronic and acute climate hazards	Full disclosure required by 30 June 2022

Source: Own elaboration based on: Klaassen, P., and Blijlevens, S. (2022), *EBA's Binding Standards on Pillar 3 Disclosures on ESG Risks*, https://zanders.eu/en/latest-insights/ebas-binding-standards-on-pillar-3-disclosures-on-esg-risks/ (accessed: 25.04.2022).

into two groups: qualitative and quantitative (Tables 2.8 and 2.9). Quantitative disclosures are presented in Table 2.8 and qualitative disclosures in Table 2.9.

Hamilton (1995), Hart&Ahuja (1996), and Blacconiere and Pattern (1993) draw attention to the relationship between the quality of the natural environment and financial institutions and the financial market or the widely perceived financial situations of individuals (banks and their clients). Banks are important in environmental risk management because they can eliminate financing to enterprises that do not meet environmental standards and that represent so-called dirty business. On the one hand, the refusal to finance enterprises with increased environmental risk is part of the process of bank credit risk management because the risk of financing affects the assets that are the subject of collateral, the financial liquidity, and, consequently, the borrower's solvency, which affects his/her financial credibility (Schmidheiny and Zorraquin, 1996). On the other hand, Heim and Zenklusen (2005) indicate a positive relationship between savings, bond profitability, and green banking. Gupta (2005) and Goldar (2007) predict that the market will increasingly reward entities that use pro-environmental practices through friendly consumption patterns (e.g., of energy, water, or other resources) (Goldnar, 2007). Rewarding entities that represent the "best practice" in environmental protection is usually expressed

TABLE 2.9 Qualitative disclosures

Risk	*Business strategy and processes*	*Governance*	*Risk management*
Environmental risk	Adjustment business strategy of institution and incorporation of ESG risk Objectives, limits, and targets for the assessment of environmental risk and performance assessment of these items Policies and procedures of environmental risk management	The responsibilities of the management body for ESG risk management The integration of ESG risk into the organizational arrangement Governance arrangements in the ESG scope Alignment of the remuneration policy with ESG risk–related objectives	Concept, methodology, management framework of ESG risk Implementation of tools and processes to control ESG risk Institutional activities, commitments, and exposures to mitigate ESG risk Description of limits of ESG risk Description of transmission channels of ESG risk

Source: Own elaboration based on: Klaassen, P., and Blijlevens, S. (2022), *EBA's Binding Standards on Pillar 3 Disclosures on ESG Risks*, https://zanders.eu/en/latest-insights/ebas-binding-standards-on-pillar-3-disclosures-on-esg-risks/ (accessed: 25.04.2022).

by lower costs of raising capital, which thereby increases access to financial markets and financing. Banks play a special role in the financial intermediation system. This role consists of estimating the risk and, depending on its valuation, determining the cost of capital and making decisions about accepting or rejecting the transaction. Therefore, banks have the option to negatively screen transactions, the effects of which may turn out to be socially and environmentally harmful. Through the negative selection mechanism, banks can actively influence market entities and, consequently, their attitudes and decisions, including those that are related to sustainable development. However, increasing the effectiveness of bank operations for sustainable development requires these institutions to adjust their business models so that they are based on building sustainable value. The conversion of traditional business models to sustainable ones is a complex process that banks need to prepare for. In the transformation of business models, the triple-bottom-line (TPL) approach is used, which consists of three components: people, planet, and profits (Fisk, 2010). The business model is usually described by the components that make up the business model canvas, which consists of analyses of areas such as key partners, key activities, value, relationships with customers, customers, key resources, ways of reaching, financial flows, and cost structures. The sustainable business model, unlike the traditional model, considers the components of the traditional model, with the difference being that it considers them at three levels: economic, social, and environmental.

2.3 Central banks and environmental sustainability

Environmental risk affects the stability and security of the financial system. Climate risk leads to climate migration and to changes in, or the inability to continue, certain economic activities, and it affects property valuations and price stability. Droughts and floods have an impact on the sizes of agricultural crops and their valuations, and the excessive exploitation of raw materials leads to their depletion and price increases. These are selected examples of environmental risk transmission. Environmental risk also affects the labor market by eliminating certain professions from the market and creating the need to establish new ones and especially in the renewable energy sector. A similar impact applies to enterprises, some of which are eliminated from the market because of environmental risk or must undergo transformation and are replaced with completely new business profiles (e.g., photovoltaics, biofuel, batteries, and the automotive industry). In sectors looking for specialists, analysts, engineers, or IT specialists who deal with renewable energy, enterprises will be subject to wage pressure because this market of professionals is still developing and there is a shortage of specialists; in turn, professions related to the so-called dirty businesses will disappear from the market (e.g., employment in the mining sector will be reduced). All the indicated change trends carry specific financial consequences and affect the liquidity and profitability of businesses as well as the prices of products and services, including basic ones, such as food and fuel. The fuel market will particularly be affected by the climate risk in connection with public policies to reduce GHG emissions, which are responsible for the greenhouse effect (Figure 2.4).

Due to smog and its consequences for human health, the smoke from coal is systematically prohibited; hence, the demand for this fuel will systematically decrease, and gas as a transition fuel will become more expensive because of the growing demand, which will translate into costs for enterprises, (e.g., the chemical sector

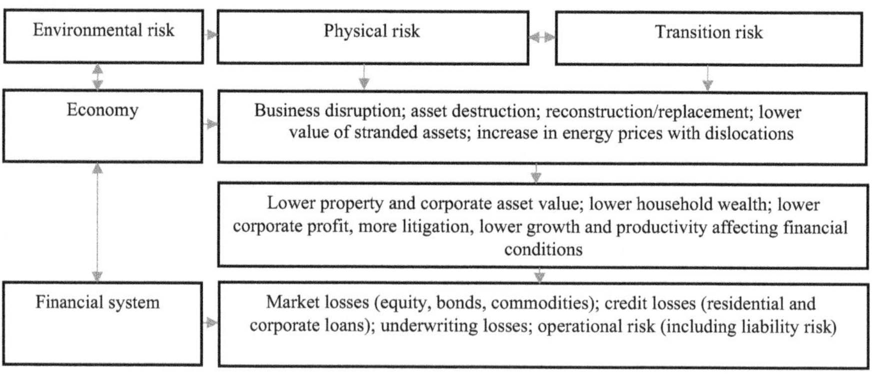

FIGURE 2.4 Climate risk, the economy, and the financial sector.

Source: Own elaboration based on: Grippa, P., Schmittmann, J., and Suntheim, F. (December 2019), Climate Change and Financial Risk, *Finance & Development* 56(4), IMF, www.imf.org/external/pubs/ft/fandd/2019/12/climate-change-central-banks-and-financial-risk-grippa.htm (accessed: 30.04.2022).

TABLE 2.10 Actions taken by central banks on climate change

Type of action	*Country example*
Assessing climate risk as a financial risk in stress tests	Brazil, Euro area, Hong Kong, Ireland, Japan, Poland, UK, Singapore
Encouraging or mandating climate-related financial disclosures	Australia, China, Euro area, Hong Kong, Japan, Singapore, Sweden, UK
Incentivizing or subsidizing green finance and/or discouraging brown investment	Brazil, China, Singapore
Setting standards and green finance/ lending (sustainability criteria) that their regulated banks will have to apply	Brazil, China, Euro area, Hong Kong, India, Japan, Kenya, Morocco, UK
Applying climate considerations to monetary policy	China
Applying green principles to own portfolio	China, France, Germany, Greece, Hong Kong, Ireland, India, Netherlands, Sweden
Measures to manage own carbon footprint beyond investments	Euro area, Ireland, Netherlands, Sweden
Where also is a debt management office issuing green bonds	China, France, Germany, Ireland, Mexico, Netherlands, Poland, UK

Source: Own elaboration based on: Jones, M., and Ranasinghe, D. (28 October 2020), Analysis: Central Banks Flexing Their Green Muscle for Climate Fight, *ESG Environment*, www.reuters.com/article/us-global-cbanks-green-analysis-idUSKBN27D1X4 (accessed: 30.04.2022).

using this type of fuel). The costs of the transformations in energy and agriculture will translate into the final prices of energy and food products and will determine the inflationary effect, until the comprehensive introduction of renewable energy sources and the assurance of a climate-neutral economy. In the case of agriculture, the costs of transformation will be related to the adoption of organic farming to eliminate the NH_3 (ammonia) that is responsible for environmental degradation and adverse effects on human health. The change in the valuation of assets and the increase in prices and wages due to climate change, as well as the wider environmental risk, determine the need to control these phenomena in terms of ensuring the stability of the financial system and considering the value of money within the context of inflation.

In this approach, central banks are responsible for the implementation of the inflation target. Central banks have a real impact on the climate risk (Table 2.10): they respond to the interest rate, and they thus determine the prices of products and services. Thus, central banks have an impact on consumption patterns and the directions of capital allocation in the economy (ECB, 2021b). The Network for Greening the Financial System (NGFS) (a group comprising 74 central banks) was launched at the Paris One Planet Summit on 12 December 2017.

Central banks are increasingly buying green bonds, which are used to fund clean energy and environmental projects, with the proceeds going to sustainable projects. The Bank of England and the Dutch Central Bank include climate

TABLE 2.11 Environmentally friendly interventions by central banks

Type of intervention	*Example*
Assessment on climate-related financial risks; macroeconomic modelling of low-carbon transition	De Nederlandsche Bank, Bank of England Only outside central banks (private sector or academia)
Support international activities on green finance	Group of 20 Green Finance Study Group, Sustainable Insurance Forum, NGFS
Disclosure of climate-related financial risks	Financial Stability Board Task Force on Climate-Related Financial Disclosures, French Energy Transition Law
Environmentally aligned prudential regulation policy	Banque of Liban, Banco Central do Brasil
Green central bank financing	Bangladesh Bank, Bank of Japan
Lending quotas	Reserve Bank of India, Bangladesh Bank
ESG factors in assets eligibility criteria	Only for own purchase, for example: DNB, Norges Bank
Green quantitative easing	Assets purchased only if they meet central bank's eligibility criteria such as European Investment Banks' bonds

Source: Own elaboration based on: *A Powerful New Force—Central Banks and Climate-Related Risks*, www.centralbanking.com/central-banks/economics/4237801/a-powerful-new-force-central-banks-and-climate-related-risks (accessed: 30.04.2022).

among their bank stress–test criteria, and the People's Bank of China accepts some green bonds as collateral. Central banks may purchase green bonds to stimulate green behavior or offer banks cheaper central bank loans on the condition that the money is lent to climate-friendly companies and projects, such as targeted long-term refinancing operations (TLTROs), which are a good example of the ECB's funding mechanism for banks (Jones and Ranasinghe, 2020). I present some other examples of environmentally friendly interventions by central banks or financial regulators in Table 2.11. In addition to the indicated pro-environmental actions taken by central banks (Table 2.11), two types of policies minimize environmental risk: climate risk–focused policies and climate finance–promoting policies. Policies that promote climate finance aim to consider externalities and the co-benefits of mitigating climate change, which might help to shift relative prices and increase investment.

The aim of using climate risk–focused tools is to correct the misconceptions about climate risks for individual financial institutions and to support reduction by changing the demand for green and high-carbon investments as well as their relative prices. Examples on the monetary policy side include the development of climate-risk assessments by central banks and the assurance that their collateral frameworks and asset portfolios adequately reflect climate risks. Some policies and instruments for climate change reduction are presented in Table 2.12. On the fiscal side, the tools needed to improve climate-risk assessment, corporate governance

TABLE 2.12 Policies and instruments for climate change reduction

Scope of policy	*Policy*	*Tools*
Financial	Redressing underpricing and lack of transparency of climate risks	Climate-related financial data and risk disclosures, green assets taxonomy, climate-related stress tests, macroprudential tools
Financial	Reducing short-term bias and improving governance framework of financial institutions	Prudential reforms, corporate governance reforms
Financial	Supporting the development of green financial institutions	Standardized taxonomy of green assets, low-carbon indices, platforms, and active issuance by authorities
Financial	Promotion of climate finance using financial regulatory tools	Green supporting/brown penalizing factors in capital requirements, minimal amount of green assets on balance sheet
Monetary	Incorporating climate risk analytics into collateral frameworks, central bank portfolio management, and QE	Developing own risk assessments, ensuring climate risks are reflected in central banks' assets portfolios
Monetary	Green QE and collateral frameworks	Better access to funding schemes for banks that invest in low-carbon projects, central bank purchases of low-carbon bonds
Monetary	Credit allocation policies	Central bank credit allocation operations, adapting monetary policy frameworks

Source: Own elaboration based on: Press Room Team (2019), *A Role for Financial and Monetary Policies in Climate Change Mitigation*, https://internationalworldofbusiness.com/a-role-for-financial-and-monetary-policies-in-climate-change-mitigation/ (accessed: 30.04.2022).

reforms, and the classification of green assets through the development of a unified taxonomy include reserve, liquidity, and capital requirements; loan-to-value ratios; credit-growth caps; climate-related-stress tests; disclosure requirements; and financial data dissemination (Press Room Team, 2019).

Conversely, financial policy instruments that actively promote climate finance revolve around "green supportive" and "brown penalizing" factors in the capital and international requirements of banks for a minimum amount of green assets on bank balance sheets (Press Room Team, 2019). The development of a strategy to mitigate climate-related risk based on proper risk management and to incorporate the risk of nonfinancial factors into the decision-making process is preceded by an analysis, during which the financial institution determines the expectations and integration of environmental factors into the decision-making process as well as the type of environmental risk; this evaluation is carried out in five steps: (1) determination of the expectations regarding the degree of integration of environmental factors; (2) identification of the risk exposure; (3) determination of the level of environmental risk that is acceptable to the bank; (4) risk response and the development of environmental policy frameworks (especially climate policy); and (5) implementation of management strategies and policies.

2.4 Conclusion

In recent years, reports and analyses (Global Risks, Deloitte, KPMG) have highlighted the importance of the increase in ESG or nonfinancial risk, and especially within the context of the impact of new technologies on the operations of financial institutions (Davis, 2022), which is primarily visible in the demand for electricity, which increases with the share of new technologies in the banking and financial sector (e.g., the development of direct service channels, the fintech market, and the digital currency market; the development of blockchain technology; the collection and processing of large datasets or big data). The increased energy demand also affects the carbon footprints of financial institutions and adversely affects the environment (resulting in greenhouse gas emissions and, consequently, increases climate risk) (Bolton and Kacperczyk, 2021). Climate change also generates a higher risk primarily because of the lack of comparable and consistent data on corporate emission levels and risk assessment tools in this regard. At the same time, the cooperation between financial institutions and entities that violate environmental standards creates the risk of reputation loss. The role of banks as financial intermediaries means that the challenges posed by ESG factors, and especially climate change for the financial system, require them to make adjustments. The scope of these activities includes the development and implementation of ESG risk–management systems, methodologies, and modelling, and the adjustment of the products and services offered in such a way as to ensure the support and promotion of good practices in the field of sustainable development.

Note

1 The Global Risks Perception Survey (GRPS), carried out since 2006, was refreshed this year to gather new and broader insights from nearly 1,000 global experts and leaders who responded.

References

Bernstein, A., Gustafson, M. T., and Lewis, R. (2019). Disaster on the Horizon: The Price Effect of Sea Level Rise. *Journal of Financial Economics* 134(2): 253–272.

Blacconiere, W., and Dennis, P. (1993). Environmental Disclosures, Regulatory Costs, and Changes in Firm Value. *Journal of Accounting and Economics*. December.

Bolton, P., and Kacperczyk, M. (2021). *Global Pricing of Carbon-Transition Risk*. 24 March. *VoxEU.org*

Breitenstein, M., Nguyen, K., and Walther, T. (2021). Environmental Hazards and Risk Management in the Financial Sector: A Systematic Literature Review. *Journal of Economic Surveys* 35(2): 512–538.

Davis, K. (2022). How Technology is Shaping the Future of Operational Risk Management. *Risk & Compliance Journal*. https://deloitte.wsj.com/articles/how-technology-is-shaping-the-future-of-operational-risk-management-1528171333 (accessed: 24.04.2022).

Degryse, H., Goncharenko, R., Theunisz, C., and Vadasz, T. (2021). *When Green Meets Green*. CEPR Discussion Paper, DP16536, Working Paper Research No 392. Brussels: National Bank of Belgium.

Deloitte. (2021). *FSOC Report on Climate-Related Financial Risks 2021*. www.2deloitte.com (accessed: 18.09.2022).

Drei, A., Le Guenedal, T., Lepetit, F., Mortier, V., Roncalli, T., and Sekine, T. (2019). ESG Investing in Recent Years: New Insights from Old Challenges. *SSRN Electronic Journal*. http://dx.doi.org/10.2139/ssrn.3683469

ECB. (2020). *Guide on Climate-Related and Environmental Risks, Supervisory Expectations Relating to Risk Management and Disclosure*. Frankfurt: ECB, p. 10. November.

ECB. (2021a). *The State of Climate and Environmental Risk Management in the Banking Sector: Report on the Supervisory Review of Banks' Approaches to Manage Climate and Environmental Risks*. Frankfurt: ECB. November 2021.

ECB. (2021b). www.bankingsupervision.europa.eu/banking/priorities/html/ssm.supervisory_priorities2022~0f890c6b70.en.html (accessed: 24.04.2022).

Equator Principles. (2006). *Final Version*. www.banktrack.org (accessed:18.09.2022).

Fatica, S., Panzica, R., and Rancan, M. (2019). *The Pricing of Green Bonds: Are Financial Institutions Special?* JRC Working Papers in Economics and Journal of Financial Stability, volume 54, 2021 accessed https://www.sciencedirect.com/science/article/pii/S1572308921000334.

Fisk, P. (2010). *People, Planet, Profit: How to Embrace Sustainability for Innovation and Business Growth*. London; Philadelphia: Kogan Page.

Fitch. (2020). *ESG in Credit 2020*. White Paper. New York. www.your.fitch.group (accessed: 18.09.2022).

Fitch. (2022). www.fitchratings.com/research/banks/where-esg-matters-for-bank-ratings-14-03-2022 (accessed: 20.04.2022).

Forbes. (2020). www.forbes.com/sites/betsyatkins/2020/06/08/demystifying-esgits-history-current-status/?sh=3e2064ed2cdd (accessed: 24.04.2022).

Global Risks Report. (2021). 16th Edition. Geneva, Switzerland: World Economic Forum. https://www.weforum.org/reports/the-global-risks-report-2021/ (accessed: 18.09.2022).

Global Risks Report. (2022). https://www.weforum.org/reports/global-risks-report-2022/ (accessed:18.09.2022).

Goldar, B. N. (2007). Impact of Corporate Environmental Performance or Profitability and Market Value: A Case Study of Indian Firms. *Institute of Economic Growth*, 5(1): 13–25.

Grippa, P., Schmittmann, J., and Suntheim. (2019). Climate Change and Financial Risk, Finance & Development. *IMF*, 56, No F. 4. December. www.imf.org/external/pubs/ft/fandd/2019/12/climate-change-central-banks-and-financial-risk-grippa.htm (accessed: 30.04.2022).

Gupta, S. (2003). *Do Stock Market Penalise Environment-Unfriendly Behaviour? Evidence from India*. Ecological Economics, vol 52, 2005, p.81–95 https://www.sciencedirect.com/science/article/abs/pii/S0921800904002897 acceessed 18.09.2022.

Hamilton, J. T. (1995). Pollution as News: Media and Stock Markets Reactions to the Toxics Release Inventory Data. *Journal of Environmental Economics and Management* 28.

Hart, S., Ahuja, G. (1996). Does It Pay to Be Green? An Empirical Examination of the Relationship Between Emissions Reduction and Firm Performance. *Business Strategy and the Environment* vol. 5(1), pages 30–37.

Heim, G., and Zenklusen, O. (2005). *Sustainable Finance: Strategy Options for Development Financing Institutions*. Zurich: EcoFact.

Johnson, H. (2008). *Risks in Banking, Chapter 3*. Washington Bankers Association. www.wabankers.com (accessed: 18.09.2022).

Jones, M., and Ranasinghe, D. (2020). *Reuters News, Central Banks Flexing Their Green Muscle for Climate Fight*. https://www.zawya.com/en/business/central-banks-flexing-their-green-muscle-for-climate-fight-r33fgqvo (accessed:18.09.2022).

Klaassen, P., and Blijlevens, S. (2022). *EBA's Binding Standards on Pillar 3 Disclosures on ESG Risks*. https://zanders.eu/en/latest-insights/ebas-binding-standards-on-pillar-3-disclosures-on-esg-risks/ (accessed: 25.04.2022).

KPMG. (2021). *ESG in Banks Effective Strategies to Use Opportunities and Mitigate Risks*. https://home.kpmg/xx/en/home/insights/2021/05/esg-risks-in-banks.html (accessed: 24.04.2022).

Martinez, R., Monaco, M., Goldblum, C., and Hales, D. (2021). *Embedding Climate Risk into Banks' Credit Risk Management. Practical Considerations*. Deloitte. https://www2.deloitte.com/xe/en/insights/industry/financial-services/climate-change-credit-risk-management.html

McKinsey, Quartely. (2022). *Five Ways that ESG Creates Value*, 2019. www.mckinsey.com/business-functions/strategy-and-corporate-finance/our-insights/five-ways-that-esg-creates-value (accessed: 24.04.2022).

Onaran, Y. (2021). ESG Risks Top the List of Near-Term Concerns for Bank Executives. *Bloomberg News*. February 02. www.bloomberg.com/professional/blog/esg-risks-top-the-list-of-near-term-concerns-for-bank-executives/ (accessed: 30.04.2022).

Press Room Team. (2019). *A Role for Financial and Monetary Policies in Climate Change Mitigation*. https://internationalworldofbusiness.com/a-role-for-financial-and-monetary-policies-in-climate-change-mitigation/ (accessed: 30.04.2022).

Schmidheiny, S., and Zorraquin, Federico J. L. (1996). *Financing Change: The Financial Community, Eco-Efficiency and Sustainable Development*. Cambridge, MA: MIT Press.

UNEP. (2019). *Addressing Climate-Related Security Risks*. https://www.unep.org/resources/toolkits-manuals-and-guides/addressing-climate-related-security-risks (accessed:18.09.2022)

USGCRP. (2017). *Climate Science Special Report: Fourth National Climate Assessment*, Vol. I [D. J. Wuebbles, D. W. Fahey, K. A. Hibbard, D. J. Dokken, B. C. Stewart, and T. K. Maycock (eds.)]. Washington, DC, USA: U.S. Global Change Research Program, 470 pp.

Wild-River, S., and Cunningham, R. (1997). *Brisbane City Council Environmental Benchmarking Study: A Report into Environmental and Related Outcomes from Brisbane City Council's* 1995–97 Implementation of the Environmental Protection Act 1994.

Wright, C., and Rwabizambuga, A. (2006). Institutional pressures, corporate reputation, and voluntary codes of conduct: An examination of the equator principles. *Business and Society Review* 111(1): 89–117.

3

ENVIRONMENTAL REGULATIONS AS A FRAMEWORK FOR ENVIRONMENTAL RISK MANAGEMENT IN BANKS

Ewa Kulińska-Sadłocha

3.1 Introduction

Since the dawn of time, humankind has been confronted with environmental risks and has sought to mitigate them. With economic development and the pillaging of natural resources, and finally with the degradation of the natural environment perceived by science and even by ordinary people, the issue of environmental risk management has objectively become increasingly important. For many years, financial institutions, including banks, have been intensifying their interest in environmental issues, related social aspects, and finally corporate governance adequate to the level of civilization development and applicable legal regulations. Over the years, the manner and scope of banks' involvement in pro-environmental activities has varied greatly. The differences resulted, inter alia, from voluntary commitments under sustainable financial initiatives and the scope and area of operations, including differences between national legal regulations on environmental protection and social issues as well as the approach of bank managers and owners to ESG issues. There is a growing importance of initiatives undertaken by various international institutions to standardize and coordinate banks' sustainable activities at regional as well as global levels. Many countries have already introduced regulations for ESG risk management with guidelines for the implementation and disclosure of results. This is determined by the need to engage banks in creating conditions and mobilizing resources for financing the transformation of the economy toward sustainable models.

The aim of the considerations in the chapter is to provide a synthetic overview of environmental regulations and banks' voluntary initiatives on ESG issues as well as EU regulations on environmental risk in the context of standardization of the environmental risk management process in a bank.

DOI: 10.4324/9781003310099-3

3.2 Legal aspects of environmental protection and their implications for banking activities

Environmental regulations are of fundamental importance not only for the state of the environment now but to counteract climate change in the future and thus contribute to protecting the health and life of society[1]. They cover the natural environment, the human-made environment, and elements of humankind's social environment relating to its living conditions (e.g., fauna, flora, water, soil, air, climate, landscape, natural resources, and cultural heritage). Environmental issues are regulated through acts of international law, community acts, and national acts (Table 3.1). The purpose of regulation is to protect the soil, air, water, and plant and animal world from the negative impact of human activity; to eliminate losses and damages caused by this activity; and to provide humankind with an environment that ensures a healthy and dignified life. Legal regulations take into account four basic principles of environmental policy: the principle of the perpetrator, the principle of prevention, the principle of cooperation, and the precautionary principle (Nowak, 2001; Rogall, 2010; Rosicki, 2010). The last principle is associated with new, increasingly complex, and difficult to fully verify threats to the environment or human health and life[2].

TABLE 3.1 Typology of environmental legislation

Regulatory level	*Description*
Acts of international law (treaties, conventions, agreements, protocols)	The acts are guided by the principles of good neighborliness and non-abuse of law and include obligations regarding, among other things, the following: – Cooperation between states in the field of the environment; – Information and consultation with states with which resources are shared on activities affecting their natural state; – Information and warning of events harmful to the environment; – Peaceful use of resources. They ensure the consistency of actions taken by individual states in the field of environmental protection. They specifically address environmental problems that are not limited by administrative boundaries, such as global warming, ozone layer depletion, and acid rain—for example, the MARPOL Convention, International Convention for the Prevention of Pollution from Ships (1973); Vienna Convention for the Protection of the Ozone Layer (1985); Espoo Convention, Convention on Environmental Impact Assessment in a Transboundary Context (1991); Convention on Biological Diversity (1992); and the United Nations Framework Convention on Climate Change, UNFCCC (1992).

Regulatory level	*Description*
Community acts of the European Union (treaty, directive, regulation, decisions, and other acts not binding on member states—for example, recommendations, opinions, resolutions, action programs)	EU environmental policy is based on Articles 11 and 191–193 of the Treaty on the Functioning of the European Union (TFEU). Combating climate change is an explicit objective of EU environmental policy, and sustainable development is an overarching objective of the EU. The EU's task is to ensure that the provisions of ratified international environmental agreements are respected in its member states. The EU is a party to 33 international environmental agreements and 14 conventions protecting specific areas (e.g., the Baltic Sea, Rhine, Danube Region, the Mediterranean, and the Alps) The EU's environmental policy and legislation relates to, among other things, combating climate change; protecting natural habitats; protecting soil and forests; keeping air and water clean; ensuring proper disposal of waste; preventing and remedying environmental damage; and protecting the environment through criminal law, recycling, and recovering parts and materials.
National acts Example: Poland (constitution, laws, regulations, orders, recommendations, codes of good practice, general and specialized programs)	The Republic of Poland shall ensure environmental protection, guided by the principle of sustainable development, while the public authorities are obliged to protect the environment and pursue policies that ensure environmental safety for present and future generations (Article 74 of the Constitution of the Republic of Poland). Before joining the EU, Poland ratified more than 20 international agreements in the field of the environment. According to the Polish Constitution, a ratified international agreement, once promulgated, constitutes part of the national legal order and is directly applicable, unless its application depends on the issuance of a law. The main national legal acts regulating environmental issues include the following: – Ustawa z dnia 27 kwietnia 2001 r. Prawo ochrony środowiska (Act of 27 April 2001, Environmental Protection Law)—the act sets out the principles of environmental protection and the conditions for using its resources, taking into account the requirements of sustainable development. – Ustawa z dnia 16 kwietnia 2004 roku o ochronie przyrody (Act of 16 April 2004, on nature protection)—the act sets specifies the objectives, principles, and forms of protection of living and inanimate nature and landscape.

(*Continued*)

TABLE 3.1 (Continued)

Regulatory level	*Description*
	– Ustawa z dnia 3 października 2008 r. o udostępnianiu informacji o środowisku i jego ochronie, udziale społeczeństwa w ochronie środowiska oraz o ocenach oddziaływania na środowisko (Act of 3 October 2008, on providing information about the environment and its protection, public participation in environmental protection, and environmental impact assessments).
	Implementing acts to the aforementioned acts containing, among others, permissible standards, rules, procedures.

Source: Own elaboration based on: Rosicki, R. (2010), Ogólna charakterystyka międzynarodowego prawa Ochrony środowiska. *Środkowoeuropejskie Studia Polityczne* (3): 79–104; MSZ, Internetowa Baza Traktatowa, https://traktaty.msz.gov.pl/umowa-3 (accessed: 18.05.2022); MKŚ, Konwencje międzynarodowe, www.gov.pl/web/klimat/konwencje-miedzynarodowe (accessed: 18.05.2022) and https://eur-lex.europa.eu/summary/chapter/20.html (accessed: 18.05.2022).

Regulations set the standards for environmental impact, oblige entities to comply with them, and provide sanctions for noncompliance (Table 3.2). An entrepreneur who causes environmental damage is responsible for it and must take the necessary preventive and remedial measures, bearing all related costs according to the "polluter pays" principle.[3]

All economic entities, including banks, as active participants of social life, are obliged to comply with the applicable laws and standards and thus minimize the negative environmental impact of their activities. Both the direct impact of environmental risk factors on banks and the negative impact of the bank on the environment are much smaller than in the case of other industries included in the activities posing a threat to the environment, such as the energy industry; mineral industry; chemical industry; production and processing of metals; waste management; large-scale production of pulp, paper, and cardboard; textile dyeing; tanneries or large-scale production of meat, dairy products, and food (Directive 2004/35/CE). The bank's financial risks (credit, market, liquidity), operational, compliance, reputation are most significantly affected by the environmental risks of its customers and counterparties as well as those associated with its capital investments.

The development of environmental legislation and regulations is in itself a factor in the rising awareness in this area while at the same time prompting appropriate action under the threat of sanctions for their disregard or noncompliance. This also applies to regulations that are relevant to the identification and assessment of key environmental risks associated with a bank's financial transactions. In particular, it is about being able to verify whether and to what extent stakeholders, especially customers, counterparties, and investors, comply with the applicable environmental regulations. Thus, financial intermediaries and especially banks implicitly become supervisors and controllers of their stakeholders' behavior. The IFC (International

TABLE 3.2 Liability for environmental damage under Polish environmental law

Type of liability	*Anticipated consequences*
Civil liability Criminal liability	– Request to restore the lawful state and to take preventive measures, in particular by setting up installations or devices protecting against the threat or violation. – To require the cessation of any activity causing danger or infringement of environmental norms. – A claim for cessation of advertising or any other form of promotion of a good or service if such advertising or other form of promotion is contrary to the promotion of a proper pattern of consumption. – Claim for reimbursement of expenses.
Criminal liability	– Fines. – Restrictions of liberty. – Imprisonment.
Administrative liability	– Imposing an obligation to limit the negative impact on the environment and its threats and to restore the environment to a proper state. – Suspension of activities to the extent necessary to prevent deterioration of the environment. – Suspension of the operation of installations. – A ban on manufacturing, importing from abroad, or marketing products that do not meet environmental protection requirements. – Order to remove the identified deficiencies within a specified period of time. – Suspension of start-up or use of a plant or installation, including a warehouse or any part thereof, if the identified deficiencies may cause a risk of an industrial accident. – An administrative fine for exceeding or breaching the conditions of using the environment.

Source: Own elaboration based on: Act of 27 April 2001, Environmental Protection Law (Ustawa z dnia 27 kwietnia 2001 r. Prawo ochrony środowiska).

Finance Corporation) recommends that the audit of financial institutions' compliance with environmental regulations should cover such areas as (IFC, 2022):

- Air emissions and air quality (emissions standards);
- Energy use and conservation;
- Wastewater and water quality (effluent discharge criteria);
- Water use and conservation;
- Hazardous materials use, handling, and disposal;
- Waste generation and disposal;
- Land contamination;
- Biodiversity and natural resources;
- Labor and working conditions;

- Occupational health and safety;
- Community health, safety, and security;
- Land acquisition and resettlement;
- Indigenous peoples;
- Cultural heritage.

When analyzing the legitimacy of the implementation of pro-environmental solutions, one must first of all take into account the different levels of development, national wealth, and/or awareness of societies, which are strong determinants of, on the one hand, accounting for global or international standards and, on the other hand, their implementation, and especially their application in domestic practice. The point is that even the best regulations are not able to force pro-environmental or pro-social actions, when a country, entity, family, or person does not have the financial resources to introduce appropriate solutions (e.g., technological ones). Taking into account the global character of the consequences of environmental destruction, one of the basic problems is financing the outlays (investment, modernization, operational, etc.). The lack of own funds in an appropriate amount for the needed actions puts the issue of external capital support and its effectiveness on the agenda. In a discriminative approach, one can assume the refusal of bank financing for projects with a harmful environmental impact. On the other hand, in the purposive approach, there is the issue of support of market conditions of assistance and sources of its financing (credit, leasing, long-term lease, handling of bond issue, etc.)

3.3 Evolution of pro-environmental initiatives and banking environmental standards

Pro-environmental initiatives and activities of banks have a history dating back to the 1970s, when attention was drawn to the growing social and environmental problems and the associated threats to civilization (IUCN-UNEP-WWF, 1980). The negative impact of economic activities on the environment was associated with pressures on the allocation of financial resources by banks in lending processes and a significant reduction in some countries in the financing of sectors considered to be hazardous to the environment (Jeucken, 2004). Individual banks began to integrate environmental considerations into their credit and investment risk management processes or monitor resource consumption to reduce operating costs (Weber, 2012). They also created positions dedicated to ecology, including environmental impact assessments of projects if they undertook the financing of them. The activation of the role of banks in supporting sustainable development and reducing environmental risks occurred after 1987 following the publication of the so-called Brundland Report (Table 3.3).

From the analysis of the sustainability initiatives and projects undertaken, it appears that there has been a succession of organized efforts to integrate environmental and social issues into the financial sector (Jeucken and Bouma, 1999; Pisano

TABLE 3.3 Selected initiatives, standards, and guidelines to activate banks on ESG

Year	*Description*
1992	**United Nations Environment Programme Finance Initiative (UNEP FI)**—partnership between the UNEP and the global financial sector in transforming finance (including banks) into sustainable finance and financing sustainable socioeconomic development.
	Rio de Janeiro Earth Summit 1992—154 countries signed an international environmental treaty to reduce the negative impact of human activities on the environment (Agenda 21). More than 100 banks from around the world signed the UNEP FI Declaration. *Banking and Environment*—a commitment to conduct business in harmony with the environment, providing opportunities for sustainable development.
1994	**United Nations Framework Convention on Climate Change, UNFCCC**—initiative aimed to stabilize the concentration of greenhouse gases in the atmosphere at a level that would prevent dangerous climate change by humans.
1996	**ISO 14001**—a voluntary international standard for environmental management systems in organizations.
1997	**Kyoto Protocol**—an international treaty, closely linked to the UNFCCC, that committed signatories to binding standards for reducing harmful emissions to combat global warming.
1999	**Dow Jones Sustainability World Index**—the first global stock exchange index of sustainable companies (the first global sustainability benchmarks).
2000	**UN Millennium Development Goals**—goals to eradicate poverty, hunger, and inequality; improve health and education; and ensure environmental sustainability and global partnership for development to be implemented worldwide between 2000 and 2015.
	UN Global Compact—an initiative to adopt and apply 10 principles in the areas of human rights, labor standards, and the environment and anti-corruption in all areas of business.
	Global Reporting Initiative (GRI)—publication of the most recognized and widely used international guidelines for reporting on sustainability issues.
2002	**Earth Summit "Rio+10" held in Johannesburg**—defining three pillars on which social and economic development should be supported: economy, society, and environment, emphasizing the need to reduce poverty and increase the commitment of states, business, politics, science, and society to implement the principles of sustainable development.
2003	**Equator Principles**—risk management guidelines, widely recognized by financial institutions, resulting in limiting funding to only those projects that will not violate the principles of social and environmental responsibility.
	The Collevecchio Declaration on Financial Institutions and Sustainability—signed by 103 nongovernmental organizations from around the world (mostly social and environmental) committing banks to act in the interest of society (support environmental protection and promote universal human rights and social justice).
2006	**UN Principles for Responsible Investment** (PRI)—a set of possible actions to integrate environmental, social, and corporate governance issues into investment practices across all asset classes.

(*Continued*)

TABLE 3.3 (Continued)

Year	*Description*
2007	**UNEP FI Declaration on Climate Change by the Financial Services Sector**—a commitment by banks to initiate action to prevent adverse climate change and to take this issue into account in current and strategic decision-making.
2009	**Global Alliance for Banking on Values** (GABV)—a collaborative network of credit institutions that aims to change the banking system to be more transparent and support sustainable socioeconomic development with a focus on the potential of individuals to build stronger communities.
2011	**UN Guiding Principles on Business and Human Rights**—global standards for preventing and responding to risks of human rights abuse in business operations.
2012	**UN Conference on Sustainable Development in Rio de Janeiro (Rio+20)**—declaration committing countries to continue efforts to build a global green economy. The need to eliminate poverty and misery and to mobilize additional financial resources, especially for developing countries, in order to reduce disparities in development in relation to rich countries was pointed out. A decision was made to develop a set of Sustainable Development Goals (SDGs) and guidelines for green economy policies were adopted.
	Sustainable Banking Network (SBN)—a collaborative network for the sustainable development of banking sectors, bringing together central banks, supervisors, and banking associations from emerging markets.
2014	**RE 100% Climate Group**—a global initiative bringing together entities that have committed to source 100% of the electricity they consume from renewable sources (by 2050 at the latest). The goal of the initiative is to accelerate the transition to a zero-carbon power grid globally.
2015	**2030 Agenda for Sustainable Development**—a universal call to action to end poverty, protect the planet, and improve the lives and prospects of everyone, everywhere. The 17 goals were adopted by all UN member states in 2015 as part of the 2030 Agenda for Sustainable Development, which set out a 15-year plan to achieve the goals.
	Paris Agreement on Climate Change—limit the rise in global temperatures in the current century to 2°C and make efforts to further limit the rise in temperatures to 1.5°C above preindustrial levels.
	EU High-Level Expert Group on Sustainable Finance (HLEG)—a group of experts advising the European Commission on financing sustainable investments as well as on protecting the stability of the financial system from environmental risks.
2016	**G20 Green Finance Study Group** (GFSG)—a research group focused on opportunities to scale up financing for sustainable development goals (mainly environmental). Reactivated as a working group (Sustainable Finance Working SFWG) in 2021 to coordinate international efforts to mobilize sustainable finance and further align the financial system with the Paris Agreement and the SDGs.

Year	*Description*
2017	**TCFD Recommendations on Climate-Related Financial Disclosure**—a set of voluntary, consistent disclosure recommendations designed to help companies provide investors, lenders, and insurers with credible information about financial risks related to climate impacts.
	Network for Greening the Financial System (NGFS)—a network of central banks working together to green the financial system.
	UNEP FI Positive Impact Initiative (PII)—principles for ensuring the positive impact of business and financial institutions on the pillars of sustainable development (economic, environmental, and social), also identifying and mitigating potential negative impacts.
2018	**EU Technical Expert Group** (TEG)—an expert group to assist the European Commission in developing a single classification system for sustainable economic activities, an EU green bond standard, a methodology for low-carbon indicators, and climate-related disclosure indicators.
2019	**UNEP FI Principles for Responsible Banking** (PRB)—a global standard for responsibility in banking.
	Poseidon Principles—a framework for integrating climate considerations into lending decisions to promote decarbonization of international shipping.
	BCBS Task Force on Climate-Related Financial Risks (TFCR)—focused on the assessment, measurement, and mitigation of climate-related financial risks (includes regulatory, supervisory, and disclosure-related elements).
2020	**EU European Green Bond Standard** (EUGBS)—a voluntary standard to help scale up and raise the environmental ambitions of the green bond market.
2021	**UNEP FI Net-Zero Banking Alliance**—a commitment by banks to align their loan and investment portfolios to net-zero emissions by 2050.
	UNEP FI Blue Finance—a commitment by banks to conduct lending and investment activities in line with Sustainable Development Goal SDG14: Life under Water.

Source: Own elaboration based on: Information contained on the UNEP FI websites (www.unepfi.org) and information on the websites of individual initiatives; Borys, G. (2000), *Ryzyko ekologiczne w działalności banku*, Warszawa: Biblioteka Menedżera i Bankowca; Kulińska-Sadłocha, E. (2009), Banki a zmiany klimatyczne, W: Brzozowska, K., and Flejterski, S. (red.), *Finanse 2009—Teoria i praktyka. Bankowość*, Szczecin: Wydawnictwo Uniwersytetu Szczecińskiego; Zioło, M. (2017), Instytucjonalny i prawny wymiar zrównoważonego rozwoju oraz finansów zrównoważonych, W: Raczkowski, K., and Zioło, M. (red.), *Strefa finansowa wobec wyzwań zrównoważonego rozwoju*, Warszawa: CeDeWu.

et al., 2012). For image reasons, plus others, banks were eager to sign declarations in this regard, and circular institutions developed bank-dedicated guidelines or policies corresponding to general environmental or sustainability standards (Jeucken, 2004).

The biggest changes in the approach of banks to environmental issues occurred after the global financial crisis of 2007–2009. Banks operating in a responsible manner, taking into account environmental and social risks, sometimes referred to as ethical, socially responsible or sustainable banks, did not suffer substantial losses, and interest in their services during the crisis increased significantly (Benedikter,

TABLE 3.4 Principles for Responsible Banking

PRINCIPLE 1: ALIGNMENT
We will align our business strategy to be consistent with and contribute to individuals' needs and society's goals, as expressed in the Sustainable Development Goals, the Paris Climate Agreement, and relevant national and regional frameworks.
PRINCIPLE 2: IMPACT AND TARGET SETTING
We will continuously increase our positive impacts while reducing the negative impacts on, and managing the risks to, people and the environment resulting from our activities, products, and services. To this end, we will set and publish targets where we can have the most significant impacts.
PRINCIPLE 3: CLIENTS AND CUSTOMERS
We will work responsibly with our clients and our customers to encourage sustainable practices and enable economic activities that create shared prosperity for current and future generations.
PRINCIPLE 4: STAKEHOLDERS
We will proactively and responsibly consult, engage, and partner with relevant stakeholders to achieve society's goals.
PRINCIPLE 5: GOVERNANCE AND CULTURE
We will implement our commitment to these principles through effective governance and a culture of responsible banking.
PRINCIPLE 6: TRANSPARENCY AND ACCOUNTABILITY
We will periodically review our individual and collective implementation of these principles and be transparent about and accountable for our positive and negative impacts and our contribution to society's goals.

Source: UNEP FI (2021): *Principles for Responsible Banking, Guidance Document*, www.unepfi.org/publications/principles-for-responsible-banking-guidance-document/ (accessed: 20.06.2022).

2011). After 2015, international financial organizations, states, central banks, and regulators began to take action to build a sustainable financial system (including a sustainable banking sector) and prepare instruments for financial institutions to actively support sustainable socioeconomic development. Cooperation networks in this area have been established (e.g., TCFD, GFSG, HLEG, NGFS, TEG, IPSF). The Basel Committee on Banking Supervision (BCBS) has started to include risks arising from ESG issues in its standards in the regulatory framework and national supervisors in the regulation of banking activities.

In September 2019, the Principles for Responsible Banking (PRBs) developed under the UNEP FI by 28 banks (including six banks with more than USD 1 trillion in assets) were adopted. The PRBs provide a global standard for responsibility in banking and indicate ways to align banks' business practices and strategies with society's goals, as expressed in the Sustainable Development Goals and the Paris Climate Agreement (Table 3.4).

Among other banking initiatives, the PRB is distinguished by its comprehensive yet framework nature, which provides opportunities for adaptation to the specific conditions of a bank's organization and operations. The principles apply to all areas of a bank's operations and levels of management (strategic, portfolio, transactional)

TABLE 3.5 Signatories of the Principles for Responsible Banking

Region	*Number of signatories banks*	*Countries most represented in the PRB (Number of banks)*
Africa and the Middle East	25	Nigeria (6) Egypt (6) South Africa (5)
North America	12	USA (7) Canada (5)
Latin America and the Caribbean	44	Ecuador (8) Mexico (8) Panama (5)
Asia Pacific	54	China (19) South Korea (10) Japan (9)
Europe	162	Norway (21) Sweden (13) United Kingdom (13)
Total	297	

Source: Own elaboration based on: UNEP FI, www.unepfi.org/banking/bankingprinciples/prbsignatories/#_ftn1 (accessed: 30.06.2022).

and focus on setting goals in areas where banks have or can have the greatest impact on society's objectives. They also require signatory banks to publicly report on the effect of negative and positive impacts and the bank's contribution to the social objectives as well as information on their progress in the implementation with involvement of key stakeholders. The consequence of failing to comply with the obligations is the removal of the bank from the list of signatories to the PRB[4].

At the end of June 2022, more than 290 banks were signatories to the PRB, and 113 were also signatories to the Net-Zero Banking Alliance, a commitment to align their lending and investment portfolios to net-zero emissions by 2050 (Table 3.5). In addition, nine joined the Blue Finance initiative (commitments to align lending and investment activities with the Sustainable Development Goal SDG14: Life under Water).

The involvement of the largest banks in the creation of PRBs and the great interest of the financial community as well as the growing pressure of the global community regarding responsible behavior stimulate the expansion of the group of interested credit institutions. However, it is worth remembering past experiences when popular declarations often did not translate into real actions. Nevertheless, all the initiatives, recommendations, and principles together form an excellent set of possible actions for mainstreaming environmental considerations into decision-making at the bank level and in individual areas of its business. By pointing out the most important environmental, social, and governance risks; the problems; and the ways to address them, they are excellent guidelines for developing a coherent strategy for a bank's sustainable development or environmental risk management.

3.4 The environmental regulatory framework for banking activities in the EU

In December 2019, the European Commission announced the *European Green Deal* (EGD), which aims to make the continent climate neutral by 2050, while in July 2021, the *Strategy for Financing the Transition to a Sustainable Economy* based on *Action Plan: Financing Sustainable Growth* was announced, also taking into account the *European Green Deal Investment Plan* assuming the mobilization of resources to finance sustainable investments in Europe over the next 10 years (Communication from the Commission to the European Parliament, 2018; 2019; 2021a and 2021b). The strategy is aimed at achieving the following objectives:

- Preferring capital flows for sustainable investment to achieve inclusive and sustainable growth,
- Managing financial risks in the context of depletion of natural resources, environmental degradation, and social issues (increasing the resilience of the financial system), and
- Promoting transparency and a long-term approach in financial and economic activities.

An element of the plan is the so-called fair transition mechanism, which takes into account the differences in the economies of individual member states (e.g., degree of dependence on the extraction and use of fossil fuels). The strategy opens up new investment opportunities, which at the same time may generate risks for economic participants—for example, in the form of materialization of new risk transmission channels related to environmental factors. In the process of transforming the economy, the European Commission emphasized the special role of financial sector entities, including banks. This involves, on the one hand, imposing new obligations on banks and creating a regulatory framework and, on the other hand, the need for banks to adapt their activities to new regulatory requirements and changes in the environment.

In 21 April 2021, the European Commission adopted a Sustainable Finance Package, which aims to improve the flow of finance for the implementation of the European Green Deal. One of the proposed measures within the package is the Corporate Sustainability Reporting Directive (CSRD). It extends the scope and reporting requirements of the Non-Financial Reporting Directive (a regulatory framework that has been mandating sizeable public interest entities to report on their sustainability performance since 2018) to additional companies, including all large listed companies. The draft provides for a common reporting framework from 2024 and requires that all information be published in companies' management reports and disclosed in digital format. Regulations supporting the transition to a sustainable economy are as follows:

- Directive 2014/95/EU of the European Parliament and of the Council of 22 October 2014 amending Directive 2013/34/EU (2021) in regard to disclosure of nonfinancial and diversity information by certain large undertakings and groups (NFRD)—the directive requires public interest entities (including banks) with more than 500 employees to report on their policies on environmental, social, labor, respect for human rights, and anti-corruption and bribery issues; business model; key risks and due diligence procedures; there is a "comply or explain why you are not complying" principle; the directive has been supplemented through the Guidelines on Reporting Non-Financial Information in 2017 and in 2019 with a supplement on climate-related disclosures.

- Regulation (EU) 2019/2088 of the European Parliament and of the Council of 27 November 2019 on sustainability-related disclosures in the financial services sector (SDFR)—the regulation lays down harmonized transparency rules on how financial market participants and financial advisers take into account environmental, social, and good governance factors in investment decisions and financial advice. It lays down rules on the consideration of sustainability objectives, generally and at the level of individual products, and aims to increase market transparency and prevent greenwashing.
- Regulation (EU) 2020/852 of the European Parliament and of the Council of 18 June 2020 on the establishment of a framework to facilitate sustainable investment, and amending Regulation (EU) 2019/2088—the regulation establishes a general framework for assessing whether an economic activity qualifies as environmentally sustainable and to what extent. It includes a system of uniform classification of sustainability measures to support investors in making investment decisions and imposes a number of reporting obligations on financial market participants (for which the SFDR and entities subject to the NFRD apply) regarding the extent to which their activities comply with the taxonomy and, in the case of financial market participants that offer green or sustainable financial products and services, an obligation to disclose the extent to which their activities contribute to the objectives of the regulation.
- Commission Delegated Regulation (EU) 2021/2139 of 4 June 2021 supplementing Regulation (EU) 2020/852 of the European Parliament and of the Council by establishing the technical screening criteria for determining the conditions under which an economic activity qualifies as contributing substantially to climate change mitigation or climate change adaptation and for determining whether that economic activity causes no significant harm to any of the other environmental objectives—the regulations further clarify the criteria for environmentally sustainable economic activity and contain technical eligibility criteria for determining the conditions under which an economic activity qualifies as substantially contributing to climate change mitigation or climate change adaptation and for determining whether that economic activity causes no significant harm to any of the other environmental objectives.

Financial sector regulation aims to ensure that individual and institutional investors can invest according to their sustainability preferences and that environmental and social considerations are integrated into risk management. Regulators such as the Basel Committee on Banking Supervision (BCBS), the European Central Bank (ECB), and the European Supervisory Authorities (ESAs) (such as EBA, ESMA, EIOPA) are increasingly working to ensure that banks are aware of ESG risks and formulate business strategies to manage and mitigate those risks and respond to new challenges such as climate, environmental, IT, and cyber risks[5]. This has resulted in numerous guidelines and reports containing technical disclosure standards and requirements (Table 3.6).

TABLE 3.6 Regulations for incorporating environmental risk into bank risk management systems

Regulations/guidelines	*Description*
BCBS. Principles for the effective management and supervision of climate-related financial risks (June 2022)	The document includes 18 principles covering corporate governance, internal controls, risk assessment, management, and reporting. Principles 1 through 12 provide banks with guidance on effective management of climate-related financial risks, while principles 13 through 18 provide guidance for prudential supervisors. The principles seek to achieve a balance in improving practices related to the management of climate-related financial risks and providing a common baseline for internationally active banks and supervisors while maintaining sufficient flexibility given the degree of heterogeneity and evolving practices in this area. The document builds on the review of the current Basel Framework, particularly the Basel Core principles for effective banking supervision (BCPs) and the supervisory review process (SRP), and draws from existing supervisory initiatives undertaken by individual prudential authorities and other international bodies.
EBA. Final draft implementing technical standards on prudential disclosures on ESG risks in accordance with Article 449a CRR (January 2022a)	The final report presents the EBA final draft ITS on Pillar 3 disclosures on environmental, social, and governance (ESG) ESG risks, which puts forward tables, templates, and associated instructions that specify the requirement in Article 449a of the Capital Requirements Regulation (CRR) to disclose prudential information on ESG risks, including transition and physical risk, addressed to large institutions with securities traded on a regulated market of any member state. The ITS includes the following: – Tables for qualitative disclosures on environmental, social, and governance risks; – Templates with quantitative disclosures on climate change transition risk; – A template with quantitative disclosures on climate change physical risk;

Regulations/guidelines	*Description*
	– Templates with quantitative information and key performance indicators (KPIs) on climate change mitigating measures, including the Green Asset Ratio (GAR) on taxonomy-aligned activities according to Regulation (EU) 2020/852 on the establishment of a framework to facilitate sustainable investment (Taxonomy Regulation), extended information on taxonomy alignment of exposures in the banking book, and other mitigating actions.
ESAs. Final report on draft regulatory technical standards with regard to the content and presentation of disclosures pursuant to Article 8(4), 9(6), and 11(5) of Regulation (EU) 2019/2088 (October 2021)	The report contains additional regulatory technical standards on sustainability-related disclosures in the financial services industry. It regulates the disclosure of information on websites, prior to entering into an agreement with a client, and information made available to a client periodically after entering into an agreement. Disclosures include, but are not limited to, the following: – Indicators of adverse sustainability impacts; – The principle of not inflicting serious harm on sustainable investments; – Products that promote environmental and social issues and invest resources in sustainable investments as well as environmentally sustainable products.
EBA. ESMA. Guidelines on the assessment of the suitability of members of the management body and key function holders (EBA/GL/2021/06 / ESMA35–36–2319) (July 2021)	The guidance clarifies the suitability requirements for members of the management body and the concepts of, among other things, the following: – That a member of the management body acts honestly and ethically and exercises independent judgment; – That the management body has adequate knowledge, skills, and experience; – Devoting adequate human and financial resources to the induction and training of members of the management body; – That diversity is accounted for in the selection of members of the management body. The guidelines pay particular attention to the need to consider, as part of the assessment of the suitability of board members (both individually and collectively), competencies in managing ESG risks and AML/CFT risks.
EBA. Report on Environmental, Social, and Governance (ESG) risks' management and supervision (June 2021)	The report includes the following: – A uniform definition of ESG risks; – Criteria, parameters, and indicators by which supervisors, banks, and investment firms can assess the impact of short-, medium- and long-term ESG risks;

(*Continued*)

TABLE 3.6 (Continued)

Regulations/guidelines	*Description*
	– Principles for integrating ESG risks in a proportionate manner into internal governance and risk management frameworks and strategies; – Proposals on how to incorporate ESG risks into the supervisory review process.
ECB. Guide on climate-related and environmental risks' supervisory expectations relating to risk management and disclosure (November 2020)	The guide outlines the ECB's understanding of the safe and prudent management of climate and environmental risks within the current prudential framework. It includes the following: – Characteristics of climate-related and environmental risks; – Supervisory expectations relating to business models and strategy; – Supervisory expectations relating to governance and risk appetite; – Supervisory expectations relating to risk management; – Supervisory expectations relating to disclosures.
EBA. Guidelines on loan origination and monitoring *(May 2020)*	The guidelines apply to all credit institutions in Europe and affect existing credit facilities, including their refinancing, as well as new credit facilities. They set out supervisory expectations on standards for taking, managing, and monitoring credit risk, as well as ensuring appropriate practices in areas such as consumer protection and anti-money laundering.

Source: Own elaboration based on: Documents discussed in the table.

In some areas of banking, regulations and guidelines have already been implemented, while in other cases, draft legal acts have been developed. A requirement was introduced for supervisory authorities to carry out specific analyses of certain ESG issues, regarding the possibility of including them in regulations, with specific proposals to be submitted to the European Commission for final consideration and regulatory action[6].

Regulators, by developing, consulting, and sharing documents, provide a basis for banks to develop appropriate approaches to managing environmental risk, or ESG risk more broadly. The new regulations pose challenges for banks, particularly in the area of quantifying environmental and community impacts, measuring a bank's exposure to sustainability risks, or measuring the impact of ESG factors on other bank risks. It is important that environmental risk—in particular, climate change risk—is comprehensively incorporated into banks' risk management strategies and policies and is treated on an equal footing with key risks for the bank, such as credit risk, market risk, or operational risk. Including environmental issues in financial advisory services or prudential requirements may increase the cost of operations for banks beyond the possible benefits and may make it more difficult for borrowers to obtain financing, especially for activities that pose a threat to the environment.

3.5 Environmental risk assessment and management

Environmental risk management (ERM) in a bank is part of the bank's risk management system. Environmental risk is of a cross-cutting nature, which means that it may affect, to different extents and through different channels, traditional financial and nonfinancial risks, such as credit, liquidity, market, operational, reputation, or compliance risk (NGFS, 2020). The integration of environmental risk into the banking risk management process requires the modification of the existing methods of identification and the measurement and control of individual risks, taking into account the causal relationships between these risks and environmental risk. Additionally, this requires a modification of the business strategy and risk management strategy and, with it, a modification of the risk management structure—in particular, a clear division of tasks and responsibilities.

Environmental risks are difficult to manage because of the following (Vermeer, 2014):

- The external occurrence of environmental risks and the significantly limited ability to directly impact them;
- The existence of a number of environmental risks, including those related to climate change, water, energy consumption, waste, and biodiversity, which are interrelated;
- The varying scale of occurrence of environmental risks due to their scope (e.g., local, national, international, global) and time horizon;
- The sudden and destructive nature;
- The lack or limited availability of environmental data and their low quality, including disclosures by banks' customers and counterparties;
- The lack of key indicators to identify and measure key environmental risks.

Banks include entities with many years of experience in environmental risk management as well as entities that have consciously ignored environmental or social risks due to their low impact on their business or lack of awareness of such impact (Zioło et al., 2021). This is why all kinds of guidelines and recommendations on environmental risk management are so important, in particular those prepared by international financial institutions or supervisory authorities, such as Principles for the Effective Management and Supervision of Climate-Related Financial Risks (BCBS), Guidelines on Loan Origination and Monitoring (EBA), and Environmental and Social Management at FIs (EBRD).

Effective environmental risk management requires the identification and assessment of events that may have a negative impact on the bank's operations. The analysis of the effects of these events, also from a financial perspective, is the starting point for planning actions that prevent the negative effects of the risk, as well as those limiting its scale. A number of methods are used to estimate environmental risk, which can be classified into one of three groups (Krogulec et al., 2018; NGFS, 2020):

- Quantitative methods: They are based on quantitative data that can be measured and on mathematical statistics and the calculus of probability. They allow us to determine a numerical value of risk—for example, expected loss, probability of default, exposure of default, loss given default, events tree analysis, fault tree analysis, failure mode and effect analysis, and stress testing.
- Qualitative methods: They are based on good practice and experience. Risks and potential consequences of risk occurrence are presented in a descriptive way—for example, structured "what if" technique, scenario analysis, preliminary hazard analysis, and risk assessment matrix.
- Quantitative-qualitative (mixed) methods: They combine elements of quantitative and qualitative methods and can help gain a more complete picture than a standalone quantitative or qualitative methods—for example, use qualitative analysis based on scenario methods to identify all risk areas and risk consequences, while using quantitative analysis to determine the cost of risk effects.

Environmental risk assessment (ERA) methodology has been widely used to identify and assess environmental risks for many years. ERA identifies potential environmental risks caused by economic operators and determines the likelihood of negative impacts on various aspects of the environment, such as living organisms, natural habitats, and ecosystems. ERA is based on two assumptions: namely, that the cost of eliminating all environmental risks is very high and that environmental management decisions are always made based on incomplete information (McIntosh and Pontius, 2017). The purpose of the ERA is to provide a quantitative and/or qualitative estimate of risk as well as information about environmental impacts.

In its framework, conducting an environmental risk assessment involves six steps (EPA, 2021):

- Step 1: Problem formulation—the most critical step where risk managers define the scope of an ERA by identifying what needs to be protected from harm.
- Step 2: Hazard characterization—examining the potential environmental hazards present in the workplace or site.
  Step 3: Exposure characterization—identifying what and who is at risk (if an ERA identifies a significant risk, the next step is to develop a management approach to reduce or eliminate the risk).
- Step 4: Risk characterization—combining hazard and exposure characterization results and then assessing the risk.
- Step 5: Documentation—recording the results of the assessment and implementing precautions.
- Step 6: Monitoring—reviewing the assessment at regular intervals.

ERA is very well described in the literature and applied in regulation and in business practice in various industries (Murray-Smith and Taylor, 2018). Although the goal of any ERA is generally the same (to identify the hazard, estimate the risk posed, and consider steps to reduce risk if necessary), there are a number of different frameworks used by different groups to conduct an ERA (McIntosh and Pontius, 2017). In the practice of banks, ERA is not yet well established, although a number of activities are being undertaken in this area[7].

Environmental factors are increasingly important to banking operations. Additionally, while banks may also be directly exposed to environmental risks, most exposures are indirect and arise from the environmental risks to which their customers and counterparties are exposed. In addition, the bank is exposed to indirect environmental risks from, among other things, rising costs of raw materials, new environmental regulations, and conflicts with other stakeholders or political conflict. It is often difficult to distinguish between local and global risks or to manage the complex interactions between different risk factors independently. In addition, assessing and managing environmental risks requires fast and easy access to environmental information, which is currently the biggest challenge for banks and supervisory institutions.

3.6 Environmental risk management in Polish banking practice—the example of the PKO BP SA Bank

At the end of April 2022, there were 30 commercial banks in Poland, including 13 with predominantly Polish capital and 17 with foreign capital. The assets of banks with a majority of domestic capital accounted for 56.3% of the assets of the entire banking sector (KNF, 2022). The review of nonfinancial information posted on banks' websites and available in published reports allows us to conclude that all commercial banks include environmental and social aspects in their management, but to a very diverse extent. In terms of scope, comprehensiveness and manner of disclosing information on ESG risk in banking activities, banks belonging to international or global financial groups, such as ING, BNP Paribas, Santander, or Citi, stand out—they have been involved in initiatives related to ESG issues in financial activities for many years and have experience in environmental risk management[8]. On the other hand, in the case of several banks with predominantly domestic capital, the disclosure of information on nonfinancial issues as part of the management report was initiated by the requirements of Directive 2014/34/EU transposed into the Polish legal system through the Accounting Act.

The analyzed banks with predominantly domestic capital most often disclose nonfinancial information in the annual report; two banks publish separate reports on bank sustainability, and three publish statements on nonfinancial information. In the case of one bank, there is perfunctory information on the website regarding charitable activities. In addition:

- For six banks, environmental risk is included only as a component of credit risk;
- For six banks, environmental risk (ESG risk more broadly) is reflected in the risk policy or risk management strategy, but to a very diverse extent;

- Four banks' disclosures to date are in line with the EU taxonomy;
- Ten banks apply GRI reporting standards, which include standards for reporting indicators in the following areas: general, economic, environmental, and social.

It should be added that three out of six banks with predominantly domestic capital listed on the Warsaw Stock Exchange are part of the responsible WIG-ESG index (Alior Bank, Bank PeKaO SA, and Bank PKO BP SA). This means that these banks meet the requirements in terms of environmental, social, economic, and corporate governance issues at the appropriate level.[9] Against the background of the analyzed banks, Bank PKO BP SA stands out, being the oldest and the largest bank in Poland in terms of assets (over 17% of the balance sheet total of the banking sector). This bank publishes the most comprehensive report, showing the impact of its business model and strategy on ESG activities undertaken and their results (Table 3.7). In 2021, the ESG risk was included in the risk management strategy at the bank and the bank's group. Additionally, PKO BP has developed and implemented an own policy for financing the carbon-intensive energy sector, the chemistry, oil and gas sector policy and policy for financing the renewable energy sector.

The bank manages the ESG risk as part of managing other types of risk. ESG risk management is supported by all committees operating at the bank in terms of their activities and competences related to ESG risk. The risk management process takes into account the double materiality perspective: the impact of ESG factors on the bank's operations, financial result, and development and the impact of the bank's activities on the society and the environment. The following have been identified among the key ESG risks:

- The risk of the noncompliance of products with the applicable standards;
- The risk of unauthorized access to customer funds;
- The risk of unauthorized access to customer information;
- The risk related to the outsourcing of services;
- The risk of financing entities whose products pose an environmental or social threat;
- The climate risk;
- The risk of a negative impact on the physical environment and social environment;
- The employee risk;
- The health and safety risk;
- The risk of the violation of human rights, including children's rights;
- The risk of corruption;
- The risk in the supply chain;
- The risk of inadequate communication.

ESG risk assessment is part of the evaluation of the borrower's business model, both for new and existing customers, and affects the terms of the lending decision. The

TABLE 3.7 Overview of the adopted ESG initiatives in 2021

Environmental	*Social*	*Corporate governance*
Assessment of the impact of environmental, social, and governance factors on the customer's creditworthiness.	Offer of special solutions that helped customers maintain financial liquidity in a pandemic situation.	Implementation of an ESG risk assessment for corporate customers to identify nonfinancial risks.
Study of the impact of lending transactions on ESG issues and classifying them (from transactions with a positive effect on ESG issues through to those with a significantly negative impact).	Transfer of almost PLN 3 million to medical facilities and helping organizations fight against the COVID-19 pandemic.	Adaptation of indicators to be achieved in the ESG area and including them in the bank group's nonfinancial goals for the following years.
Purchase of guarantees of origin for the electricity from water sources in a RES installation (68.9 GWh). Reduction in CO_2 emissions of 49,539 tons.	Provision of assistance under the PFR's anti-crisis shields and the BGK's tools.	Updating the procurement policy, keeping the ESG principles in the purchasing process.
Continuation of activities on the implementation of the Energy Management System in accordance with ISO50001.	Development of organizational tools and solutions facilitating communication with customers and ensuring their convenient service.	Preparation of a Supplier Code of Ethics.
Conducting an energy efficiency audit and identifying tasks that should lead to a reduction in energy consumption.	Implementation of remote work solutions and digital services to ensure safety of the bank's employees and customers and adaptation of medical care to the pandemic situation.	Conducting an ESG survey among the bank's key suppliers in order to determine the level of familiarity with ESG issues.

Source: PKO BP SA, Podsumowanie ujawnień ESG w 2021 roku, www.pkobp.pl/relacje-inwestorskie/esg-w-grupie-pko-banku-polskiego/podsumowanie-ujawnien-esg/ (accessed: 27.06.2022).

bank has put in place tools to estimate the nonfinancial risks of corporate clients and to effectively assess and control them. The risk estimation process begins with the creation of a risk map, which allows for the initial identification of ESG risks in a given business. Sources of further information include the borrower's annual reports and press releases and client interviews. The client interview is conducted on the basis of a prepared questionnaire, the purpose of which is to identify in-depth ESG risks in the client's business and to identify potential risk areas.

Based on the assessment of the sectoral economic outlook, the bank creates a list of industries subject to sectoral limits and sets their nominal limits in the overall loan portfolio structure by industry. When granting or reviewing its financing, the bank analyses the impact of climate change risk as well as the related legal and regulatory changes on each entity's ability to service debt. A synthetic measure of creditworthiness is a customer's internal rating, which reflects (among others) the exposure to climate change risk. The bank performs stress tests for the deterioration of the risk profile of the entire loan portfolio subject to various types of risks. The bank's current lending policy also includes no new exposures to the coal and lignite mining sector. The bank has committed that its exposure to green finance as a proportion of its assets will remain at least three times higher than that to high-carbon sectors.

The bank complies with EU and national regulations on ESG issues. PKO BP disclosed information as part of the global initiative CDP Disclosure Insight Action for the first time in 2020 and presented a preliminary assessment of risks and opportunities resulting from climate change, in line with the classification by TCFD (Task Force on Climate-Related Financial Disclosures). In terms of risks, PKO BP identified:

- Regulatory risk associated with the prices of emission rights and extension of the ETS system to other sectors;
- Regulatory risk associated with the extension of the scope of reported emissions and making the reporting of greenhouse gas emissions obligatory rather than voluntary across the supply and value chain;
- Risk associated with the financing of investment projects that use new eco-friendly technologies that may not succeed in the market;
- Risk of an increase in the frequency and severity of unusual weather conditions.

The bank is not a signatory to voluntary sustainable banking initiatives. In 2019, the bank signed the Environmental Responsibility Charter of Entrepreneurs and Employers in Poland (*Karta Odpowiedzialności Ekologicznej Przedsiębiorców i Pracodawców w Polsce*), in which it pledged to strive for climate neutrality and achieve the goals of a circular economy (Pracodawcy RP, 2019)[10]. PKO BP has an ESG 4 Institution Risk Rating from Sustainalytics (20.7/100), an MSCI Rating (A), a FTSE Russell Rating (3.7/5), and a V.E Rating (47/100). PKO BP, like other Polish banks, is characterized by a high exposure to air pollution (smog), which is one of Poland's biggest developmental challenges. It is caused, among other things, by EU policies and regulations, as well as the growing ecological awareness of society.

3.7 Conclusion

Environmental regulations are constantly developing and cover an increasingly wide range of issues in their multitude, comprehensiveness, and complexity (e.g., regulations often referring to acts outside of environmental regulations) create problems related to their interpretation and practical application. Not complying with the regulations is connected with bearing legal, financial, or image consequences of entities whose activity significantly influences the environment or human health. In environmental policy and its regulations, there has been a shift from a threat-based to a risk-based approach. This is due, among other things, to the fact that for a number of environmental issues, elimination of risk is not possible or necessary to protect people and the environment and that a certain level of risk in a given scenario is considered acceptable after weighing the benefits. In addition, environmental risks are increasingly turning into systemic risks, posing a potential threat to financial stability.

ESG risk issues in banks are the subject of many self-regulatory initiatives, soft law (guidelines, best practices, recommendations), and legal regulations. Many banks have made voluntary commitments to take action to prevent adverse climate change and to consider climate risk in their decision-making (e.g., UNEP FI. Declaration on Climate Change by the Financial Services Sector; RE 100% Climate Group, Poseidon Principles, UNEP FI. Net-Zero Banking Alliance) or have committed to voluntary environmental guidelines in lending and investment activities (e.g., Equator Principles, UN Principles for Responsible Investment, UNEP FI. Positive Impact Initiative, UNEP FI. Blue Finance). The multitude of existing nonbinding standards and guidelines in the market, including those related to the reporting of ESG issues, significantly hinders the comparability of information published by financial institutions and thus the assessment of their credibility. The supervisors' endeavor to develop universally binding standards for disclosures on ESG issues is an initiative that, in the long run, should facilitate a reliable assessment of banks' actual exposure to environmental risk and the incorporation of the results of that assessment in lending and investment decisions.

It is critical for banks to build resilience to the impact of environmental risk in their business strategies and risk management processes. Banks must actively manage and monitor their environmental risk exposures at both the customer and portfolio levels. Assessing and managing environmental risk requires quick and easy access to environmental information, which is currently the biggest challenge for banks and supervisors. The solution will be fostered by the development of new information and communication technologies as well as the increasing involvement of regulators, rating agencies, and academia.

Notes

1 For several years, environmental protection law has been treated as a special branch of law, and its distinctiveness within the legal system is often emphasized (Przybojewska, 2018).

2 The precautionary principle originates from German law and was incorporated into the legal regulation of air protection in the 1970s. This principle entered the international legal order through the Rio Declaration in 1992 and was introduced to the EU in 1992 by the Maastricht Treaty as one of the basic principles of environmental policy (Michalak, 2017).

3 The principle "polluter pays" is embedded in legislation in the EU (Environmental Liability Directive) (Directive, 2004/35/CE), the United States (Comprehensive Environmental Response, Compensation and Liability Act (CERCLA), 1980), and Western

Australia (Contaminated Sites Act, 2003). In 2011, China brought in specific pollutant discharge standards for the rare earths industry (Keith-Roach, 2016).

4 The following banks have been removed from the signatory list because of noncompliance with membership requirements: First City Monument Bank (Nigeria) and Keystone Bank (Nigeria).

5 European Union banking prudential regulations are based on Basel standards (BCBS), within which ESG risk shall be considered. Some of these requirements are defined by regulations developed by the European Commission and passed by the European Parliament, and some by guidelines formulated by the European Banking Authority.

6 August 2, 2022, marked the end of the open public consultations conducted by the EBA regarding the integration of ESG risk into prudential supervision for credit institutions. The Discussion Paper (DP) was issued in relation to the mandates in Article 501c of Regulation (EU) No 575/2013, i.e. the Capital Requirements Regulation (CRR), and in Article 34 of Regulation (EU) 2019/2033, i.e. the Investment Firms Regulation (IFR), for the EBA to provide reports on the topic. This DP provides an initial assessment of how the framework interacts with environmental risks and poses questions on whether adaptations are required to effectively address such risks. The analysis is focused on exposures related to assets and activities associated with environmental objectives/impacts. Those related to social objectives/impacts will be considered in the next steps (EBA, 2022b).

7 Most ERA models for commercial banking business assess the impact of environmental factors on credit risk metrics, such as probabilities of default (PD) and Loss Given Default (LGD). These models—including transition risk models and physical risk models—work by first estimating the environment-related losses or changes in some metrics that constitute explanatory variables for the loan-related risk models and then using these results as inputs for banks' credit risk models to generate adjusted risk measures including PD, LGD, and credit ratings. Thus, the adjusted risk metrics produced from the second step have incorporated environmental factors—that is, translated environmental risks into credit risks (NGFS, 2020).

8 Standards and solutions on ESG issues developed, binding, and improved at the group level are implemented by all group entities, taking into account the specific nature and regulatory framework applicable in the country where they operate.

9 The WIG-ESG Index is derived largely from reports by Sustainalytics, a research firm (Morningstar Company) that provides ESG data for the world's largest investment and index companies. Sustainalytics' methodology is based on measuring an industry's exposure to specific risks related to ESG criteria. It also evaluates how an entity manages ESG risks. The basis of the assessment is the analysis of information published on the companies' websites, their annual reports, and reports containing nonfinancial data.

10 The Environmental Responsibility Charter for Entrepreneurs and Employers in Poland is the Polish contribution to the Marrakech Business Action for Climate (MBA4C) initiative. MBA4C is an agreement of 47 employers' associations and business organizations from around the world supporting their countries in the implementation of the 2015 Paris Agreement. Poland is represented by the largest employers' association, Employers of Poland.

References

BCBS. (2022). *Principles for the Effective Management and Supervision of Climate-Related Financial Risks*. Bank for International Settlements (online). www.bis.org/bcbs/publ/d532.pdf (accessed: 25.06.2022).

Benedikter, R. (2011). *European Answers to the Financial Crisis: Social Banking and Social Finance*. Stanford, Spice: Freeman Spogli Institute for International Studies. www.researchgate.net/publication/248388817_Social_Banking_and_Social_Finance.

Borys, G. (2000). *Ryzyko ekologiczne w działalności banku*. Warszawa: Biblioteka Menedżera i Bankowca. Zarządzanie i Finanse.

Communication from the Commission to the European Parliament, the Council, the European Economic and Social Committee and the Committee of the Regions. (2018). *Action Plan: Financing Sustainable Growth*. https://eur-lex.europa.eu/legal-content/EN/TXT/PDF/?uri=CELEX:52018DC0097&from=EN (accessed: 20.09.2022).

Communication from the Commission to the European Parliament, the Council, the European Economic and Social Committee and the Committee of the Regions. (2021a). *EU Taxonomy, Corporate Sustainability Reporting, Sustainability Preferences and Fiduciary Duties: Directing finance towards the European Green Deal*. https://eur-lex.europa.eu/legal-content/EN/TXT/PDF/?uri=CELEX:52021DC0188&from=EN (accessed: 19.10.2022).

Communication from the Commission to the European Parliament, the Council, the European Economic and Social Committee and the Committee of the Regions. (2019). *The European Green Deal*. https://eur-lex.europa.eu/resource.html?uri=cellar:b828d165-1c22-11ea-8c1f-01aa75ed71a1.0002.02/DOC_1&format=PDF (accessed: 20.09.2022).

Communication from the Commission to the European Parliament, the Council, the European Economic and Social Committee and the Committee of the Regions. (2021b). *Strategy for Financing the Transition to a Sustainable Economy*. https://eur-lex.europa.eu/resource.html?uri=cellar:9f5e7e95-df06-11eb-895a-01aa75ed71a1.0001.02/DOC_1&format=PDF (accessed: 19.10.2022).

Directive 2004/35/CE of the European Parliament and of the Council of 21 April 2004 on Environmental Liability with Regard to the Prevention and Remedying of Environmental Damage. https://eur-lex.europa.eu/legal-content/EN/TXT/?uri=celex%3A32004L0035.

EBA. (2020). *Guidelines on Loan Origination and Monitoring*. www.eba.europa.eu/sites/default/documents/files/document_library/Publications/Guidelines/2020/Guidelines%20on%20loan%20origination%20and%20monitoring/884283/EBA%20GL%202020%2006%20Final%20Report%20on%20GL%20on%20loan%20origination%20and%20monitoring.pdf (accessed: 25.06.2022).

EBA. (2021). *Report on Environmental, Social and Governance (ESG) Risks Management and Supervision*. June 23. www.eba.europa.eu/sites/default/documents/files/document_library/Publications/Reports/2021/1015656/EBA%20Report%20on%20ESG%20risks%20management%20and%20supervision.pdf (accessed: 25.06.2022).

EBA. (2022a). *Final Draft Implementing Technical Standards on Prudential Disclosures on ESG Risks in Accordance with Article 449a CRR*. www.eba.europa.eu/sites/default/documents/files/document_library/Publications/Draft%20Technical%20Standards/2022/1026171/EBA%20draft%20ITS%20on%20Pillar%203%20disclosures%20on%20ESG%20risks.pdf (accessed: 25.06.2022).

EBA. (2022b). *The Role of Environmental Risks in the Prudential Framework*. Discussion Paper. EBA/DP/2022/02. https://www.eba.europa.eu/sites/default/documents/files/document_library/Publications/Discussions/2022/Discussion%20paper%20on%20the%20role%20of%20environmental%20risk%20in%20the%20prudential%20framework/1031947/Discussion%20paper%20on%20role%20of%20ESG%20risks%20in%20prudential%20framework.pdf (accessed: 19.10.2022).

EBA.ESMA. (2021). *Final Report on Joint ESMA and EBA Guidelines on the Assessment of the Suitability of Members of the Management Body and Key Function Holders Under Directive 2013/36/EU and Directive 2014/65/EU*. www.eba.europa.eu/sites/default/documents/files/document_library/Publications/Guidelines/2021/EBA-GL-2021-06%20Joint%20GLs%20on%20the%20assessment%20of%20suitability%20%28fit%26propoer%29/1022127/Final%20report%20on%20joint%20EBA%20and%20ESMA%20GL%20on%20the%20assessment%20of%20suitability.pdf (accessed: 25.06.2022).

ECB. (2020). *Guide on Climate-Related and Environmental Risks, Supervisory Expectations Relating to Risk Management and Disclosure*. Frankfurt: European Central Bank. November. www.bankingsupervision.europa.eu/ecb/pub/pdf/ssm.202011finalguideonclimate-relatedandenvironmentalrisks~58213f6564.en.pdf (accessed: 25.06.2022).

EPA. (2021). *The NRC Risk Assessment Paradigm*. United States Environmental Protection Agency. www.epa.gov/fera/nrc-risk-assessment-paradigm (accessed: 27.06.2022).

ESAs. (2021). *Final Report on Draft Regulatory Technical Standards with Regard to the Content and Presentation of Disclosures Pursuant to Article 8(4), 9(6) and 11(5) of Regulation (EU) 2019/2088*. Joint Committee of the European Supervisory Authorities. October 22. www.esma.europa.eu/sites/default/files/library/jc_2021_50_-_final_report_on_taxonomy-related_product_disclosure_rts.pdf (accessed: 25.06.2022).

IFC. (2022). *Review Environmental and Social Regulatory Framework*. First for Sustainability. Financial Institutions: Resources, Solutions and Tools. https://firstforsustainability.org/risk-management/managing-environmental-and-social-risk-2_2/implementing-an-esms/review-environmental-and-social-regulatory-framework/ (accessed: 20.09.2022).

IUCN–UNEP–WWF. (1980). *World Conservation Strategy: Living Resource Conservation for Sustainable Development*. www.iucn.org/content/world-conservation-strategy-living-resource-conservation-sustainable-development.

Jeucken, M. (2004). *Sustainability in Finance. Banking on the Planet*. Delft: Eburon, pp. 15–17.

Jeucken, M., and Bouma, J. (1999). The Changing Environment of Banks. In *GMI Theme Issue: Sustainable Banking: The Greening of Finance*, No. 27. Greener Management International, pp. 20–35.

Keith-Roach, M. (2016). Legislation and Best Practice in the Emerging European Rare Earth Element Industry. In *Rare Earths Industry. Technological, Economic, and Environmental Implications*, I. Borges De Lima (ed.), Elsevier, pp. 279–291. https://www.researchgate.net/publication/299390404_Environmental_Legislation_and_Best_Practice_in_the_Emerging_European_Rare_Earth_Element_Industry (accessed: 20.09.2022).

KNF. (2022). *Dane miesięczne sektora bankowego—kwiecień*. www.knf.gov.pl/publikacje_i_opracowania/dane_statystyczne/bankowy?articleId=56224&p_id=18

Krogulec, E., Sawicka, K., Zabłocki, S., and Falkowska, E. (2018). Ocena ryzyka środowiskowego w zakresie zanieczyszczenia wód podziemnych i gruntów w rejonie robót górniczych. *Górnictwo Odkrywkowe. No. 2/2018*. Wrocław: Instytut Górnictwa Odkrywkowego, pp. 51–52.

Kulińska-Sadłocha, E. (2009). Banki a zmiany klimatyczne. In *Finanse 2009—Teoria i praktyka. Bankowość*, W. K. Brzozowska and S. Flejterski (red.). Szczecin: Wydawnictwo Uniwersytetu Szczecińskiego, pp. 175–182.

McIntosh, A., and Pontius, J. (2016). *Science and the Global Environment. Case Studies Integrating Science Global Environment*. Elsevier, Boston.

Michalak, M. (2017). Zasada przezorności w Unii Europejskiej—hamulec postępu czy najbardziej racjonalna droga? *Studia Prawnoustrojowe* 37. Uniwersytet Warmińsko-Mazurski, s. 45–56.

MKŚ. (2018). *Konwencje międzynarodowe*. Warszawa: Ministerstwo Klimatu i Środowiska. www.gov.pl/web/klimat/konwencje-miedzynarodowe (accessed: 18.05.2022).

MSZ. (2022). *Internetowa Baza Traktatowa*. Warszawa: Ministerstwo Spraw Zagranicznych. https://traktaty.msz.gov.pl/umowa-3 (accessed: 18.05.2022).

Murray-Smith, R., and Taylor, D. (2018). Policy, Regulations, and Risk Assessment. In *Environmental Contaminants, Health Care and Environmental Contamination*, Alistair B. A. Boxall and Rai S. Kookana (eds.). Elsevier, Amsterdam, pp. 239–260.

NGFS. (2020). *Overview of Environmental Risk Analysis by Financial Institutions*. www.ngfs.net/sites/default/files/media/2020/09/23/overview_of_environmental_risk_analysis_by_financial_institutions.pdf (accessed: 26.06.2022).

Nowak, Z. (2001). *Zarządzanie środowiskiem*. Część 1. Gliwice: Wydawnictwo Politechniki Śląskiej, pp. 228–280.

Pisano, U., Martinuzzi, A., and Bruckner, B. (2012). *The Financial Sector and Sustainable Development: Logics, Principles and Actors*. ESDN Quarterly Report No 27. December. www.sd-network.eu/quarterly%20reports/report%20files/pdf/2012-December-The_Financial_Sector_and_Sustainable_Development.pdf.

Pracodawcy RP. (2019) *Karta Odpowiedzialności Ekologicznej Przedsiębiorców i Pracodawców w Polsce*. https://pracodawcyrp.pl/upload/files/2019/11/karta-odpowiedzialnosci-ekologicznej-polskiego-biznesu-v2.pdf (accessed: 27.06.2022).

Proposal for a Directive of the European Parliament and of the Council amending Directive 2013/34/EU, Directive 2004/109/EC, Directive 2006/43/EC and Regulation (EU) No 537/2014, as Regards Corporate Sustainability Reporting. (2021). https://eur-lex.europa.eu/legal-content/EN/TXT/PDF/?uri=CELEX:52021PC0189&from=EN (accessed: 20.09.2022).

Przybojewska, I. (2018). Wykładnia rozszerzająca prawa ochrony środowiska jako szczególnej gałęzi prawa. *Studia prawnicze KUL* 2(74): 67–69.

Rogall, H. (2010). *Ekonomia zrównoważonego rozwoju*. Poznań: Wydawnictwo Zysk i S-Ka, pp. 219–223.

Rosicki, R. (2010). Ogólna charakterystyka międzynarodowego prawa Ochrony środowiska. *Środkowoeuropejskie Studia Polityczne* (3): 79–104.

UNEP FI. (2021). Principles for Responsible Banking. Guidance Document. www.unepfi.org/publications/principles-for-responsible-banking-guidance-document/ (accessed: 20.09.2022).

Ustawa z dnia 16 kwietnia 2004 roku o ochronie przyrody. Dz. U. 2004 Nr 92. poz. 880. https://eli.gov.pl/api/acts/DU/2004/880/text/U/D20040880Lj.pdf (accessed: 20.09.2022).

Ustawa z dnia 27 kwietnia 2001 r. Prawo ochrony środowiska. Dz. U. 2001 Nr 62. poz. 627. https://eli.gov.pl/api/acts/DU/2001/627/text/U/D20010627Lj.pdf (accessed: 20.09.2022).

Vermeer, A. (2014). As Climate Change Continues to Accelerate, Businesses Must Assess and Manage Their Environmental Risk. In *A New Guide to Managing Environmental Risk*. Duke Corporate Education. www.dukece.com/insights/new-guide-managing-environmental-risk/ (accessed: 26.06.2022).

Weber, O. (2012). *Sustainable Banking—History and Current Developments*. https://ssrn.com/abstract=2159947.

Zioło, M. (2017). Instytucjonalny i prawny wymiar zrównoważonego rozwoju oraz finansów zrównoważonych. In *Strefa finansowa wobec wyzwań zrównoważonego rozwoju*, W. K. Raczkowski and M. Zioło (red.). Warszawa: CeDeWu, pp. 59–83.

Zioło, M., Spoz, A., and Kulińska-Sadłocha, E. (2021). *Zrównoważone rynki finansowe. Perspektywa krajowa i międzynarodowa*. Warszawa: PWE.

4

QUANTITATIVE METHODS AND IT IN ENVIRONMENTAL RISK MODELLING

Iwona Bąk and Maciej Oesterreich

4.1 The quantitative methods used in environmental risk assessment and evaluation

Both quantitative and qualitative methods are used to study, analyse and predict the level of risk. Among the former, fault tree analysis (FTA) and event tree analysis (ETA) are the most commonly distinguished methods (Robu et al., 2007; Tejaswi and Samuel, 2017; USACoE, 2018).

4.1.1 Fault tree analysis

The fault tree analysis method determines the logical relationships between causes, so-called elementary events and their effects (abnormal conditions) and quantifies the likelihood of adverse events.

The FTA analysis includes both qualitative and quantitative components. The former is always performed (tree diagram), and the latter is feasible only when information about the probability of occurrence of the events included in the tree is available.

As part of the analysis, it is necessary to do the following (Borysiewicz et al., 2000, p. 48; Kabir, 2017):

- Define the top event (initiating events);
- Determine the structure of the faulty tree (intermediate events);
- construct a faulty tree;
- Identify the primary events leading to the top event;
- Determine the likelihood of an initiating event;
- Determine the 'minimum tree cross-sections' (minimum sets of elementary events leading to a top event);
- Calculate the probability of occurrence of a top event;
- Analyse the results in order to determine the dominant elementary events;

DOI: 10.4324/9781003310099-4

- Perform a sensitivity analysis that checks how changing the probability of damage of one element from the set of minimal sections influences the probability of top event occurrence.

The basic tool in the FTA analysis is a tree diagram (a faulty tree). Its construction starts with a top event and passes through intermediaries to elementary events. Their interrelationships are represented by logical gateways (Rusin and Wojaczek, 2012; Bakeli and Hafidi, 2020). The most common designations used in constructing a tree diagram are shown in Table 4.1.

TABLE 4.1 The most common designations used in the construction of a tree diagram

Event symbols	
Top event 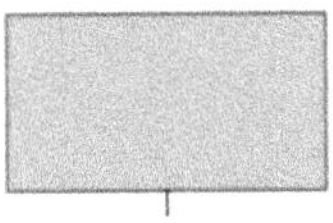	The subject of the analysis is often a catastrophic event causing the entire system to fail.
Intermediate event 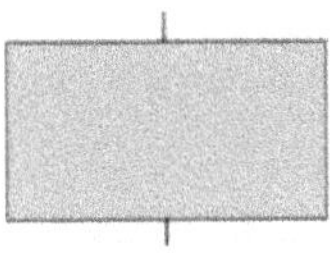	Indirect events are events caused by one or more other elementary or intermediate events.
Basic event 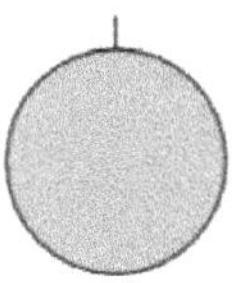	An elementary event that affects the occurrence of a top event.
Underdevelopment event 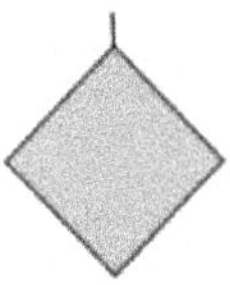	This symbol is used for events that cannot be classified as basic (or intermediate) and for which no information is available to create a separate sub-tree.
Event transfer (in, out) 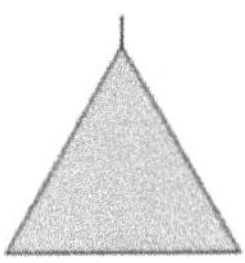 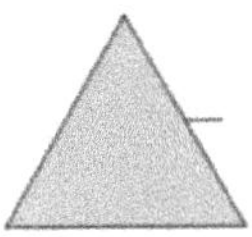	The transfer event is used when the error tree is too large to fit, for example, a document. It allows you to replace one large part of the tree with one symbol and discuss its further part in a separate diagram.

(*Continued*)

TABLE 4.1 (Continued)

Event symbols	
Conditional event 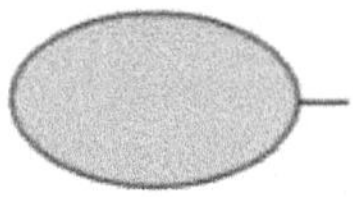	Conditional events are those that act as a condition for the INHIBIT gateway.
House events 	The external event usually expected to occur. These events may or may not occur, so they are likely to be 1 or 0, respectively.
Gate symbols	
AND gate 	An output event will only occur if all input events occur.
Priority AND gate 	An output event will only occur if all input events occur in a specific order.
OR gate 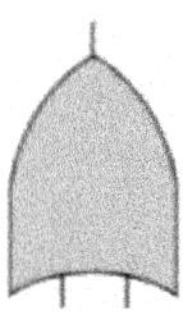	An output event will occur when one of the input events occurs.
XOR gate 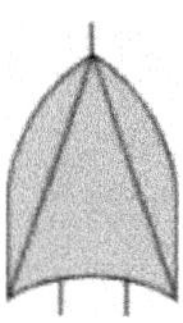	An output event will occur when exactly one input event occurs.
k/*N* or VOTING gate 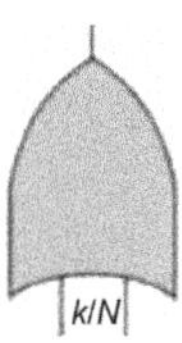	An output event will occur when *k* input events occur.

Event symbols	
INHIBIT gate 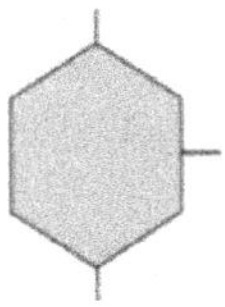	An output event will happen when the input and conditional events occur.

Source: Own elaboration according to LimbleCMMS, 2021.

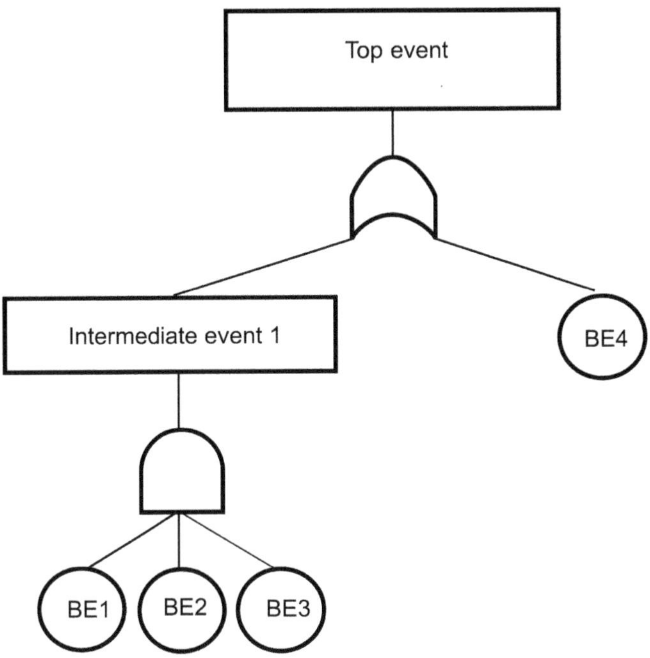

FIGURE 4.1 An example of a faulty tree.

Source: Own elaboration.

An example of a faulty tree is shown in Figure 4.1.

The disadvantages of the fault tree analysis include the following (Tejaswi and Samuel, 2017):

- The need to use a complicated mathematical apparatus, especially for a very complex tree diagram;
- Inability to accurately determine the influence of the human factor, which is often underestimated or overestimated;
- The immediate impact of the investigator's experience on the quality of the results obtained.

TABLE 4.2 Examples of uses of FTA and ETA methods

Source	*Description*
Gatfaoui, 2004	The author models the lifetime of companies (using French firms as an example) while examining the related empirical probabilities of failure to meet their obligations. For that purpose, he uses FTA analysis.
Chu and Feng, 2009	The article presents a combination of FTA and architecture-centric systems analysis to analyse the architecture of IT systems used in e-business.
Ye, 2016	The paper discusses the methods of identifying credit risk used by Chinese commercial banks. The advantages and disadvantages of selected methods (including FTA) were discussed. The author made several suggestions regarding the identification and management of credit risk.
Hao, 2013	In this paper, the author aimed to build a method to control and mitigate the impact of operational risk for banks associated with the occurrence of major events in domestic and international markets. The ETA method and Bayesian network were used for this purpose.
Kim et al., 2013	The paper proposes to use FTA and (FMEA) methods to evaluate and improve the security of the IC card payment system.
Gordon, 2014	The author focuses on using incident response trees built using ETA to measure the risk of incidents affecting the security of online financial services.
Santos et al., 2014	The article develops the extension of the I-O model using the ETA method to assess the propagation of the effects of disasters in interdependent sectors of the economy using inoperability and economic loss metrics.
Kim et al., 2015	The paper proposes a process model for improving the software security of a mobile banking information system by applying FTA and FMEA analysis.
Henriques de Gusmão et al., 2018	The paper proposes a model that integrates FTA analysis, decision theory and fuzzy theory to determine the current causes of cyber-attack prevention failures and the vulnerability of a given system. The constructed model was applied to assess the cybersecurity risks associated with attacks on enterprise systems and evaluate the possible consequences.

Source: Own elaboration.

The FTA has been successfully applied, among other things, in the banking and financial institutions sectors, as shown in Section 4.1.2 (Table 4.2).

4.1.2 Event tree analysis

The event tree analysis (ETA) method is an inductive logic model that identifies the possible outcomes of a given initiating event. This event is most likely to result in an accident or incident. The combination of the initiating event and the fitness/failure in the process under analysis defines the individual sequence of emergency events (Aven, 2003, p. 11; Lacasse, 2008). There are two basic forms of event tree analysis (Hong et al., 2009):

- Pre-event—used to determine sets of initiating events and assess the probability of their occurrence;
- Post-event—used to analyse an abnormal situation and identify imperfections in the process under investigation.

In the context of the ETA analysis, there are six main steps (Borysiewicz et al., 2000, p. 51):

1 The identification of the initiating event that may lead to an abnormal situation;
2 The identification of the barriers intended to mitigate the effects of the initiating event;
3 Event tree structure;
4 A description resulting from the construction of a contingency sequence tree;
5 The determination of minimum tree cross-sections;
6 The development of documentation.

ETA is the basis for creating a probabilistic process model (facility) for hazard analysis. This model is depicted as a tree representing the chronological (logical) progression of events begun by an initiating event. Each branch represents a separate sequence of relationships between that event and the barriers. Figure 4.2 shows an example of the event tree.

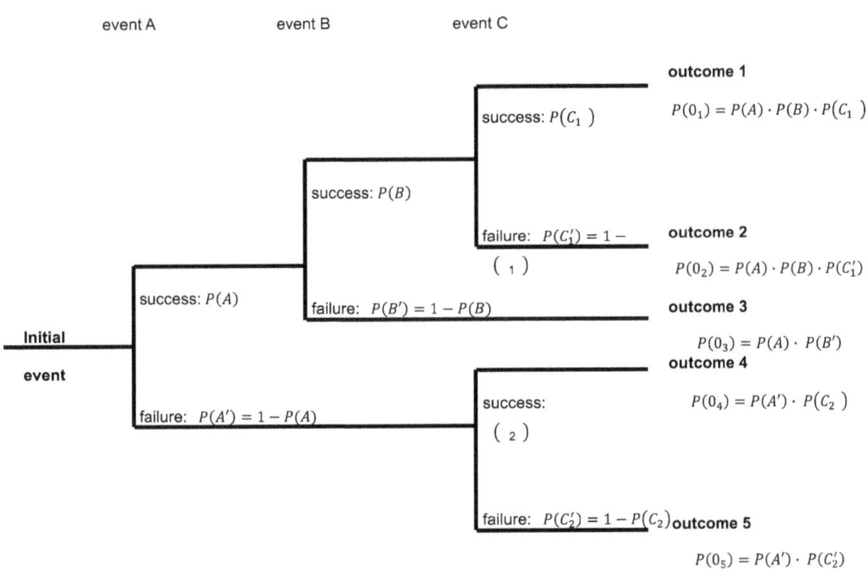

FIGURE 4.2 An example of an event tree.

Source: Own elaboration.

The ETA method also has its limitations, which include the following (Tejaswi and Samuel, 2017):

- An inability to apply to complex processes;
- Accurate identification of the initiating event is required; if the event is not identified, it can lead to misleading results.

Although FTA and ETA methods in risk analysis are primarily associated with strictly engineering problems, they are also used in the banking, finance, business management, and economic research sectors (Table 4.2).

4.2 IT tools, software-supporting environmental risk analysis, databases, data engineering and big data

Many programmes are available on the market that support risk analysis through different methods. However, this subsection focuses on integrated environments that combine many different tools, including those used in the financial sector. A description of selected environments is presented here:

- ALD Software Suite
- Relyence Tool Suite
- Isograph Reliability Workbench
- Kyriba Enterprise Liquidity Management Platform
- MX.3
- D&B Finance Analytics

4.2.1 ALD Software Suite

ALD Software Suite has been used to analyse safety and reliability in many leading entities, including THALES, BAE Systems, Lockheed Martin, NASA, MBDA, SAGEM and more (ALD, 2022a). Table 4.3 provides information about the modules in the package with a brief description.

4.2.2 Relyence Tool Suite

The Relyence Reliability Suite is a complete set of analytical tools and services for risk management, designed for many industries, including aerospace, automotive, defence, health, mining, telecommunications and others. Table 4.4 shows the basic modules available in the package.

4.2.3 Isograph Reliability Workbench

Isograph Reliability Workbench provides an integrated environment to support risk analysis. The use of an integrated database ensures a high degree of security

TABLE 4.3 Main ALD Software Suite modules

Module	*Description*
RAM Commander	Reliability and safety software that covers engineering tasks related to reliability of electronic, electromechanical and mechanical systems. RAM Commander modules: Reliability Prediction, RBD, Fault Tree Analysis, Event Tree Analysis, FMECA and Testability Analysis, Process & Design FMEA and more.
FavoWeb	FavoWeb FRACAS is a web-based and user-configurable Failure Reporting, Analysis and Corrective Action System (FRACAS) of ALD Software that captures information about equipment or a process throughout its life cycle, from design to production, testing and customer support. ALD also provides FavoWeb as a cloud-based SaaS application.
D-LCC	Life Cycle Cost (LCC) analysis and Total Cost of Ownership evaluation are the basis for decision-making for various industries and equipment: from IT systems to submarines. LCC analyses the total ownership costs of various design alternatives and system components over the projected life cycle of a system.
SCAT	Sneak Circuit Analysis Tool (SCAT) automatically identifies potential sneak paths, power-to-power ties and design concerns. It focuses on portions of the circuitry, such as a circuit card assembly or a subsystem, power distribution or complete designs.

Source: ALD, 2022a, 2022b.

TABLE 4.4 Main components of the Sequence Tool Suite

Module	*Description*
FMEA	Failure mode and effects analysis
FAULT TREE	Fault tree analysis for risk assessment
RBD	Reliability block diagram modelling
WEIBULL	Life data analysis using Weibull techniques
FRACAS	Failure reporting, analysis and corrective action system
RELIABILITY PREDICTION	Standards-based failure rate and MTBF analysis
MAINTAINABILITY PREDICTION	Maintainability analysis based on mil-hdbk-472
ALT	Accelerated life testing analysis

Source: Relyence, 2022.

TABLE 4.5 Main modules of Isograph's Reliability Workbench

Module	*Description*
Reliability Prediction	Predicts the reliability of electronic and mechanical components using MIL-217, Quanterion 217 Plus, SN29500, IEC 61709, FIDES, Telcordia TR/SR, IEC TR 62380, GJB299C and NSWC.
FMECA	Full framework and reporting facilities to allow users to construct FMECAs and FMEAs to MIL-STD-1629A, GJB 1391–92, BS 5760 Part 5, AIAG & VDA, SAE J1739, ARP5580 and similar standards as well as customise the FMEA or FMECA to the user's requirements.
RBD	A powerful system reliability analysis tool that allows reliability block diagram analyses to be performed in an integrated environment.
FaultTree+	Provides CCF analysis, importance analysis, uncertainty and sensitivity analysis facilities. The event tree model may be created independently of the fault tree model or may use the gate results of fault tree analysis as the source of event tree probabilities.
Weibull Analysis	Used to analyse historical failure data and produce failure distributions that will be used as inputs to the failure models used in a fault tree analysis or a reliability block diagram (RBD) analysis.
Markov Analysis	Exhibits strong dependencies between component failures.
Reliability Growth	Measures how a system's reliability changes over time during the testing process. The discovery of system failures leads to system improvements during testing and debugging. Test data is analysed using a reliability growth model to demonstrate how reliability is improving.
Reliability Allocation	Reliability allocation sets reliability goals for individual subsystems to meet a system reliability target. Reliability values may be allocated using a variety of methods based on complexity, criticality, achievable reliability or other factors that are deemed appropriate.
System Safety Assessment	Provides the framework for recording the hazards and failures associated with a system and demonstrating that the resulting safety requirements are met. Failures may be linked to probabilistic verification models such as fault trees, RBDs, Markov models and FMECAs in an integrated environment.

Source: Isograph, 2022.

and reliability. Table 4.5 provides brief information about the main modules in the package.

4.2.4 Kyriba Enterprise Liquidity Management Platform

The Kyriba Enterprise Liquidity Management Platform offers solutions that ensure transparency, control, productivity and financial decision-making based on reliable

TABLE 4.6 Main modules of the Kyriba Enterprise Liquidity Management Platform

Module	*Description*
Treasury Management System	Control of different bank accounts Protect against fraud Manage in-house-banking Financial transactions management
Payments	Improving overall payment efficiencies and, further, reducing opportunities for fraud
Connectivity	Cloud connectivity to all internal systems and financial partners
Working Capital	Payment system across 195 programmes in 27 currencies for suppliers in 86 countries around the world and trusted by seven major financial institutions
FX Risk Management	Toolkits to collect data from ERP systems and spreadsheets for the analysis of exposures and reliable risk analysis

Source: Kyriba, 2022.

TABLE 4.7 Main modules of MX.3

Module	*Description*
Sales and Trading	Risk-based pricing and structuring to real-time portfolio and P&L analysis
Treasury	Covers all services connected with managing funding, liquidity and banking book risk management
Enterprise Risk Management	Management of market, credit, XVA and liquidity risk with a particular focus on FRTB, CVA capital charge, SA-CCR and cleared and bilateral OTC margining regulatory solutions
Operations and Finance	Toolkit to high automation along the full processing cycle of bilateral and cleared trades
Investment Management	Solution that allows investment managers to monitor their positions, risk, cash and security inventories in real-time

Source: Murex, 2022.

and credible data. Entities gain access to new products and services combined with the integration of the entire enterprise with banks, ERP systems, third-party systems as well as internal datasets. A description of the platform modules is presented in Table 4.6.

4.2.5 MX.3

MX.3 is a third-generation integration platform serving more than 57,000 users: banks, asset managers, insurance companies, pension funds, hedge funds, corporations and companies in more than 60 countries. A description of the platform modules is presented in Table 4.7.

TABLE 4.8 Key D&B Finance Analytics modules

Module	*Description*
Credit Information	The platform also makes it possible to monitor customers' current situation and react quickly if necessary. It also allows for comprehensive customer portfolio management.
Receivables Management	Supports invoicing, payment, recovery and cash flow management processes. Enables automation of selected procedures by acting according to predefined scenarios, in line with risk-based strategies.

Source: D&B, 2022.

4.2.6 D&B Finance Analytics

D&B Finance Analytics is a platform based on the D&B Data Cloud database and supported by artificial intelligence systems. It is a comprehensive solution that improves the financial operability of the company and allows to reduce operating costs, thanks to the high automation of activities. At the same time, it enables easy risk management, increased operational efficiency and overall improvement of business efficiency. A description of the platform modules is presented in Table 4.8.

4.3 The panel data analysis and multivariate regression model in finding relationships among types of banks and the impact of environmental factors on banks' risk management and modelling process on sustainable value

The report of the Centre of Sustainable Finance (CCSF, 2016) presents information on the tools and techniques used to assess environmental risk by banks, financial institutions and insurance companies. The model approach (at various stages of implementation) was recorded for four entities, and detailed information is presented in Table 4.9.

A characteristic feature of the models used by banks and financial and insurance institutions is their closed and internal character. They are primarily used within analytical units for specific applications. Their design is often adjusted and adapted to the current economic and social situation as well as the requirements of market regulators (Basel III (Poppensieker et al., 2018) and IFRS 9 (Maggi et al., 2017)).

The value-at-risk (VaR) measure is one of the universal tools used by banks and financial institutions. It is often one of the components of internal risk models (Trenca, 2009).

TABLE 4.9 Use of selected models by financial institutions and banks

Country	*Entity*	*Application*
Germany	Global investors and Allianz Climate Solutions	Firm-level modelling of carbon and energy regulation under different scenarios
India	YES BANK	Trucost's environmentally extended input-output model (EEIO) and the India Natural Capital Model, commissioned by GIZ and BMZ
South Africa	Santam	Scenario analysis and systems models
Global	S&P Global Ratings and Swiss Re	Probabilistic modelling, with sovereign credit risk analysis

Source: Own elaboration according to CCSF, 2016.

4.3.1 Value-at-risk (VAR)

Value-at-risk (VaR) is the aggregate measure of risk, the largest probable loss the company will incur over a given period with a given level of confidence. Therefore, this measure represents the maximum amount (risk value) an investor may lose in a given period with a certain probability (Varcholová and Rimarčík, 2003). This measure has become an essential risk management tool for financial institutions (Abad et al., 2014).

In the literature on the subject, many studies can be found related to methods for determining VaR, the most common of which include the following (Manganelli and Engle, 2001; Abad et al., 2014):

- Nonparametric methods: historical simulation, nonparametric density estimation methods;
- Parametric method: volatility models, density functions, higher-order conditional time-varying moments;
- Semi-parametric methods: volatility-weight historical simulation, filtered historical simulation, CAViaR model, extreme value theory, Monte Carlo method.

Mathematically, the risked value can be written as (Krawczyk, 2006):

$$P\left(V_t \le \left(V_0 - VaR\right)\right) = \alpha \tag{1}$$

where:

V_0—the current value of the portfolio;
V_t—a random variable expressing the value of the portfolio after the period t;
α —the given probability level.

The determination of the VaR shall be as follows:

$$VaR = V_0\left(1 - e^{\theta(\alpha)}\right)\sqrt{t} \tag{2}$$

$$\theta(\alpha) = \mu - \lambda\sigma \tag{3}$$

where:
μ —the average rate of return on the distribution;
λ —the distribution function of the normal distribution for a given level of significance α ;
σ —the standard deviation of the rate of return.

The above formulae show that the value of the VaR for a given probability level α VaR can also be recorded as (Yanenkova et al., 2021):

$$VaR^{\alpha} = EL_{\alpha} + UL_{\alpha} \tag{4}$$

where:
EL_{α} —expected loss, the expected loss in the event of default by the borrower;
UL_{α} —unexpected loss, deviation from the average expected loss level (the degree of risk of the loan portfolio).

The value can be calculated using the formula: EL_{α}

$$EL_{\alpha} = \sum_{i=1}^{N}\left(PD_i \cdot CD_i \cdot \left(1 - RR_i\right)\right) \tag{5}$$

where:
PD_i —probability of default, the probability that a contractor fails to meet the terms of a contract within a specified period;
CD_i —credit exposure, the value of assets at risk at the time of default;
RR_i —recovery rate, the amount of loss compensation that can be recovered in the event of default by the borrower through the exercise of guarantees, collateral, and so on.

In turn, UL_{α} , is determined as follows:

$$UL_{\alpha} = VaR^{\alpha} - EL_{\alpha} \tag{6}$$

The advantages of the VaR method include (Krawczyk, 2006):

- universality, enabling direct comparisons of risks in different business areas;
- estimation of the probability of a loss greater than the assumed amount;
- consideration of interdependencies of price changes of various assets, which makes it possible to measure the degree of risk reduction resulting from diversification.

In contrast, the following are considered disadvantages of VaR (Macroption, 2022):

- A false sense of security;
- VaR does not measure the worst-case loss;
- Difficulty in applying to large portfolios;
- Lack of additivity of VaR;
- Dependence on input data and assumptions made;
- Different VaR methods lead to different results.

The first of the disadvantages relates to the nature of the risk and its highly subjective assessment. Others are mostly based on the unpredictability of future events and their scale. It is also difficult to blame the method for the insufficient quality of the results in the case of the lack of up-to-date data or its inaccuracy, which are the basis for the analysis. On the other hand, in the case of the problem of rapid obsolescence of VaR assessments (Damodaran, 2007), especially when extrapolating it to future periods, its quality can be improved using, for example, the method based on the means of the square root rule (Blake et al., 2000), GARCH(1,1) model or extreme value theory (Odening and Hinrichs, 2003)

The undeniable disadvantage of VaR, however, is the fact that the selected method of its estimation has a direct impact on the obtained results. To increase the accuracy of the risk level assessment, especially for institutions using high confidence levels in their models, a conditional value-at-risk (CVaR) (Dargiri et al., 2013) can be used. Its additional advantage over VaR is also its greater ease of application to investment portfolios (Sarykalin et al., 2014).

4.3.2 *Probability of default model (PD)*

In the construction of the measure EL_α (expected loss), a measure of the probability of debtor insolvency (PD) is used. For its estimation, logistic regression is often used. For such a model, the logarithm of the odds ratio is defined as (Jacobs, 2021):

$$ln\left(\frac{P(\omega_1 \mid x)}{P(\omega_2 \mid x)}\right) = \theta^T x \tag{7}$$

where:

$x = (x_1,\ldots,x_k) \in R^k$ —*k*-dimensional explanatory variable matrix;

$\theta = (\theta_1,\ldots,\theta_k) \in R^k$ —*k*-dimensional parameter vector.

It is assumed that $P(\omega_1 \mid x) + P(\omega_2 \mid x) = 1$ where:

$$P(\omega_1 \mid x) = \frac{1}{1 + \exp(-\theta^T x)} = \sigma(-\theta^T x) \tag{8}$$

The function $\sigma(-\theta^T x)$ is the same as a logistic sigmoid taking any real value in the range $\langle 0,1 \rangle$.

For the estimation of the parameters of such a model, the highest reliability method is used, for which the formula gives the reliability function:

$$P(y_1,\ldots,y_N \mid \theta) = \prod_{n=1}^{N} \left(\sigma(-\theta^T x_n)\right)^{y_n} \left(1 - (-\theta^T x_n)\right)^{1-y_n} \tag{9}$$

A negative logarithmic likelihood function (or cross-entropy error) is also used to facilitate computational calculations:

$$L(\theta) = -\sum_{n=1}^{N} y_n ln\left(\sigma(-\theta^T x_n)\right) + (1 - y_n) ln\left(1 - \sigma(-\theta^T x_n)\right), \tag{10}$$

whose minimum value is reached with respect to θ using Newton's iterative method (scheme).

In line with the guidance provided by the methodological study created by 16 banks gathered around UNEP FI and the Acclimatise consulting firm (UNEP FI, 2019) for borrowers with climate change risks (agriculture, energy sector), a recalculation of the PD value is recommended. Its value may vary depending on the assumed time range (the '20s and '40s of the 21st century) and the adopted climate scenarios (2°C and 4°C). The calculations shall specifically acknowledge (NGFS, 2020):

- Estimates of climate change impact (temperature and precipitation) on production (agriculture and energy) and prices (agriculture) by economic sector and region/country, based on relevant (peer-reviewed) studies;
- Estimates of the impact of extreme weather events on production losses (the percentage of crop loss in the agricultural sector, a downturn in electricity production or reduced levels in the energy sector).

The impact of these changes and phenomena will be equivalent to the percentage loss of income for all borrowers within a given sector and region/country.

Similar recommendations were also made for the loan-to-value ratio (LTV) meter.

4.3.3 *Loan-to-value ratio (LTV)*

The LTV ratio can be used to determine the risk of granting different secured credit products and is determined according to the formula (Wong et al., 2011):

$$LTV = \frac{MA}{APV}, \tag{10}$$

where:

MA—mortgage amount;
APV—appraised property value.

Its essence is based on comparing the loan amount to the collateral value. The lower its value, the higher the level of collateral (usually the value of a real estate) concerning the loan value and the lower the level of risk for the financial institution.

The way to determine the optimal LTV is discussed in the paper by Lin (2014). In turn, the article by Bian et al. (2018) provides an analytical link between the value of the property and the LTV meter, indicating that it is being burdened with the risk of an underestimation of the credit risk.

According to the methodological guidance in the Network for Greening the Financial System (NGFS, 2020) report, the value of the LTV measure, like PD, needs to be updated. It estimates the impact of extreme climate events affecting the property value. Their impact on the value of properties (in the bank's portfolio) by sector is then calculated, which is the basis for analysing the change in the bank's LTV level. The bank calculates the average remaining mortgage term for its portfolio and then multiplies this value by the probability of the risks occurring during this period.

4.4 The role of simulation methods in environmental risk modelling in banking

In a paper by (Wu and Olson, 2013), the authors conducted a broad literature review on using simulation methods in risk assessment. They have identified the following types of application directions:

1. Engineering risk analysis based on optimisation tools;
2. Performance assessment under uncertainty;
3. Decision-making and industry modelling in uncertainty;
4. Portfolio management;
5. Game-based risk analysis;
6. Decisions on credit scoring;
7. Data mining in corporate risk management;
8. Agent-based supply chain risk management;
9. Other decision-making methods and corporate risk management applications.

Within the banking sector, simulation methods are widely used:

1. In the analysis of the resilience of the banking system to unpredictable events:
    - Barnhill and Souto (2009) presented a portfolio simulation methodology to assess the correlated effects of market risk, private and sovereign credit risk and interbank insolvency risk. To this end, they analysed 28 Brazilian

banks under two scenarios. Research shows that banks with more diversified government portfolios and business and consumer loans are generally more profitable and better suited to potential government insolvency.

- In the paper by Kyritsis et al. (2015), the authors, using simulation methods, examined the sustainability and probability of survival of firms and banks in Greece in the case of prolonged crises in the post-2007 and post-2011 periods. The study was complemented by DEA analysis to determine the efficiency of banks and selected firms under different scenarios.
- In contrast, Chavarria et al. (2014) used a numerical simulation of the banking system to identify its vulnerabilities, which is helpful in assessing the validity of different potential responses from the regulator's perspective. An example based on the banking system of a Latin American country was used to demonstrate the advantages of this approach. It was confirmed that the probability of developing cascades of bank failures is proportional to the extent to which banks are linked within the network. At the same time, the authors pointed out that the examination of the banking system by analysing individual bank failures can give a misleading picture of the resilience of the entire system.
- Gleeson et al. (2013) presented a simulation-based method for event analysis in banking network models, allowing for the initiation of cascades when one or more banks become insolvent and including the identification of liquidity risk effects. Theoretical results were compared to Monte Carlo simulations and can be used to assess the stability of a given banking network topology.
- The study of the Czech Central Bank (Hausenblas et al., 2012) assessed the contamination resilience of the Czech banking system, considering the size and structure of interbank exposures and the balance sheet and regulatory characteristics of individual banks in the network. The simulation results suggest that the potential for contamination due to credit losses on interbank exposures was rather limited.

2 To conduct stress tests of banking systems:

- The Bank of Finland's report (Leinonen, 2005), consisting of 11 separate studies, analyses payment and settlement systems using simulation techniques, mostly based on the BoF-PSS1 or BoF-PSS2 payment and settlement system simulators provided by the bank. The studies focused on ensuring liquidity requirements, settlement speed, congestion and methods for resolving it, liquidity economics, systemic risk and the impact of shocks on system performance. The research involved banking systems located in several countries.

3 To improve the effectiveness of the measures, methods and models used in banks:

- In Wang et al. (2017), the authors tested the effectiveness of using the Monte Carlo method to determine VaR for the Chinese banking sector. This method proved to be effective in the absence of unexpected market crashes.

4.5 The limitations of environmental risk modelling—the IT and quantitative methods perspective

According to Gurjar and Mohan (2002), the limitations of quantitative methods used in QRA relate to five aspects, such as the following:

- Completeness—the inability of a mathematical model to fully describe a real phenomenon;
- Model quality—it is not possible to thoroughly verify the quality of the models;
- Accuracy/uncertainty—problem with access to data, their rapid obsolescence, the appearance of new factors not included in models and that influence the probability of occurrence of phenomena;
- Reproducibility—many quantitative methods used in risk assessment require considerable experience from the researcher, and therefore, the results obtained are subject to a certain degree of subjectivity, resulting in low reproducibility;
- Incomprehensibility—results obtained by QRA methods are often difficult to interpret and therefore difficult to implement and use.

It should be noted that the human factor often comes into play when analysing the above limitations. According to Renn (1985) and Stroie (2011), it is important as far as it defines the exact scope of the risk analysis to be carried out as well as its degree of acceptability.

At the same time, certain limitations may result from the specificity of the problem being analysed. For example, Molnar et al., 2021 focused on the problem of limitations of QRA methods concerning the pharmaceutical sector (production of active pharmaceutical ingredients) and indicated that these might arise from the following:

- Selection of active ingredients for analysis;
- Management of toxicity data;
- Specifications of habitats;
- Length of the exposition;
- Overestimating the model under a worst-case scenario;
- Ignoring the effects of mixing different components.

For this reason, it is essential to use IT tools appropriately adapted to the assigned problem (Hillson, 2020; Kumar and Fragkos, 2020). As the tools used must often be adapted to the individual requirements of the entities, they involve high purchase costs and, due to the complexity of the analyses, also maintenance costs.

References

Abad, P., Benito, S., and López, C. (2014). A Comprehensive Review of Value at Risk Methodologies. *The Spanish Review of Financial Economics* 12: 15–32. https://doi.org/10.1016/j.srfe.2013.06.001

ALD. (2022a). *ALD Reliability and Safety Tools*. https://aldservice.com/Reliability-products/ald-reliability-and-safety-tools-overview.html (accessed: 24.05.2022).

ALD. (2022b). *ALD Software Architecture*. www.aldsoftware.com/download/ald/White Papers/ALD_Software_Architecture.pdf (accessed: 24.05.2022).

Aven, Terje. (2003). *Foundation of Risk Analysis*. West Sussex, England: John Wiley & Sons.

Bakeli, Tarik Hafidi, and Adil Alaoui. (2020). *Fault Tree Analysis (FTA) Based Approach for Construction Projects Safety Risk Management*. Proceedings of the 5th NA International Conference on Industrial Engineering and Operations Management Detroit, MI, USA, 10–14, August. www.ieomsociety.org/detroit2020/papers/434.pdf (accessed: 30.05.2022).

Barnhill, Theodore Jr, and Souto Marcos. (2009). *Systemic Bank Risk in Brazil: A Comprehensive Simulation of Correlated Market, Credit, Sovereign, and Interbank Risks*. International Monetary Fund. www.elibrary.imf.org/downloadpdf/books/071/20952-9781484368589-en/ch008.pdf (accessed: 22.05.2022).

Bian, Xun, Lin, Zhenguo, and Liu, Yingchun. (2018). House Price, Loan-to-Value Ratio and Credit Risk. *Journal of Banking & Finance* 92: 1–12. https://doi.org/10.1016/j.jbankfin.2018.04.006

Blake, David, Cairns, Andrew, and Dowd, Kavin. (2000). Extrapolating VaR by the Square-Root Rule. *Researchgate.net*. www.researchgate.net/publication/238231953_Extrapolating_VaR_by_the_Square-Root_Rule (accessed: 29.06.2022).

Borysiewicz, Mieczysław, Andrzej, Furtek, and Sławomir, Potempski. (2000). *Poradnik Metod ocen ryzyka związanego z niebezpiecznymi instalacjami procesowymi*. Otwock and Świerk: Instytut Energii Atomowej.

CCSF. (2016). *Environmental Risk Analysis by Financial Institutions—A Review of Global Practice. An Input Paper for the G20 Green Finance Study Group*. Cambridge Institute for Sustainability Leadership. www.cisl.cam.ac.uk/system/files/documents/environmental-risk-analysis.pdf (accessed: 20.05.2022).

Chavarria, Esteban, Cifuentes, Arturo, and Hawas, Francisco Javier. (2014). *A Numerical Simulation Approach to Study Systemic Risk in Banking Systems*. https://dx.doi.org/10.2139/ssrn.2539020

Chu, Wang, and Feng, Yanli. (2009). *Fault Tree Based Architectural Analysis for E-Business Systems*. Proceedings of the Second Symposium International Computer Science and Computational Technology (ISCSCT '09), Huangshan, China, 26–28 December, 052–057. http://citeseerx.ist.psu.edu/viewdoc/download?doi=10.1.1.404.828&rep=rep1&type=pdf (accessed: 15.05.2022).

D&B. (2022). *D&B Finance Analytics*. May 30. www.dnb.com/products/finance-credit-risk/dnb-finance-analytics.html\.

Damodaran, Aswath. (2007). Value at Risk (VaR). *Stern.nyu.edu*. https://pages.stern.nyu.edu/~adamodar/pdfiles/valrisk/ch7.pdf (accessed: 29.06.2022).

Dargiri, M. N., Shamsabadi, H. A., Thim, C. K., Rasiah, D., and Sayedy, B. (2013). Value-at-Risk and Conditional Value-at-Risk Assessment and Accuracy Compliance in Dynamic of Malaysian Industries. *Journal of Applied Sciences* 13(7): 974–983. https://dx.doi.org/10.3923/jas.2013.974.983

Gatfaoui, Hayette. (2004). *From Fault Tree to Credit Risk Assessment: A Case Study*. EERI Research Paper Series 5. https://econwpa.ub.uni-muenchen.de/econ-wp/em/papers/0509/0509002.pdf (accessed: 15.05.2022).

Gleeson, James P., Hurd, T. R., Melnik, Sergey, and Hackett, Adam. (2013). Systemic Risk in Banking Networks Without Monte Carlo Simulation. In *Advances in Network Analysis and Its Applications*, R. Kranakis (ed.). Berlin Heidelberg: Springer, pp. 27–56. https://dx.doi.org/10.1007/978-3-642-30904-5_2

Gordon, Dan. (2014). Using Incident Response Trees as a Tool for Risk Management of Online Financial Services. *Risk Analysis* 34(9). https://dx.doi.org/10.1111/risa.12195

Gurjar, Bhola Ram, and Mohan, Manju. (2002). Environmental Risk Analysis: Problems and Perspectives in Different Countries. *RISK: Health, Safety & Environment* 13(1): 3. https://scholars.unh.edu/risk/vol13/iss1/3/ (accessed: 15.05.2022).

Hao, Xiaoling. (2013). *Operational Risk Control of Commercial Banks based on Bayesian Network*. Proceedings of the 2013 the International Conference on Education Technology and Information System (ICETIS 2013), Sanya, China, 21–22, June. https://doi.org/10.2991/icetis-13.2013.209

Hausenblas, Václav, Kubicová, Ivana, and Lešanovská, Jitka. (2012). *Contagion Risk in the Czech Financial System: A Network Analysis and Simulation Approach*. CNB Working Paper Series 14. www.cnb.cz/export/sites/cnb/en/economic-research/.galleries/research_publications/cnb_wp/cnbwp_2012_14.pdf (accessed: 12.05.2022).

Henriques de Gusmão, Ana Paula, Mendonça Silva, Maisa, Poleto, Thiago, Camara e Silva, Lucio, and Cabral Seixas Costa, Ana Paula. (2018). Cybersecurity Risk Analysis Model Using Fault Tree Analysis and Fuzzy Decision Theory. *International Journal of Information Management* 43: 248–260. https://doi.org/10.1016/j.ijinfomgt.2018.08.008

Hillson, David. (2020). Quantitative Risk Analysis: Strengths and Weaknesses. *multibriefs.com*, December 03. http://exclusive.multibriefs.com/content/quantitative-risk-analysis-strengths-and-weaknesses/business-management-services-risk-management (accessed: 15.05.2022).

Hong, Eun-Soo, Lee, In-Mo, Shin, Hee-Soon, Nam, Seok-Woo, and Kong Jung-Sik. (2009). Quantitative Risk Evaluation based on Event Tree Analysis Technique: Application to the Design of Shield TBM. *Tunnelling and Underground Space Technology* 24: 269–277. https://dx.doi.org/10.1016/j.tust.2008.09.004

Isograph. (2022). *Reliability Workbench*. www.isograph.com/software/reliability-workbench/ (accessed: 24.05.2022).

Jacobs, Michael Jr. (2021). Validation of Corporate Probability of Default Models Considering Alternative Use Cases. *International Journal of Financial Studies* 9(4): 63. https://doi.org/10.3390/ijfs9040063

Kabir, Sohag. (2017). An Overview of Fault Tree Analysis and Its Application in Model Based Dependability Analysis. *Expert Systems with Applications* 77: 114–135. http://dx.doi.org/10.1016/j.eswa.2017.01.058

Kim, Myong-Hee, Jin, Eun-Ji, Park, and Man-Gon. (2013). Fault Tree Analysis and Fault Modes and Effect Analysis for Security Evaluation of IC Card Payment Systems. *Journal of Korea Multimedia Society* 16(1): 87–99. http://dx.doi.org/10.9717/kmms.2013.16.1.087

Kim, So Young, Kim, Myong Hee, and Park, Man-Gon. (2015). Fault Tree Analysis and Failure Mode Effects Analysis for Software Security Improvements in Mobile Banking Information Systems. *Journal of Korea Multimedia Society* 18(11): 1342–1350. http://dx.doi.org/10.9717/kmms.2015.18.11.1342

Krawczyk, Ewa. (2006). Zastosowanie modelu ryzyka Value at Risk (VaR) opartego na metodzie Monte Carlo do rynku nieruchomości. *Zeszyty Naukowe SGGW—Ekonomika i Organizacja Gospodarki Żywnościowej* 58: 117–133. https://sj.wne.sggw.pl/pdf/EIOGZ_2006_n58_s117.pdf (accessed: 20.05.2022).

Kumar, Santhosh, and Fragkos, Grigorios. (2020). Quantitative Vs Qualitative Cyber Risk Management Approach. *digital14.com*, November 30. www.digital14.com/insights/blogs/cyber-risk-management (accessed: 16.05.2022).

Kyriba. (2022). *The Kyriba Enterprise Liquidity Management Platform*. www.kyriba.com/resource/optimize-liquidity-reduce-risk-unlock-growth/ (accessed: 30.05.2022).

Kyritsis, Costas, Rekleitis, Panagiotis, and Trivelas, Panagiotis. (2015). Simulation for the Stability and DEA Risk Analysis of Greek Banks within a Prolonged Duration of the Debt Crisis. *Procedia Economics and Finance* 33: 376–387. https://dx.doi.org/10.1016/S2212-5671(15)01722-0

Lacasse, Suzanne. (2008). Event Tree Analysis of Åknes Rock Slide Hazard. In *Proceedings of the 4th Canadian Conference on Geohazards: From Causes to Management*, J. Locat, D. Perret, D. Turmel, D. Demers, et S. Leroueil (eds.). Québec: Presse de l'Université, p. 594.

Leinonen, Harry (ed.). (2005). Liquidity, Risks and Speed in Payment and Settlement Systems—A Simulation Approach. *Bank of Finland Studies* E31. https://helda.helsinki.fi/bof/bitstream/handle/123456789/9355/118263.pdf?sequence=1&isAllowed=y (accessed: 22.05.2022).

LimbleCMMS. (2021). *What is Fault Tree Analysis and How to Perform It.* https://limblecmms.com/blog/fault-tree-analysis/ (accessed: 10.05.2022).

Lin, Li. (2014). Optimal Loan-to-Value Ratio and the Efficiency Gains of Default. *Annals of Finance* 10: 47–69. https://doi.org/10.1007/s10436-013-0232-7

Macroption. (2022). *Value At Risk (VAR) Limitations and Disadvantages.* www.macroption.com/value-at-risk-var-limitations-disadvantages/#so-many-problems-should-you-still-use-var (accessed: 23.05.2022).

Maggi, Filippo, Natale, Alfonso, Pepanides, Theodore, Risso, Enrico, and Schröck, Gerhard. (2017). IFRS 9: A Silent Revolution in Banks' Business Models. *Mckinsey.com*, April 13. www.mckinsey.com/business-functions/risk-and-resilience/our-insights/ifrs-9-a-silent-revolution-in-banks-business-models (accessed: 18.05.2022).

Manganelli, Simone, and Engle, Robert F. (2001). *Value at Risk Models in Finance.* ECB Working Paper 75. www.ecb.europa.eu/pub/pdf/scpwps/ecbwp075.pdf (accessed: 12.05.2022).

Molnar, Eva, Fodor, Istvan, Svigruha, Reka, and Pirger Zsolt. (2021). Issues, Challenges, Directives, and Limitations Concerning the Improvement of Environmental Risk Assessment of Pharmaceutically Active Compounds. *Ecotoxicology and Environmental Safety* 216: 112212. https://doi.org/10.1016/j.ecoenv.2021.112212

Murex. (2022). *MX.3.* www.murex.com/en (accessed: 30.05.2022).

NGFS. (2020). *Overview of Environmental Risk Analysis by Financial Institutions.* Network for Greening the Financial System, September. www.ngfs.net/sites/default/files/medias/documents/overview_of_environmental_risk_analysis_by_financial_institutions.pdf (accessed: 23.05.2022).

Odening, Martin, and Hinrichs, Jan. (2003). Using Extreme Value Theory to Estimate Value-at-Risk. *Agricultural Finance Review* 63(1): 55–73. https://dx.doi.org/10.1108/00215000380001141

Poppensieker, Thomas, Schneider, Roland, Schneider, Sebastian, and Stackebrandt, Lennart. (2018). Basel III: The Final Regulatory Standard. *Mckinsey.com*, April 18. www.mckinsey.com/business-functions/risk-and-resilience/our-insights/basel-iii-the-final-regulatory-standard (accessed: 18.05.2022).

Relyence. (2022). *The Relyence Product Line Up.* https://relyence.com/products/ (accessed: 24.05.2022).

Renn, Ortwin. (1985). Risk Analysis: Scope and Limitations. In *Regulating Industrial Risk: Science, Hazards and Public Protection*, H. J. Otway, and M. Peltu (eds.). London: Butterworths, pp. 111–127. https://elib.uni-stuttgart.de/bitstream/11682/7340/1/ren80.pdf (accessed: 20.05.2022).

Robu, Brîndușa Mihaela, Căliman, Florentina Anca, Bețianu, Camelia, and Gavrilescu, Maria. (2007). Methods and Procedures for Environmental Risk Assessment. *Environmental*

Engineering and Management Journal 6(6): 573–592. www.researchgate.net/publication/322921157_Methods_and_procedures_for_environmental_risk_assessment (accessed: 6.05.2022).

Rusin, Andrzej, and Wojaczek, Adam. (2012). Application of Fault Tree Analysis in the Maintenance Intervals Planning for Power Unit Systems. *Archiwum Energetyki* 152(3–4): 95–106. https://yadda.icm.edu.pl/baztech/element/bwmeta1.element.baztech-4ca2cb31-5dc3-4835-9df4-5fbad27ad0c7/c/Rusin.pdf (accessed: 15.05.2022).

Santos, Joost R., Yu, Krista Danielle S., Pagsuyoin, Sheree Ann T., and Tan, Raymond R. (2014). Time-Varying Disaster Recovery Model for Interdependent Economic Systems Using Hybrid Input–Output and Event Tree Analysis. *Economic Systems Research* 26(1): 60–80. https://dx.doi.org/10.1080/09535314.2013.872602

Sarykalin, Sergey, Serraino, Gaia, and Uryasev, Stan. (2014). Value-at-Risk vs. Conditional Value-at-Risk in Risk Management and Optimization. *INFORMS TutORials in Operations Research*. https://doi.org/10.1287/educ.1080.0052

Stroie, Elena Ramona. (2011). Advantages and Disadvantages of Quantitative and Qualitative Information Risk Approaches. *Chinese Business Review* 10(12): 1106–1110. www.davidpublisher.com/Public/uploads/Contribute/555d6fdde07cc.pdf (accessed: 15.05.2022).

Tejaswi, D., and Samuel, Christopher. (2017). Techniques for Environmental Risk Assessment: A Review. *Rasayan Journal of Chemistry* 10(2): 499–506. http://dx.doi.org/10.7324/RJC.2017.1021657

Trenca, Ioan. (2009). The Use in Banks of Value at Risk Method in Market Risk Management. *Analele Ştiinłifice Ale Universitălii "Alexandru Ioan Cuza"* 56: 186–196. http://anale.feaa.uaic.ro/anale/resurse/16_F12_Trenca.pdf (accessed: 18.05.2022).

UNEP FI. (2019). *Annual Overview 07/2018–06/2019*. www.unepfi.org/wordpress/wp-content/uploads/2019/09/UNEP-FI-Annual-Overview-2019-.pdf (accessed: 22.05.2022).

USACoE. (2018). *Risk Assessment—Quantitative Methods*. www.iwr.usace.army.mil/Portals/70/docs/risk/Risk_Assessment_Quantitative_Methods_dft.pdf?ver=2018-07-03-134519-250 (accessed: 10.05.2022).

Varcholová, Tatiana, and Rimarčík, Marián. (2003). Value-at-Risk Methods and Models and Their Application. *BIATEC* 11: 32–34. www.nbs.sk/_img/documents/biatec/bia10_03/32_34.pdf (accessed: 18.05.2022).

Wang, Dehong, Song, Jianbo, and Lin, Yongzhao. (2017). Does the VaR Measurement Using Monte-Carlo Simulation Work in China?—Evidence from Chinese Listed Banks. *Journal of Financial Risk Management* 6(1): 66–78. https://dx.doi.org/10.4236/jfrm.2017.61006

Wong, Tak-Chuen, Fong, Tom, Li, Ka-Fai, and Choi, Henry. (2011). Loan-to-Value Ratio as a Macroprudential Tool—Hong Kong's Experience and Cross-Country Evidence. *Systemic Risk, Basel III, Financial Stability and Regulation*. http://dx.doi.org/10.2139/ssrn.1768546

Wu, Desheng Dash, and Olson, David L. (2013). Computational Simulation and Risk Analysis: An Introduction of State of the Art Research. *Mathematical and Computer Modelling* 58(9–13): 1581–1587. https://doi.org/10.1016/j.mcm.2013.07.004

Yanenkova, Iryna, Nehoda, Yuliia, Drobyazko, Svetlana, Zavhorodnii, Andrii, and Berezovska, Lyudmyla. (2021). Modelling of Bank Credit Risk Management Using the Cost Risk Model. *Journal of Risk and Financial Management* 14: 211. https://doi.org/10.3390/jrfm14050211

Ye, Nan. (2019). *The Credit Risk Identification of Commercial Banks in China*. Proceedings of the 2nd International Symposium on Social Science (ISSS 2016), Xi'an City, China, 29–30. November. https://doi.org/10.2991/isss-16.2016.10

5

ENVIRONMENTAL RISK MODELLING AND DECISION-MAKING PROCESSES

Anna Spoz

5.1 The decision-making process in environmental risk modelling in light of selected theories (prescriptive and descriptive decision-making models)

The issue of decision-making is part of the decision theory, which includes the analysis and support of decision-making processes. The decision-making process includes a logically related group of thought operations, arranged in an appropriate order, which allows the assessment of the decision situation and the selection of the most favorable solution variant.

Decision-making conditions that affect the ease of making decisions depend on the type of decision-making situation. In a certain (deterministic) situation, in which the undertaken action clearly determines the result, the decision-maker can predict with great accuracy the effect of the decision made. In conditions of uncertainty due to the inability to determine the factors influencing the decision situation and the probability of their occurrence, the consequences of the decisions made cannot be predicted. Referring to Frank Knight, we have to deal with uncertainty if the calculus of probability cannot be applied in the analysis of an uncertain situation. The last type of decision-making condition relates to risk—that is, to a situation in which the result of actions cannot be precisely predicted and uncertainty is felt. Therefore, risk is the potential volatility of events. Risk arises from making decisions about the future; therefore, actions taken under risk conditions mean making decisions in the absence of complete information.

The factor that triggers the decision-making processes is the problematic situation. Problems that are the subject of decision-making processes can be categorized into well-structured problems and unstructured problems. Structured problems are those that have been quantified so well that mathematical models can be used to solve them. In this case, methods from the area of operations research are applicable,

DOI: 10.4324/9781003310099-5

and the most frequently used instruments include linear programming, dynamic programming, integer programming, game theory, Bayesian decision-making theory, mass service theory, and probability theory.

Unstructured problems are those that, due to the lack of clearly defined, quantitative relationships, require a qualitative approach. In this case, the heuristic method is used. Heuristics are practical methods of conduct based on experience and intuitive assessment of reality. The subjectivism of this method makes it more unreliable, and the adopted solution does not guarantee the achievement of the assumed and optimal results. This group of methods includes brainstorming, synectics, lateral thinking, and the Delphi method.

Each decision-making process consists of several phases, and these phases are defined differently by different authors. Generally, within the decision-making process, we can distinguish the phase of identifying the decision problem, solving the decision problem, making the decision, and implementing the decision (Holska, 2016). Decision-making models, depending on the type of answers provided, can be divided into normative (prescriptive decision-making models) and descriptive-explanatory decision-making models (descriptive decision-making models). Normative decision-making models are based on the assumption that the decision-maker is a rational being and strives to obtain all information that is relevant to the decision-making process and the selection of the best alternative. The evaluation of each of the alternatives is based on two variables—that is, the subjective utility of the assumed results (comparing the expected benefits and the assumed costs) and the estimated probability that the selection of a specific alternative will lead to a specific result (Brown, 1990). Various procedures can be used to estimate the two variables. The need to collect much information and then perform many mathematical calculations makes these models difficult to apply.

In response to the imperfections of normative models, a second group of descriptive decision-making models has emerged. Their purpose is to explain how decisions are actually made and what the actual course of the decision-making process is. In this case, researchers usually adopt the inductive nature of the procedure by describing and explaining the real course of decision-making processes. Within this group of models, we can distinguish between models of limited rationality by focusing on the interpretation of decision-makers' behavior and limitations resulting from human cognitive disabilities and heuristic models characterized by departing from the principles and norms adopted in rational action in order to stimulate creativity (Redziak, 2013).

The prescriptive decision model combines the advantages and minimizes the disadvantages of normative and descriptive models. It leads to the selection of satisfactory decisions with realistic goals but while accounting for the limitations of decision-makers and corresponding to the intuitive ways in which decisions are made by individuals. It is based on a pragmatic value—that is, the ability to facilitate decision-makers in making decisions (Bell et al., 1988)

The environmental risk results from the potential negative impact of changes in the environment (climate change, loss of biodiversity, or environmental pollution) on the activities of entities or invested assets (EBA, 2021). The multitude of factors influencing the emergence of environmental risk and the variety of possible effects of the actions taken make prescriptive multi-criteria models extremely useful in decision-making processes. Decision-making analyses are widely used to identify and solve problems related to the growing importance of ESG factors, especially environmental ones, on the activity of an entity on the market (Zamanifar and Hartmann, 2021).

5.2 The impact of environmental risk on the decision-making process of banks and enterprises

The importance of environmental factors as risk factors for the world economy increases every year. This is confirmed by the Global Risks Report 2021, according to which as many as four of the five major global threats in terms of probability and three of the five most important risks for the global economy in terms of impact are related to the environment and include climate action failure, extreme weather, human environmental damage, biodiversity loss, and natural resources crises (Global Risks Report, 2021). Environmental risk affects, albeit to a different extent, individual market entities (Figure 5.1).

Exposure of business entities to environmental risk is determined by many factors, which can generally be divided into external (geographic location and legal

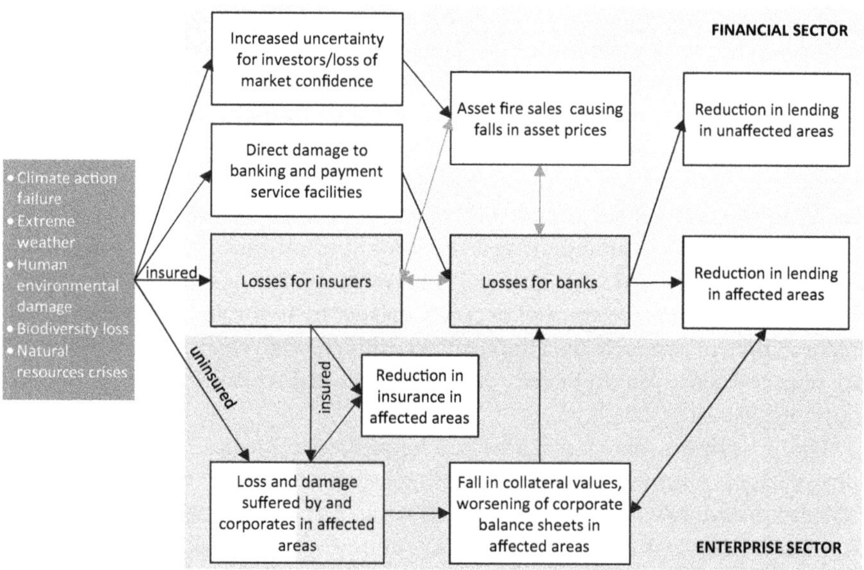

FIGURE 5.1 The impact of environmental risk on entities from the financial sector and enterprises.

Source: Own elaboration based on: Cambridge Centre for Sustainable Finance, 2016.

regulations in the industry in which the economic entity operates) and internal (resulting from the organizational structure of the entity and its business strategy) factors. Due to the interconnection between individual market entities, environmental risk affects economic entities both directly and indirectly. For example, a change in the value of assets held by investors in capital markets may result from both the frequency and intensity of extreme weather phenomena and may be dictated by a change in the preferences of investors investing in pro-ecological projects and/or limiting or eliminating entities from sectors with high environmental harmfulness from their portfolio—for example, mines.

Environmental risk is also increasingly affecting the activities of insurers. On the one hand, the intensity and unpredictability of weather changes increases customer interest in insurance against weather phenomena, thus contributing to an increase in insurers' revenues on this account. On the other hand, the amount and value of claims paid is growing year by year. Enterprises are interested in reducing the risk accompanying the commercial transactions carried out as well as insuring the company's property against losses resulting from unpredictability or intensity of weather phenomena. Losses incurred by entities will translate into profitability and solvency of entities indirectly determining their ability to repay their credit obligations and the possibility of incurring new ones, and therefore, they will also affect entities of the financial sector.

The growing importance of environmental risk on the activities of modern business entities makes its effective identification, valuation, and management increasingly important for their efficient functioning and the creation of shock-resistant business models. Therefore, environmental aspects are increasingly accounted for in the economic decisions made.

5.3 The integration of ESG factors into the decision-making process in the banking sector

Environmental risk is particularly important for financial institutions due to their role as financial intermediaries and equity raising agents (Zioło, 2019). Taking into account the fact that the environmental risks of transmission to financial risks, the correct identification of E&C risk and its subsequent management is extremely important from the point of view of the stability of individual financial institutions and the entire financial sector (NGFS, 2020).

The growing awareness of the importance of environmental risk for the banking sector translates into the activities of its entities. In 2017, the Paris One Planet Summit launched the Network for Greening the Financial System (NGFS). It is an organization associating central banks and supervisory authorities that want to actively contribute to the development of environmental and climate risk management in the financial sector and share best practices in this area (NGFS, 2020). In November 2020, the European Central Bank (ECB) issued the "Guide on Climate-Related and Environmental Risks," which provides guidance on how financial institutions should take into account C&E risks in the process of formulating and implementing a business strategy and entity management model, including risk management.

The study shows that the ECB expects financial institutions to analyze the impact of environmental risk on their business environment and then include the obtained information in their strategy of operation in the short, medium, and long term. The business environment covers a wide range of trends and factors that shape the business conditions in which an institution operates or may operate. These factors include both macroeconomic variables (GDP, inflation) and the competitive environment, policy and applicable legal regulations, and technologies, as well as social (including demographic) and geopolitical changes. All these areas can be affected by environmental risk. Therefore, the ECB expects that financial institutions will map in detail such influences on their business environment and take them into account in the implemented strategy.

The analysis of the impact of environmental factors on the activities of financial institutions should be carried out in the short, medium, and long term. All these three time horizons should be reflected in the adopted business strategy (MAS, 2020).

Institutions are expected to adequately document their climate and environmental risk assessments—for example, by regularly monitoring significant or emerging risks. The way in which institutions will respond to changes in their business environment and the resulting changes in the level of environmental risk over time should translate into the resilience of their business model.

Business strategy is the main tool for positioning an institution in the business environment in order to generate acceptable returns consistent with its risk appetite. The level of environmental risk should be accounted for in the process of determining the risk appetite by an individual. The method of managing environmental risk by bank clients translates into the size of the bank's risk. According to the guidelines, financial institutions should require a client with a higher environmental risk to take appropriate steps to manage the risk within the prescribed period. These activities may include the client's commitment by the bank to develop a sustainable transformation strategy or in cooperation with the client in this regard. The bank may also through its actions (e.g., by reducing the cost of a loan) stimulate customers to take actions aimed at reducing the environmental risk. On the other hand, in relation to customers who improperly manage environmental risk, the bank should consider taking into account the additional cost in the valuation of the loan, the application of credit exposure limits, and reassessment of its relationship with its clients.

At the portfolio level, the bank should develop quantitative and qualitative tools and metrics to monitor and assess exposure to environmental risk. Environmental and climate risk should be integrated into the entity's risk management model, and the assignment of responsibility for its management within the organization should follow the three lines of defense model. The ECB expects that financial institutions for which this risk turns out to be significant will assess and verify the applied stress tests in order to reflect this risk in their baseline and adverse scenarios (ECB, 2020). The bank should develop scenario analysis and stress testing capabilities to assess the impact of significant environmental risk on its risk profile and business strategies and test its resilience to financial losses. The bank should identify and simulate plausible risk scenarios, taking into account the linkages between environmental risk and other types of risk. The results of the scenario analysis and stress tests should be fed into the process of reviewing banks' environmental risk management policies and practices. The bank should also adequately document the key features of scenario analysis and stress testing, including the selection of scenarios, the validity of the assumptions made, and the assessment of results (MAS, 2020).

Environmental risk can be incorporated into the decision-making processes of financial institutions through financial instruments that can be adapted to take into account environmental factors. Financial institutions have to take into account two types of approaches to environmental risk assessment in their activities. The first is to understand the impact of environmental factors on the valuation of financial assets and liabilities and the risks associated with them. The second is to translate environmental risk factors into quantitative measures that will facilitate risk management in an entity and in making investment decisions. A valuable recognition of the impact of a given environmental risk on an entity should facilitate and accelerate investors' decision-making.

The suitability of risk analysis tools and related indicators depends primarily on the asset classes and environmental risks to which financial institutions are directly and/or indirectly exposed. Creating and implementing policies and procedures will have an indirect impact on financial institutions. An example of an immediate threat may be the physical impact of climate change on real economy assets or the transition to a low-carbon economy. If companies are not prepared for the physical effects of climate change or the transition to a low-carbon economy, they can face credit, market, business, and legal risks. Within each of these risks, financial instruments used to assess the environmental risk can be distinguished (Figure 5.2).

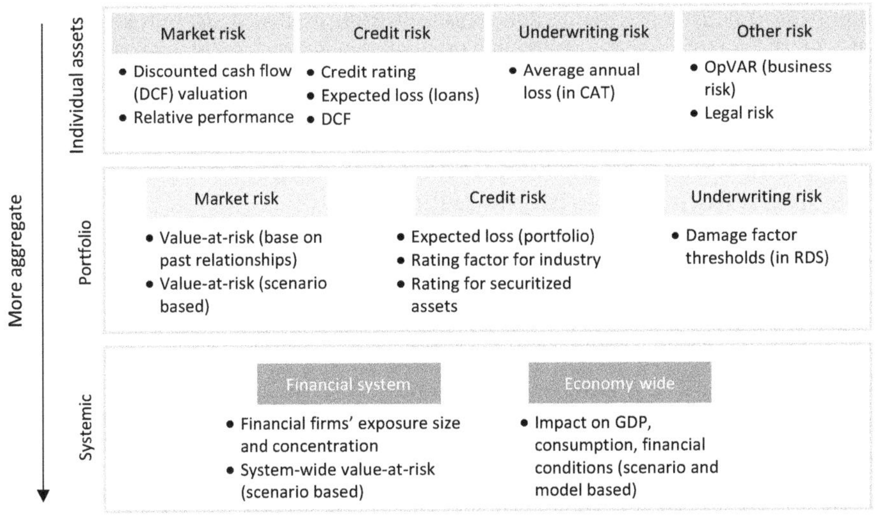

FIGURE 5.2 Toolbox for environmental risk assessment.

Source: GFSG, 2017.

It needs to be emphasized that analyses should be carried out at different levels within a single organization—for example, at the level of individual assets, at the portfolio level, and at the macroeconomic or systemic level (Enhancing Environmental Risk . . . 2017).

In November 2021, the ECB published a report containing the conclusions of the review of the state of climate and environmental risk management in financial institutions. The study shows that financial institutions have started the process of adjusting to the supervisor's recommendations, although the scope of this process and its advancement in individual banks vary. The largest entities did the best in this regard. Of all institutions whose asset base exceeds EUR 500 billion, 80% have at least partially met the expectations of the ECB.

Institutions focused mainly on the issue of risk management, with less emphasis on the process of its identification and mitigation. Many institutions have incorporated C&E risk into their procedures and policies. In all surveyed entities, the C&E risk was included in the credit policies. This kind of risk was reflected in the procedures for assessing the impact of potential climate change and environmental degradation on the institutions' business environment. Certain actions have also been taken to assign responsibility for environmental risk management. A few institutions (less than 20%) developed key indicators for risk identification and classification and set limits on these indicators. Only about 10% of institutions analyze the impact of C&E risk on their macroeconomic and competitive environment. Few banks analyze the impact of climate change and environmental degradation on the macroeconomic situation and the competitive environment in the market.

Financial institutions made the least progress in the areas of internal reporting as well as market and liquidity risk management and stress testing. Less than one-third of institutions meet the expectations in this regard at least partially. Lack of reporting data is often cited as the cause of insufficient progress by institutions in identifying and managing C&E risks. However, few actors took any action in this regard (ECB, 2021).

5.4 Review and comparison of decision support methods in environmental risk modelling

Due to the growing impact of environmental risks on business entities, environmental aspects are increasingly accounted for in decision-making processes. The diversity of factors determining the exposure of entities to environmental risks makes regulators, financial institutions, and enterprises use comparative risk assessment (CRA) and multi-criteria decision analysis (MCDA) methods in the decision-making process. Both these methods make it possible to compare alternatives that can differ significantly in terms of potential impacts. Table 5.1 shows a comparison of the CRA and MCDA methods.

In the case of the CRA method, the basis is to build a two-dimensional decision matrix that includes assessments of alternative solutions according to various criteria. Unfortunately, the CRA method does not have a structured method of

TABLE 5.1 Comparison of comparative risk assessment and multi-criteria decision analysis methods

Elements of decision-making process	*Comparative risk assessment*	*Multi-criteria decision analysis*
Define problems	Stakeholder input collected after the problem is defined by decision-makers and experts. Problem definition is possibly refined based on stakeholder.	Stakeholder input incorporated at beginning of problem formulation stage. Often provides higher stakeholder agreement on problem definition. Thus, proposed solutions have a better chance at satisfying all stakeholders.
Generate alternatives	Alternatives are generated through formal involvement of experts in more site-specific manner.	Alternatives are generated through involvement of all stakeholders including experts. Involvement of all stakeholders increases likelihood of novel alternative generation.
Formulate criteria by which to judge alternatives	Criteria and sub-criteria are often defined.	Criteria and sub-criteria hierarchies are developed based on expert and stakeholder judgment.
Gather value judgments on relative importance of criteria	Quantitative criteria weights are sometimes formulated by the decision-maker, but in a poorly justified manner.	Quantitative criteria weights are obtained from decision-makers and stakeholders.
Rank/select final alternatives	Alternative chosen by aggregation of criteria scores through weight of evidence discussions or qualitative considerations.	Alternative chosen by systematic, well-defined algorithms using criteria scores and weights.

Source: Linkov et al., 2006.

aggregating the results based on criteria in order to determine the optimal alternative solution. This property is shared by the MCDA. This method helps decision-makers evaluate and select alternatives, based on multiple criteria using systematic analysis. This method is used to evaluate alternative solutions on the basis of many, potentially contradictory, or even disproportionate, criteria in a decision problem.

MCDA can be naturally linked to the adaptive management paradigm. Adaptive management assumes uncertainty in the knowledge of managers about the system, and consequently, adaptive management is not based on the selection of one best policy, but rather, on the dynamic observation of the occurring changes and emerging alternatives in order to obtain information about the effects of various modes of action.

The use of MCDA in decision-making practice requires the following (Dodgson et al., 2009):

1. Determining the decision context—at this stage, a decision must be made whether or not to use the MCDA method to make a decision (i.e., assessment whether using the analysis will provide relatively more value than not performing it). Next, MCDA goals must be set and policymakers and key players identified. A key player is anyone who can make a significant contribution to the MCDA. This stage also identifies stakeholders, who are people deciding on financial or other investment.
2. Identifying the options to be assessed—it is very important to take a holistic approach to the choice of options. When the options are predetermined, there is a strong temptation to follow this. It is very common for options to be formulated on a "go/no-go" basis, which limits the applicability of all alternatives.
3. Defining goals and criteria—evaluating an option means assessing the consequences of choosing it. The consequences of the decision are equal in terms of various criteria, so at this stage, you should choose which criteria should be accounted for from the point of view of the decision to be made.
4. Assessing the expected performance of each option against criteria—you need to find a value related to the consequences of each option for each criteria. To do this, describe the alternative consequences of each option, score the options on the criteria, and analyze the consistency of the results in each of the criteria.
5. Assigning a weight to each criterion to reflect their relative importance for the decision—the assigned weight of the criterion illustrates the range of the option difference and the significance of this difference.
6. Combining weights and scores for each option to get an overall value—at this stage, overall weighted scores at each level in the hierarchy and overall weighted scores should be calculated.
7. Checking and analyzing the results achieved—there are several ways to analyze the results. One is to rank the options in order, with the top-tier option determined by the weighted average of all preference scores. The combined results also show how much better one option is than another. Another way

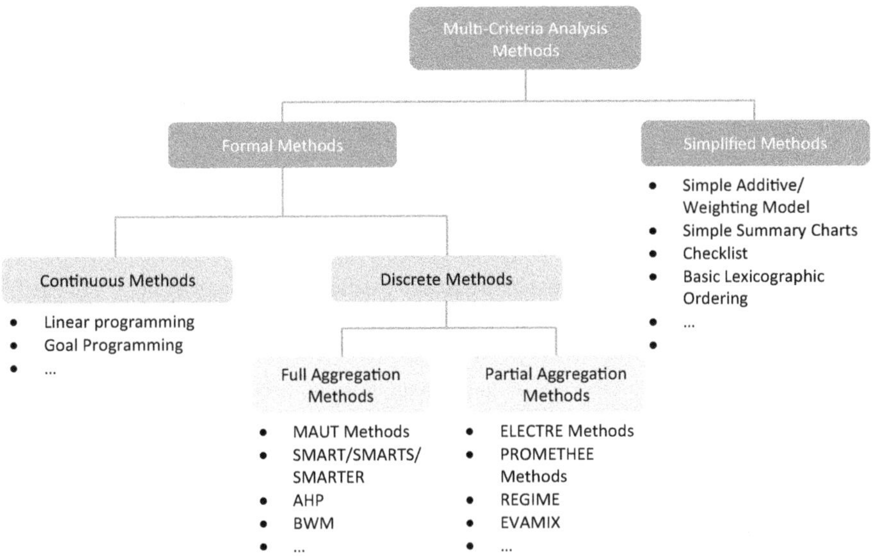

FIGURE 5.3 Classification of MCDA methods.

Source: Dean, 2020b.

could be to present the options with a value tree and display the options in a two-dimensional graph to show the major trade-offs.

8. Performing a sensitivity analysis—at this stage, you should look for answers to whether other preferences or weights affect the overall order of options. Then analyze the advantages and disadvantages of the selected options and compare the pairs of options. You should also look for new options that may be better than those originally considered.

Various classifications of MCDA methods can be found in the literature on the subject. For the purposes of this study, the division of MCDA methods proposed by Dean (2018) will be quoted (Figure 5.3).

Regarding the multitude and variety of MCDA methods and tools, the main groups of MCDA methods and their characteristics will be discussed in this study.

According to the classification proposed by Dean (2020a), MCDA methods can be divided into formal and simplified. Formal MCDA methods, which include the continuous method and discrete method, are based on extensive procedures and the adoption of a series of fairly rigorous (and often arbitrary) rules and advanced mathematical principles. Computer support is often needed to implement such methods. The first group of methods distinguished within the formal method is the continuous method. This group of methods is most often used to support decision-making processes in which there are a very large or infinite number of alternative solutions, although they do not have to be known from the beginning. This category includes linear programming and goal programming.

The second group of MCDA methods distinguished under the formal method is the discrete method. This group of methods is used in decision-making processes where the alternatives to be assessed are limited in number and are relatively well developed at the beginning of the analysis. Within discrete methods, the full aggregation method and partial aggregation method can be distinguished. The division is based on a different approach to the analyzed problem. The full aggregation method aims at synthesizing the results of alternatives against all the different criteria into one global result. This group of methods includes, among others, methods of multi-attribute utility theory (MAUT), SMART/SMARTS, or AHP. The undoubted advantage of the full aggregation method is the full compensation between the criteria. It is worth remembering, however, that sometimes high scores on selected criteria may compensate for a low score on one or more criteria. Therefore, an alternative that scores well on all criteria may have the same overall performance as a solution that scores exceptionally high on many criteria but performs very poorly on other criteria (Dean, 2020b). In opposition to the full aggregation method, a partial aggregation method was developed, including ELECTRE methods, PROMETHEE methods, and REGIME. These methods challenge the existence of a complete system of preferences for any decision problem and focus on finding relationships that surpass the set of alternatives. The purpose of this group of methods is to determine the degree of dominance of one option over the other. Particular methods within this group differ in the type of data and information used (quantitative and qualitative) and the rules and procedures within which the dominance of individual alternatives is established.

Another group of MCDA methods are simplified methods. This group includes, among others, simple additives, charts, checklists, and so on. The simplicity of this methods makes it easy and quick to use, attracting a large number of users. However, these methods can, and it is very likely that they will, lead to many inconsistencies and flaws in the process of analyzing the choice of alternatives to solve a given problem (Dean, 2020a).

5.5 The usefulness of the MCDA method to assess the role of environmental factors in the decision-making process of banks

MCDA has been accepted as an important decision-making tool in the implementation of environmental projects (Linkov et al., 2006; Cegan et al., 2017). Due to the possibility of using qualitative and quantitative data, it is extremely useful in the context of environmental risk modelling.

As part of its environmental risk management, the entity must choose one of the options—that is, termination, mitigation, transfer, use, or tolerating the risk. Choosing a specific alternative requires analyzing a number of factors of different natures, from technical and economic criteria to social and ethical issues, and the capabilities of the individual. The decision-making process is therefore complex

Adapting the MCDA methodology for environmental risk management			
General MCDA Steps	Risk Assessment	Selection of Alternatives	Strengths
1. Definition of the problem	What is distribution of risk?	What are spatial effects of alternatives?	Implemented by decision-makers; actual questions reflecting the needs of public authorities are addressed.
2. Identification of stakeholders problem	This step can be run as a single-stakeholder process or as a group process Stakeholders can include companies, banks, insurers, business partners.		Able to include views from multiple stakeholders.
3. Identification of alternatives	Identify risk determinants	Identify potential choices and alternatives	Allows comparison between a large range of criteria.
4. Identification of criteria alternatives	Identyfikacja kryterów ważnych z punktu widzenia rozpatrywanego procesu decyzyjnego		Able to integrate multiple considerations or criteria.
5. Evaluation of alternatives	Calculation of the effects of each alternative on all criteria.		Synthesis of current knowledge using both quantitative and qualitative data.
6. Weighting of criteria	Ranking of the criteria in order of importance		Enables exploration of disciplinary, organizational, cultural preferences and values.
7. Decision analysis alternatives	Application of MCDA decision rule and analysis of results		Captures complexity. Exploration and comparison of an alternative's efficiency. Enhances transparency and social acceptability.
8. Choosing a good achievable goal	Simulations of extreme effects on ranking and assessment of the robustness of results		Allow exploration of the relative importance of criteria and effect on the efficiency ranking alternative.

FIGURE 5.4 The use of the MCDA method for environmental risk management.

Source: Compilation based on Hongoh, 2011.

and requires consideration of the effects of alternative solutions. MCDA provides a practical way to compare decision options based on adopted criteria (Figure 5.4).

Banks play a very important role in the economy as an intermediary and a provider of capital. Their decisions on environmental issues will directly or indirectly affect the behavior of other economic entities. Banks as lenders or participants in the capital market may support the implementation of projects that fit into the concept of sustainable development or limit access to external financing or increase the cost of financing for entities whose activities have a significant negative impact on the environment. Banks also play an important role in the implementation of pro-environmental projects financed from public funds.

When making decisions based on qualitative and financial data, financial institutions must take into account the interests of various stakeholder groups. It is also important to compare the costs with the benefits for each of the analyzed decisions. Most often, the optimal solution will be the alternative that will allow one to obtain the highest surplus of benefits over costs, while the benefits and costs should be considered not only from the financial point of view, but also from environmental and social aspects. For many decision problems, MCDA can help distinguish between the different benefits associated with different environmental risk management options.

A crucial advantage of MCDA is the ability to take into account possible areas of conflict between decision-makers and stakeholders. It should be noted that the necessity to establish common criteria and weights may make it difficult to use this method in practice, on the one hand, but on the other hand, it will oblige the interested parties to focus on the reasons and goals of the other group.

MCDA methods allowed for the development of practical ways of comparing decision alternatives, assuming a multiplicity of criteria for assessing these options (Kiker et al., 2005). It combines criteria and results in a matrix, thereby integrating risk and uncertainty levels. In this way, it is possible to make an assessment (ranking) of alternatives, which will support the decision-maker in making the decision. At this point, however, it should be emphasized that MCDA is not a way to indicate which alternative is the best, but rather a way to understand how alternatives differ from one another and what effects choosing a particular alternative may have. It is also a perfect way to structure decision-makers' discussions in the decision-making process.

Like any method, MCDA has some disadvantages. The most important of them is the possibility of manipulating the result of the decision. The adopted parameters and functions needed to calculate the results (e.g., criteria and weights) may influence the obtained result. MCDA models should be used carefully and should be based on qualitative and quantitative data that are adequate in quality and quantity. The large amount of data, both in terms of the material and information required to start the process, and the cooperation of stakeholders make the application of these methods difficult in practice. For this reason, MCDA is better suited for long-term planning than during an emergency.

MCDA methods, used to solve multivariate problems (for which different units of measurement are used to describe the alternatives), do not always produce adequate results when analyzing one-dimensional problems.

Another limitation of MCDA methods is the lack of causality determination. They provide and organize knowledge for a given problem but do not give a clear picture of causal relationships. MCDA methods should therefore also be seen as an aid to the decision-making process for the decision-maker, and not as a decision-making tool.

5.6 Conclusion

The multi-criteria support of decision-making departs from the search for the best (optimal) solution in favor of supporting the person who makes the decision by helping in the analysis of the value system (preferences) and the consequences of the adopted value system and ensuring the consistency of decisions with the system of goals and values and, through certain recommendations, decision proposals and the analysis of their consequences. According to Bellman and Zadeh (1970), many decisions made in the real world take place in an environment in which the goals, limitations, and consequences of possible actions are not exactly known. A useful decision model must therefore handle incomplete and uncertain information (Ribeiro, 1996).

The undoubted advantage of the MCDA method is the ability to include many stakeholder perspectives as well as uncertain, subjective, and qualitative information in the decision-making process. For this reason, this method is extremely useful in supporting decision-making processes in the field of environmental risk modelling. For banks, due to their roles in the financing system of the economy as a whole and as its individual entities, multi-criteria methods of decision-making allow them to analyze the decision-making problem and account for the potential effects of the decisions made.

References

Bell, D. E., Raiffa, H., and Tversky, A. (1988). Descriptive, Normative, and Prescriptive Interactions in Decision Making. In *Decision Making*, D. E. Bell, H. Raiffa, and A. Tversky (eds.). New York: Cambridge University Press, pp. 9–30.

Bellman, R. E., and Zadeh, L. A. (1970). Decision-Making in a Fuzzy Environment. *Management Science* 17(4): B-141.

Brown, M. T. (1990). *Working Ethics: Strategies for Decision Making and Organizational Responsibility*. San Francisco, CA: Jossey-Bass Publishers. ISBN: 1555422802.

Cambridge Centre for Sustainable Finance. (2016). *Environmental Risk Analysis by Financial Institutions: A Review of Global Practice*. Cambridge, UK: Cambridge Institute for Sustainability Leadership.

Cegan, J. C., Filion, A. M., Keisler, J. M., and Linkov, I. (2017). Trends and Applications of Multi-Criteria Decision Analysis in Environmental Sciences: Literature Review. *Environment Systems and Decisions* 37(2): 123–133.

Dean, Marco. (2020a). Multi-Criteria Analysis. In *Advances in Transport Policy and Planning*, Vol. 6, Niek Mouter (ed.). Academic Press, pp. 165–224. https://doi.org/10.1016/bs.atpp.2020.07.001

Dean, Marco. (2020b). Participatory Multi-Criteria Analysis Methodologies: Comprehensive, Inclusive, Transparent and User-Friendly? An Application to the Case of the London Gateway Port. *Research in Transportation Economics* 88: 100887.

Dean, Marco, and Hickman, R. (2018). Comparing Cost-Benefit Analysis and Participatory Multicriteria Analysis Methodologies. In *Decision-Making for Sustainable Transport and Mobility: Multi Actor Multi Criteria Analysis*, G. Baudry, and C. Macharis (eds.). Cheltenham, UK: Edward Elgar Publishing, pp. 100–119.

Dodgson, J. S., Spackman, M., Pearman, A., and Phillips, L. D. (2009). *Multi-Criteria Analysis: A Manual*. London: Department for Communities and Local Government. ISBN 9781409810230.

EBA. (2021). *EBA Report on Management and Supervision of ESG Risks for Credit Institutions and Investment Firms*. EBA/REP/2021.18. Paris, France: European Banking Authority. https://www.eba.europa.eu/sites/default/documents/files/document_library/Publications/Reports/2021/1015656/EBA%20Report%20on%20ESG%20risks%20management%20and%20supervision.pdf (accessed: 19.09.2022).

ECB. (2020). *Guide on Climate-Related and Environmental Risks, Supervisory Expectations Relating to Risk Management and Disclosure*. November. www.bankingsupervision.europa.eu/ecb/pub/pdf/ssm.202011finalguideonclimate-relatedandenvironmentalrisks~58213f6564.en.pdf (accessed: 10.06.2022).

ECB. (2021). *The State of Climate and Environmental Risk Management in the Banking Sector: Report on the Supervisory Review of Banks' Approaches to Manage Climate and Environmental Risks*. November. www.bankingsupervision.europa.eu/ecb/pub/pdf/ssm.202111guideonclimate-relatedandenvironmentalrisks~4b25454055.en.pdf (accessed: 11.06.2022).

Enhancing Environmental Risk Assessment in Financial Decision-Making. (2017). https://g20sfwg.org/wp-content/uploads/2021/07/Enhancing_Environmental_Risk_Assessment_in_Financial_Decision-making.pdf (accessed: 7.06.2022).

GFSG. (2017). *G20 Green Finance Synthesis Report 2017*. Indonesia: G20 Green Finance Study Group.

Global Risks Report. (2021). 16th Edition. Geneva, Switzerland: World Economic Forum. https://www.weforum.org/reports/the-global-risks-report-2021/ (accessed: 18.09.2022).

Holska, A. (2016). Teorie podejmowania decyzji, [w] *Zarządzanie, organizacje i organizowanie–przegląd perspektyw teoretycznych*, K. Klincewicz (red.). Warszawa: Wydawnictwo Naukowe Wydziału Zarządzania Uniwersytetu Warszawskiego.

Hongoh, Valerie, Hoen, A. G., Aenishaenslin, C. et al. (2011). Spatially Explicit Multi-Criteria Decision Analysis for Managing Vector-Borne Diseases. *International Journal of Health Geographics* 10: 70. https://doi.org/10.1186/1476-072X-10-70

Kiker, G. A., Bridges, T. S., Varghese, A., Seager, T. P., and Linkov, I. (2005). Application of Multicriteria Decision Analysis in Environmental Decision Making. *Integrated Environmental Assessment and Management: An International Journal* 1(2): 95–108.

Linkov, I., Satterstrom, F. K., Kiker, G., Batchelor, C., Bridges, T., and Ferguson, E. (2006). From Comparative Risk Assessment to Multi-Criteria Decision Analysis and Adaptive Management: Recent Developments and Applications. *Environment International* 32(8): 1072–1093. https://dx.doi.org/10.1016/j.envint.2006.06.013

Monetary Authority of Singapore. (2020). *Guidelines on Environmental Risk Management (Banks)*. September. www.mas.gov.sg/-/media/MAS/Regulations-and-Financial-Stability/Regulations-Guidance-and-Licensing/Commercial-Banks/Regulations-Guidance-and-Licensing/Guidelines/Guidelines-on-Environmental-Risk—Banks/Guidelines-on-Environmental-Risk-Management-for-Banks.pdf (accessed: 5.06.2022).

NGFS. (2020). *Overview of Environmental Risk Analysis by Financial Institutions*. Network for Greening the Financial System, Technical document, September. www.ngfs.net/sites/default/files/medias/documents/overview_of_environmental_risk_analysis_by_financial_institutions.pdf (accessed: 19.09.2022).

Redziak, Z. (2013). *Podstawy teorii podejmowania decyzji*. Warszawa: Wydawnictwo Akademii Obrony Narodowej.

Ribeiro, R. A. (1996). Fuzzy Multiple Attribute Decision Making: A Review and New Preference Elicitation Techniques. *Fuzzy Sets and Systems* 78(2): 155–181.

Zamanifar, M., and Hartmann, T. (2021). A Prescriptive Framework for Recommending Decision Attributes of Infrastructure Disaster Recovery Problems. *Environment Systems and Decisions* 41: 633–650. https://doi.org/10.1007/s10669-021-09824-0

Zioło, M., Filipiak, B. Z., Bąk, I., and Cheba, K. (2019). How to Design More Sustainable Financial Systems: The Roles of Environmental, Social, and Governance Factors in the Decision-Making Process. *Sustainability* 11(20): 5604.

6

THE SPREAD OF ENVIRONMENTAL RISK AND THE WAY TO ANALYZE THE ISSUE

Anna Spoz

6.1 The network approach in banking

6.1.1 The network theory

Network theory has long been used in many fields of science, including sociology, biology, epidemiology, computer science, physics, and economics. This theory is based on the fact that real-world objects are interconnected to form networks. Objects form network nodes, also called vertices, and the connections between them are called edges. Most real-world networks are very complex, as they consist of many types of objects that are related in various ways. Traditional analysis of such networks is very difficult, while the network approach allows, using numerical methods, to effectively study them in terms of their functioning as well as response to external impacts or changes in structure. In the network approach, the model representing the real-world system is analyzed. Network models are useful for several reasons. First is the intuitiveness, so the complex relationships of the studied phenomena can be visually understood. There is also much theoretical work in this field, which provides a solid background for the conceptual interpretation of the network topology. Finally, there are many computational tools available, making it easier to create and manipulate network models (Martinez-Jaramillo, 2012).

Considering the issue of information spreading in the network, one of the most important theories related to it—namely, the Granovetter's (1973) weak ties theory—should be mentioned. Granovetter's approach differed from that of earlier works. He was looking for an explanation of how the spread of information in small areas of the network (micro scale) influences the spread of information in wide-area networks (macro scale), where the small groups together build the large one. In small networks, where there are primarily strong connections between nodes, information disseminates easily and directly through these strong connections. In

DOI: 10.4324/9781003310099-6

wide complex networks there are so-called bridges—that is, strong connections between nodes that are also connections between subnets. In theory, macro-scale diffusion should run through these bridges. In practice, it turned out that diffusion takes a different route, through the so-called weak ties, which represent weak relationships. The advantage of weak ties theory is that the information easily spreads to nodes that are not connected directly to the starting node. The diffusion has even wider scope thanks to weak ties because there are many of them. However, it is not favorable for the spread of negative phenomena, yet taking this theory into account, it is possible to take actions to limit the diffusion of risk in the banking system or financial system in general.

The next important network theory is the structural hole theory that has found applications in empirical research on networks within and between organizations. It allowed to explain issues at the level of the entity and its organization (at the employee level). Information is a key resource in organizations; therefore enterprises rich in structural holes have a better ability to manipulate information to achieve their goals (Labun and Wittek, 2014). Burt (1992) proved that networks influence the career development of individual employees in a company. According to the results of his research, the configuration of network connections that creates opportunities for intermediation and entrepreneurship increases the career chances of actors competing for promotion in organizations (Burt, 1992; Labun and Wittek, 2014).

According to this theory, in social networks, access to favorable structural positions is not evenly distributed among all actors. While some actors are in the center of a single tightly intertwined group, other group members may be at the intersection of multiple groups with access to multiple links. Structural gaps offer benefits in two aspects: information and control. Information benefits come in three forms: access, time, and referral. A network rich in structural holes provides access to information sources from many noninteracting parts of the network. They also increase the likelihood of receiving information earlier than other people in less favorable online positions (timing) and of direct speech (i.e., they have a positive opinion about the main people in their own networks) (Labun and Wittek, 2014).

Structural holes also offer control benefits, resulting from the possibility of either playing two unrelated games against each other or bringing them together. In both situations, the third party may reap the benefits.

The structural hole theory also assumes that actors will actively develop information and control the benefits of existing structural holes and manage the constraints of no structural holes. To this end, they use one of three strategies—that is, they can withdraw from contact by reducing the network, they can expand their network by adding a contact competitor to their network, or they can leave the network unmodified but, knowing its limitations, manage them properly (Burt, 1992).

Constructing a model that accurately reflects the real system and produces reliable test results is therefore crucial. Using the model, the structure of the system can be analyzed, but it is in most cases used to study the spread of various factors or phenomena across the network. Such an analysis is performed by simulation, where the model is influenced by an external factor and then the behavior of the network is analyzed. Due to how disease spreads in nature, the factor that spreads through the web is often called contagion. The simulation results can provide a variety of different information, such as the speed at which a factor is spreading in the network, the degree to which network nodes adopt this factor, the influence of particular model parameters on propagation, or the dependence of the propagation of the phenomenon on the type of nodes affected.

Thanks to its universality, the network approach allows one to analyze various systems from areas and domains that are completely different. Typical examples of the use of the network approach are research on the spread of diseases among the population or viruses in computer networks and dissemination of knowledge (e.g., in some communities or among scientists) as well as the analysis of the implementation of innovations by some entities under the influence of other entities (e.g., in the enterprise sector) or adopting pro-ecological behavior (in society or among enterprises). The analysis of the spread of various phenomena in financial systems is also a common application of the network approach.

Network models can take many forms and can be built using a variety of approaches and methods. The simplest ones are in the form of graphs, but in practice, even studying a network composed of objects of the same type requires more complex models due to the existence of many types of connections in the real systems that are modeled. Additionally, there are different approaches to modelling the same systems. Sometimes it is assumed that the nodes are connected randomly (random network), but sometimes the degree of nodes (the degree of a node in the network is determined by the number of its connections with other nodes) has the power law distribution, and then the network has the form of the so-called scale-free network. Some researchers believe that such a structure describes the real systems in the best way (Hein et al., 2006; Barabási and Bonabeau, 2003). This type of network is characterized by the presence of a very small group of nodes (so-called hubs) that have a large number of connections, well above the average for the network, while the rest of the vast majority of nodes have very few connections. Examples of such networks are: the internet, World Wide Web, protein regulatory network, or airline networks. Banking systems, in some countries, where a few large banks dominate are other examples of scale-free networks. The way the network functions and reacts to changes depends on the structure of this network.

To build a model of network, various methods of defining and parameterizing nodes and connections can be used. One of parameters describing a node is a degree, while connections have weights assigned. Weights may be assigned depending on the purpose. For example, in similarity-based networks, the connections between nodes represent their similarity, so weights are related to this

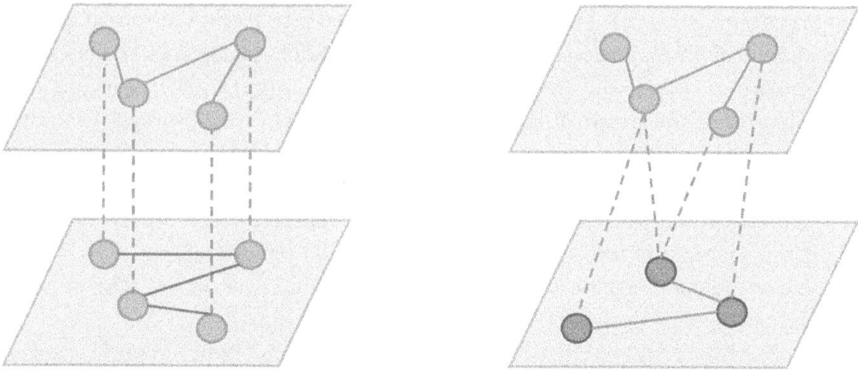

FIGURE 6.1 Examples of multilayer networks: multiplex network on the left and interconnected network on the right.

measure. In turn, in the network filtering method, the threshold method can be used, which allows one to select only nodes with significance determined on the basis of correlation or distance to other nodes, exceeding the set threshold (Battiston et al., 2010). Different types of networks can be used to discover and analyze hierarchical structures such as management networks and stock ownership networks. In turn, the links between banks or between banks and companies form transactional networks. Models are not designed to perfectly reflect real systems and are often simplified to best fit the needs of the analysis.

Building models of complex systems with various types of nodes and connections between them—that is, complex networks—requires the use of appropriate methods. For such networks, multilayer models are often developed to better represent real systems. In a multilayer network, nodes are arranged on different layers, and connections occur between nodes on the same layer (intralayer edges) and between nodes on different layers (interlayer edges) (Kinsley et al., 2020). The two main types of multilayer networks are multiplex networks and interconnected networks (Figure 6.1). In the first type of network, interlayer edges can only connect nodes representing objects of the same type on different layers. In the second type of network, interlayer edges can connect nodes representing objects of various kinds. Multiplex networks are therefore useful for analyzing different kinds of relationships between objects of the same type, as each layer represents a different type of relationship. Interconnected networks, on the other hand, group objects of the same type on individual layers, but they are different on each of the layers.

It is worth noting here that the connections between nodes can be directed or undirected. Directed connections show the directions of interaction between nodes—for example, a loan is a connection from the node representing the bank to the node representing the company: the borrower. On the other hand, undirected connections may illustrate the existence of a connection between nodes when the direction of interaction is not defined or irrelevant.

6.1.2 Models for the banking system

The analysis of the banking system most often concerns two kinds of networks. The first represents the interbank market, and the second represents banks lending to businesses (Battiston et al., 2010). Dependencies between banks and firms resulting from credit relations are strong; thus, the network of banks and firms based on loans and credits is important for the understanding and quantification of systemic risk in the financial system and economy (De Bandt and Hartmann, 2000). If a large company is in financial difficulties, the lending banks also have a problem and must take action that in turn affects other companies that are customers of those banks. In this way, a domino effect spreads phenomena or factors across the network.

Banks together with nonfinancial companies that are bank customers constitute a complex system with many types of connections. Therefore, for most cases a multilayer model is the best choice for analyzing the spread of environmental risk in this system. On the other hand, the type of multilayer model in this case will depend on what relationships will be considered. If various types of connections between banks and companies are considered, then the multiplex network model can be used, in which there will be both banks and companies on each layer, but each layer will be dedicated to only one type of relation. However, when analyzing only one type of relation between banks and firms, a two-layer model can be used, with the first layer for banks and their interrelationships and the second for companies and their relationships. Interlayer edges will in this case represent the relationship between banks and firms.

To analyze only a bank sector separate from nonfinancial companies, the multilayer network model will also work well. In particular, the multiplex network model can be used, but the nodes on each layer will represent only banks. There would still be one type of connection within one layer. In such a model, the connection may represent different types of liabilities between banks. For example, on the first layer, long-term liabilities representing loans can be placed; on the second layer, short-term liabilities representing the liquidity network; and on the third layer, financial assets representing portfolios (Montagna and Kok, 2016). There can be many such layers, depending on the needs of the analysis. Individual layers may, for example, represent different industrial sectors, such as in the Luu and Lux study (2018), who treated each of the 60 industries as a separate layer. Thanks to this, they were able to analyze the differences between companies from various industries.

Analyzing the interbank market, it is important to remember that while some statistical properties tend to differ from actual networks, four features are specific, or even unique, to interbank networks. These features affect the way interbank networks are analyzed and interpreted (Langfield and Soramäki, 2016):

- Links between banks are often directed. For example, if one bank lends to another bank, the first bank is exposed to the default of the second bank, while the second bank may be exposed to the first bank's willingness to renew the loan. In both cases, the direction of the link is important for the economic interpretation.

- The linkages between banks are always weighted in the way that linkages are associated with a monetary amount. If one bank grants a loan to another bank, the size of that loan determines the significance of those banks' exposures.
- It is characteristic for the interbank network that it consists of a multiplicity of different types of connections. Banks carry out hundreds of different types of mutual transactions, including many variants of deposits, repurchase agreements, prime loans, and derivatives. In addition, banks are linked due to their exposure to common risk factors. Different relationships have different economic interpretations: for example, a repurchase agreement that is fully secured and (in many jurisdictions) distance bankruptcy implies a different level of exposure from an unsecured loan.
- Banks have heterogeneous balance sheet characteristics. Any two banks will be of different sizes, and their compositions of assets and liabilities will be different. The heterogeneous features of the balance sheet imply heterogeneity in the inherent resistance of banks to external shocks.

When modelling and analyzing financial systems, also a slightly different approach based on the so-called financial macro network can be adopted. Contrary to the financial micro network, where nodes are single entities (banks or firms), the macro network includes sectors—for example, the banking sector, nonfinancial companies sector, investment fund sector. The links between them are represented by aggregated relationships based on various financial instruments for entire sectors. Such instruments may include bond, equity, loans, insurance, and pension guarantees. In a micro network, links are also financial instruments, but individual for each pair of entities (Stolbova et al., 2018).

After determining what type of model for the banking system will be used for the analysis, the model is constructed based on the assumptions and available data. In practice, the available data is rarely complete, especially for specific economies, or show inconsistency, which may be, for instance, caused by tax havens (Zucman, 2013). Therefore, despite lack of data, various methods are used to generate model and its parameters under certain assumptions. The missing information should be estimated, but it is always connected to the risk of adding noise from the estimation methodologies (Starnini et al., 2019). For example, individual connections between nodes on a selected layer may be randomly generated based on the knowledge of the total number of connections of a given node (Montagna and Lux, 2013). Another assumption, based on actual observations, is that large banks have many connections with firms. The size of the bank can be determined on the basis of information from the financial balance sheet, and then based on the size, the number of connections can be generated in accordance with the adopted probability distribution.

6.2 Using the network approach to analyze the spread of environmental risk in the banking sector

6.2.1 The goal of analyzing the spread of environmental risk in the banking sector

As mentioned earlier, network models are most often used to study the spread of phenomena or factors. Understanding the mechanisms and effects of the spread of phenomena in networks allows drawing conclusions about the vulnerabilities of networks to external factors. In the context of analyzing financial systems, the aim is very often to find out their resistance to shock—that is, an unfavorable phenomenon that causes disturbances in the functioning or structure of the system. Shocks may be, for instance, political instability, fiscal contraction, banking crisis, introducing new policy by regulators, or climate change. Based on the results of the analysis, we can know the mechanisms of shock propagation and draw conclusions about the weaknesses of the system. The aim of the research is developing tools to prevent the spread of the impact of negative phenomena, which environmental risk undoubtedly is.

Additionally, an important outcome of the analysis is identification of key actors or systemically important agents. These are nodes with a disproportionally high impact on some aggregate statistic of interest (Acemoglu et al., 2016).

6.2.2 Transmission channels in the financial networks

The basis for risk transmission channels in the financial system may be the existence of chains of financial contracts. Two types of transmission channels can be distinguished. The first type of channel manifests itself through changes in the valuation of securities. The simplest case of risk transmission in this case is the propagation of shock through equity. The holder's assets change their value in proportion to the change in the market value of the issuer's equity. Another case is the valuation adjustments of debt securities along the counterparty chain. The second type of risk propagation channel results from changes in investment and savings decisions in the chain of entities linked by financial agreements (Stolbova et al., 2018). The examples of transmission cases are presented in Table 6.1.

6.2.3 Scenarios of risk spreading in financial system

The spread of risk in the network of banks and companies depends on many factors, such as the financial status of individual participants in the system, their balance sheet, and the distribution of connections between them. Thanks to the simulation using the real network model, it is possible to find out how different structures of connections between nodes affect the financial stability of the entire network, what the share of individual banks or companies is in the spread of risk, the time it will take for the risk affecting one node to spread in the network, and the effects of

TABLE 6.1 Types of risk transmission channels based on financial contracts

Financial contract type	*Type of transmission channel*	*Examples*
Equity holdings	Securities valuation	An increase (decrease) in market value of a firm's equity increases (decreases) the value of the shareholder's asset.
Debt securities holdings	Securities valuation	A decrease in equity (difference between assets and liabilities) of a debt security issuer decreases the market value of this debt security that in turn decreases the asset of holder of this debt security.
Loans	Securities valuation	A decrease in creditworthiness of a firm induces a decrease in the value of the lending bank's assets.
Deposit, loans, bonds, equity holdings	Changes in savings/ investment decisions	A shock on a bank asset induces depositors to withdraw their funds (bank run). This, in turn, leads to a decrease in the creditworthiness of the bank.

Source: Stolbova et al., 2018.

this. Thanks to the simulation, we may study how the risk spreads in the network depending on which node will be directly exposed to the environmental risk. In the initial phase of the simulation, a selected node is exposed to the risk: a bank or a company. Depending on the effect of the risk, different scenarios can occur in the next stages. For example, if a bank or company does not suffer serious consequences, related facilities may not be affected either. However, even if the risk implications for a given node are not strong, they can spread to a node that is not as resilient and cause it to default. For example, if a large bank, as a result of unfavorable environmental conditions, incurs some losses, this does not have to result in its collapse, but it may limit the loan offer for its clients. Among these clients, there may be a small company that will not be able to fulfill orders without a loan and will lose financial liquidity and eventually collapse. In turn, this may cause a breakdown in related companies that are customers of other banks. After many simulation steps, as a result of the domino effect in the network, the initial negative impact of environmental risk on one of the nodes will spread. Therefore, if the impact of the risk on the first node is not extinguished in this node, there is a good chance that the effects of this risk will be amplified as a result of spreading in the network. The cumulative effects of a crash across multiple smaller nodes can go back to the starting node and cause it to default this time. This could be explained by the existence of feedback loops in the system, as discussed in Section 6.2.6. Of course, the first node affected by the risk may also break down, and then the negative impact of the risk will spread faster, especially if this node has many connections.

As can be seen from the simulation scenario described, the resistance of the network to risk depends largely on the resilience of its nodes. Therefore, maintaining system stability is not easy, and as research of network resilience shows, two extreme results are often obtained. The first is the complete extinction of the negative effects of the influence on the first node on which the external factor acted directly. Then the effects of its influence do not spread. The second case is a complete breakdown of the entire network as a result of the external factor influence spreading to all nodes of the network (Lux, 2016).

Banking systems with a scale-free network structure exposed to risk behave in a different way. In such networks, the default of a node representing a small- or medium-sized bank does not affect the stability of the system, as the negative impact on other nodes is easily absorbed by the network. Hence, the effects of the risk do not spread. The situation is completely different when the impact of risk is directed to the hub node—that is, a large bank, strongly influencing the system. If such a situation becomes insolvent, the negative effects spread like a wave propagating in water, which means that they simultaneously affect all nodes connected to the hub. Scale-free networks are therefore immune to the domino effect, as even the default of many small nodes does not threaten the stability of the network, but they are not immune to threats directed at large nodes. Therefore, if the analyzed system has a scale-free network structure, it is the hubs that should be protected against the negative impact of risk.

6.2.4 When a risk becomes a systemic risk

No matter if a risk impacts one node of a network or many nodes simultaneously, the shock may be transmitted further, thereby resulting in systemic risk. Systemic risk affects the entire network. By analogy, systemic risk in the real world is risk that affects the entire economy, a sector of the economy, the economy of a country, or other system of large scale. The results of spreading the shock show that if it is applied to all nodes in the network, the systemic effect is transferred very quickly. On the other hand, if the shock affects directly only a few nodes, it only produces an idiosyncratic effect. If the node is able to continue to transmit shock, there will be a systemic effect. The convalescence period for nodes affected by systemic shock may be an order of magnitude longer than the time needed to induce shock (Mitic, 2020).

6.2.5 Parameters of spreading

A key element in the analysis of the spread of phenomena in networks is the selection of propagation parameters. The diffusion parameters can be used to influence the behavior of the model during the propagation simulation. The comparison of simulation results for different values of parameters allows one to draw broad conclusions and develop recommendations for real systems. The diffusion parameters may be, for example, the probability of environmental risk occurrence, its impact strength, the node's threshold of resistance to risk, the risk exposure time per node, and the number of simulation steps as well as the initial state of the node.

For example, if the probability of a risk occurring is set as high, many nodes may experience it, and its negative effects will spread quickly across the network. On the other hand, a change in the resistance threshold of nodes may result in more frequent extinction of the negative effects of risk in a given node. By changing the impact time of the environmental risk, it is possible to determine the values at which the risk will not spread over the entire network.

In the spread analysis, changes in the structure of the network during the simulation can also be used, thanks to which it is possible to show how important the structure of the model is for the simulation results. This can be done, for example, by deactivating individual layers in the network. Such operations reveal how important it is to use a multilayer network, because considering only one layer takes into account only one type of relation and may lead to underestimating the significance of the risk impact on the entire system.

6.2.6 Feedback loops in risk spreading

When considering the propagation of the risk impact in the banking system, an important role is played by feedback loops. This concept explains some nonlinear changes in the behavior of the system that occur over time. It is especially useful when the banking system is considered together with the corporate sector. Then the influence of feedback loops is more visible. The presence of feedback loops in the analyzed system can manifest itself through time delays between the external factor and the appearance of effects in the network; critical points, exceeding which may cause a complete change of the system characteristics; and the presence of reinforcing mechanisms (Stolbova et al., 2018).

Feedback loops can be divided according to whether they have a reinforcing effect on the negative effects of risk or a compensatory effect: reinforcing feedback loops and balancing feedback loops. Another method of division takes into account the origin of the loop—that is, its beginning; for example, feedback loops originating from banks may have the form: bank-bank (self-loops), bank-firms-banks, but also banks-government-banks. Feedback loops can also consist of more items, but research shows that short loops have the greatest impact on spread. The longer the feedback loop, the smaller is the impact of an additional exposure to the risk impact amplification—thus, the explanatory power of the feedback loop (Stolbova et al., 2018). Feedback loops can also start in the corporate sector—for example, firms-firms, firms-banks-firms. Here also their strength depends on their length, as is the case with bank-originating loops.

6.4 The role of networks in reducing the negative effects of environmental risk on banks and their impact on the activities of enterprises

An analysis of risk spread across a bank's network provides information on factors that should be accounted for when designing and implementing an effective and environmentally risk-aware risk management system. These factors include the following (Stolbova et al., 2018):

- The structure of the financial system and the relationship between the financial system and the real economy (e.g., companies, government).
- The way the shock generated by the negative impact of climate risk spreads through a network of interconnected financial entities (i.e., transmission channels) and then to real economy sectors and entities. The interconnectedness of financial institutions can amplify shocks and significantly reduce the accuracy of estimating the probabilities of default (Battiston et al., 2016a, 2016b), thus increasing the complexity of the risk assessment.
- The existence of reinforcing and balancing feedback loops and their effects through indirect and direct shock transmission channels.

The use of multilayer networks to analyze the spread of environmental risk in a banking system shows how important it is to consider this system holistically. Taking into account only the isolated relationships between banks or between banks and nonfinancial companies results in underestimating the risk of risk spreading on the network. By considering the multiple layers of banks' relations with banks or also with companies and the links between the layers, it is possible to observe the behavior of the system in response to an external factor such as environmental risk. The analysis of the model's behavior under the influence of risk provides information on which model parameters and propagation parameters are the most important for the stability of the system. Thanks to this, the network approach to the banking system allows to develop and take actions to limit the negative effects of risk.

One of the general rules is to make the network diffusion rate lower than the threshold rate for nodes in order to limit the spread of the negative phenomenon. This can be achieved by applying appropriate safeguards against risk. To this end, banks should have an efficient risk management system that accounts for environmental risk. Moreover, banks' policies should assume avoiding cooperation with such actors who do not apply adequate safeguards against risk themselves and at the same time whose activities involve a high exposure to environmental risk.

In the analysis of network resistance to the impact of risk, the default of the bank is the case when its equity falls below the level required by regulations. Hence, if many banks in the banking system keep capital low, the system is very sensitive to environmental risks (as well as other threats). The conclusion is that equity capital should be higher to increase the resilience of the system. As for companies, a way to increase their resilience to risk is to increase their resilience to the loss of external financing (Lux, 2016). In this matter, an important role is played by regulators who, through the requirements for the banking sector, can force banks to keep equity capital at a higher level. In turn, support programs should be developed for the business sector.

Important and useful information comes from the assumption that actors of economic systems, including banks, may be able to recover to the condition before the shock, if they respond to its impact. In the context of a credit default, the entity is more likely to reemerge as a new one. In an economic context, sovereign states can recover economically, and there are examples for that (Mitic, 2020). There can be different models for recovery. For instance, Mitic (2020) proposed two approaches: soft recovery and hard recovery. In the first, agents try to adapt their behavior in order to move toward a pre-shock state. This might be achieved by building up sufficient reserves or by cutting costs. Agents interact "as normal" but are under pressure to move away from the shocked state. The model specifies that in any interaction, if the result is that the affected agent moves toward the pre-shock state, a move in that direction proceeds with a certain relaxation gain. This models the state where an "adverse" outcome is immediately rejected and an effort is made to fix the situation. Informally, this recovery mode is called "lazy," because in any interaction, there is no initial intention to move toward the pre-shock state. In the hard recovery approach, a target state is given, and an agent tries to work actively toward the target. In principle, the target for agent can be any state: for example, the pre-shock state. To move in the direction of the target, again a relaxation augmentation factor is used, but in a different way than it was used in the soft recovery mode. The result is an extended (in time) geometric relaxation of the shocked state. The aforementioned described models for recovery show that, in the simulation of network reaction to the shock, effective mechanism for recovering from shocked state can be applied.

6.5 Conclusions

The influence of banks on the corporate sector has been extensively researched and described. Obviously, the greatest is the financial impact related to the activities of banks. Access to credit and other resources offered by banks is essential for businesses to operate and develop. However, in addition to affecting companies through credit relationships, the impact of banks on businesses is also due to factors such as banks ESG policies, banks' implementation of sustainable development, and related behaviors and actions. These include the implementation of a risk management system that accounts for environmental risk. The implementation of such systems by banks has an indirect impact on their customers. Accounting for environmental risk in the bank's operations may impose limitations on related companies due to the fact that banks do not want to cooperate with clients whose activities expose the bank to increased risk of that kind. This, in turn, can encourage companies to operate in accordance with the principles of sustainable development.

The use of a network approach to analyze the spread of environmental risk in the banking system allows one to assess the system's resistance to the negative effects of this type of risk. The inclusion of enterprises forming a complex multilayer network with banks in the analysis significantly extends the benefits of the analysis. The results obtained from simulations carried out with the use of the network model can be used to develop recommendations and regulations, allowing one to reduce the negative effects of the risk impact on the entire financial system.

References

Acemoglu, Daron, Asu Ozdaglar, and Alireza Tahbaz-Salehi. (2016). Networks, Shocks, and Systemic Risk. In *The Oxford Handbook of the Economics of Networks,* Y. Bramoullé, A. Galeotti, and B. Rogers (eds.). Oxford, UK: Oxford University Press.

Barabási, Albert-László, and Eric Bonabeau. (2003). Scale-Free Networks. *Scientific American* 288(5): 60–69.

Battiston, S., Caldarelli, Guido, D'Errico, Marco, and Gurciullo, Stefano. (2016a). *Leveraging the Network: A Stress-Test Framework Based on DebtRank*, 22 February. https://ssrn.com/abstract=2571218 or http://dx.doi.org/10.2139/ssrn.2571218

Battiston, S., Glattfelder, J. B., Garlaschelli, D., Lillo, F., and Caldarelli, G. (2010). The Structure of Financial Networks. In *Network Science*. London: Springer, pp. 131–163.

Battiston, S., et al. (2016b). The Price of Complexity in Financial Networks. *Proceedings of the National Academy of Sciences* 113(36): 10031–10036.

Burt, R. S. (1992). *Structural Holes: The Social Structure of Competition*. Cambridge, MA: Harvard University Press.

De Bandt, O., and Hartmann, P. (2000). *Systemic Risk: A Survey*. Working Paper No. 3535. Frankfurt: European Central Bank. https://www.ecb.europa.eu/pub/pdf/scpwps/ecbwp035.pdf

Granovetter, Mark S. (1973). The Strength of Weak Ties. *American Journal of Sociology* 78: 1360–1380.

Hein, Olivier, Schwind, Michael, and König, Wolfgang. (2006). Scale-Free Networks. *Wirtsch. Inform* 48: 267–275. https://doi.org/10.1007/s11576-006-0058-2

Kinsley, Amy C., et al. (2020). Multilayer and Multiplex Networks: An Introduction to Their Use in Veterinary Epidemiology. *Frontiers in Veterinary Science* 7: 596.

Labun, A., and Wittek, R. (2014). Structural Holes. In *Encyclopedia of Social Network Analysis and Mining*, pp. 2075–2083. https://dx.doi.org/10.1007/978-1-4614-6170-8_263

Langfield, Sam, and Soramäki, Kimmo. (2016). Interbank Exposure Networks. *Computational Economics* 47: 3–17. https://doi.org/10.1007/s10614-014-9443-x

Luu, D. T., and Lux, T. (2018). *Multilayer Overlaps and Correlations in the Bank-Firm Credit Network of Spain*. Economics Working Paper No. 2018–04. Kiel: Kiel University, Department of Economics.

Lux, Thomas. (2016). A Model of the Topology of the Bank–Firm Credit Network and Its Role as Channel of Contagion. *Journal of Economic Dynamics and Control* 66: 36–53.

Martinez-Jaramillo, Serafin, Kabadjova, Biliana, Bravo-Benitez, Bernardo, and Solorzano-Margain, Juan. (2012). *Systemic Risk Analysis by Means of Network Theory: An Empirical Study of the Mexican Banking System*. Technical Report (Working Paper). Mexico City, Mexico: Banco de México.

Mitic, Peter. (2020). Systemic Shock Propagation in a Complex System. *Soft Computing* 24: 13667–13685. https://doi.org/10.1007/s00500-019-04466-6

Montagna, Mattia, and Kok, Christoffer. (2016). *Multi-Layered Interbank Model for Assessing Systemic Risk*. ECB Working Paper No. 1944. August 26. https://ssrn.com/abstract=2830546 or http://dx.doi.org/10.2139/ssrn.2830546

Montagna, Mattia, and Thomas, Lux. (2013). *Hubs and Resilience: Towards More Realistic Models of the Interbank Markets*. Kiel Working Papers 1826. Kiel, Germany: Kiel Institute for the World Economy.

Starnini, Michele, Marián, Boguñá, and Ángeles Serrano, M. (2019). The Interconnected Wealth of Nations: Shock Propagation on Global Trade-Investment Multiplex Networks. *Scientific Reports* 9: Article number: 13079.

Stolbova, Veronika, Irene Monasterolo, and Stefano Battiston. (2018). A Financial Macro-Network Approach to Climate Policy Evaluation. *Ecological Economics* 149: 239–253.

Zucman, Gabriel. (2013). The Missing Wealth of Nations: Are Europe and the U.S. Net Debtors or Net Creditors? *The Quarterly Journal of Economics* 128(3): 1321–1364. August. https://doi.org/10.1093/qje/qjt012

7

INCORPORATING ENVIRONMENTAL RISK IN BANKS' BUSINESS MODELS

Beata Zofia Filipiak

7.1 Introduction

Does the integration of environmental, social, and sustainability criteria become an important aspect of banks' activities and their risk assessment? The answer to this question is important not only from the point of view of climate change, but also from the point of view of business models and the values they create and offer as well as their customers and stakeholders.

Some analyses have reported that a correlation exists between commercial borrowers' sustainability performance and credit risks (Weber et al., 2015). It is demonstrated that the sustainability criteria improve the prognostic validity of banks (EBC, 2021; KPMG, 2021). ESG, and in particular, environmental risk, directly affects the profitability of the business, as financial institutions may decide to resign from providing services to a given sector defined as "dirty business" due to the increased risk of its service, reputation risk, and credit risk (Drei et al., 2019). Environmental risk also affects the operational risk of the bank, as it affects the value of receivables.

Banks should take into account the incorporation of climate—and environmental risks in their activities. Due to the occurrence of ESG risk, and in particular with high exposure to environmental risk related to climate change, they should pay particular attention to: (1) direction of changes in business model and strategy; (2) development of procedures to integrate ESG risk and environmental risk into governance and risk appetite processes; (3) changing risk management attitude to incorporate climate-related and environmental risks into their risk management framework, with a view to identifying, assessing, managing, and monitoring these risks over a sufficiently long-term horizon; (4) change the value system in business models. An important aspect, therefore, is to change the business models of banks so as to take into account the environmental factor but also to lead the way toward innovative banking models and sustainability.

DOI: 10.4324/9781003310099-7

The main aim of this chapter is to discuss the impact of environmental risk on banks' business models. The chapter is organized as follows: Section 7.1 introduces the chapter; in Section 7.2, theoretical aspects of environmental risk and its impact on the construction of the bank's triple business model are presented. Section 7.3 discusses different approaches and development of archetypes of bank business models. Section 7.4 discusses the mechanism of building lasting value in the bank's business model. Section 7.5 points to tools supporting building banking business models and environmental risk. Section 7.6 presents good and bad practices of banks in the context of implementing their business models and the problem of environmental risk. The last section concludes the chapter.

7.2 Environmental risk and its impact on the construction of the bank's triple business model

Climate change is affecting business (i.e., clients of banking institutions) and financial institutions (including the financial market), including banks (Breitenstein et al., 2021). Climate change implies doing business with SDGs and ESG factors in mind (Ziolo et al., 2021), and especially the environmental factor will affect the business in the future. It becomes imperative to identify the risks that are associated with both climate change, and in particular with the environmental factor, commonly known as the "E" factor. Due to the fact that the risk power of the environmental factor "E" will not weaken, but will only increase (Breitenstein et al., 2021), it is necessary to prepare not only for changes in banking but also to prepare a risk management plan that deals with the impact of the environmental factor on business and on banking risk. Thus, it becomes necessary to change business models.

Taking into account that the classically understood business model expresses the business logic of a specific company or institution, when referring it to banking activity, it must be extended to include specific stability conditions (Powell and Vo, 2020) and thus the specificity of this activity on the market (Osterwalder et al., 2005; Ziolo et al., 2021). A banking business model is a conceptual tool that contains a set of elements and relationships between these elements, as well as a specific type of value that the bank offers to its customers, and the way it operates, relationships with other business environments and stakeholders, including partners and partners, which allow you to run your business and create this value (Ziolo et al., 2021).

There is also a view in the literature that business models are also understood to have agency, to shape action within a financial institution, by stimulating employees to take action upon the business model (Mason and Spring, 2011). The literature on the subject combines business models with ESG risk. Therefore, it can be indicated that it is possible to adopt the Schaltegger et al. (2016) approach for banks and order:

> a business model for sustainability helps describing, analyzing, managing, and communicating (1) a company's sustainable value proposition to its customers,

and all other stakeholders, (2) how it creates and delivers this value, (3) and how it captures economic value while maintaining or regenerating natural, social, and economic capital beyond its organizational boundaries.

When a bank runs its business by accounting for sustainability, it accounts for the interests of direct and indirect stakeholders (Freeman, 1984), by considering the three most common dimensions of sustainability: people, planet, and profit (Fisk, 2010; Schutten, 2016). When running a banking business, one should take into account the external and internal principles as a fourth P, displaying the underlying values, or principles, for implementing sustainability (Marrewijk and Were, 2003; Schutten, 2016). The external and internal principles concern both the traditional rules of running a business resulting from the applicable law as well as the rules related to the implementation of stability and sustainability. Thus, the bank must see the problem more broadly and account for "the external and internal principles" related to its operations as well as its customers and stakeholders. It should be noted that one of the basic values in the concept of sustainability is the environment and environmental risk. Environmental risk as one of the basic components of nonfinancial risk factors referred in the acronym ESG (environmental, social, governance) affects conventional banking risks such as credit risk, market risk, operational risk, and others (Breitenstein et al., 2021).

Banks adapt to numerous changes and the needs of clients and stakeholders, which means that they are still in the midst of an era of fundamental change. A necessary change that requires a continuous adaptation process is in line with the idea of sustainability—in particular, the limitations resulting from the environmental risk "E," which has pushed banking institutions to rethink and adapt their business models. Some of the drivers are as follows (Sebbag and Denaye, 2017):

1. Economic uncertainty: After the recent financial crisis, the situation is highly risky due to the problems faced by economies as a result of COVID-19, and it is additionally reinforced by the instability and decisions of world powers in the face of the war in Ukraine. The economic landscape in the Eurozone and many countries around the world remains challenging. The continuing trend in many countries is low economic growth, high levels of NPLs, and a high inflation factor.
2. Political instability: Lack of political unity, Brexit, numerous aid packages for Ukraine, and the exclusion of Russian banks from the SWIFT system causes uncertainties in the current political landscape. In Europe, many European member states this year may feel destabilized as a broad-based rise in populism is taken into account. In view of the crisis and war in Ukraine, it is difficult to manage environmental risk when war is brutally destroying the environment. In addition, new decisions on energy solutions are necessary that can be taken at the political level to protect the environment.
3. Competitive landscape: As the digital revolution completely reshapes the provision of financial services and spurs the emergence of new entrants ("fintech"),

the established order in the banking sector is challenged; in the face of the challenges of the war in Ukraine, optics are changing, and the need to finance new technologies is growing. This transformation must be made with the use of renewable energy.

4. Regulatory environment: In the face of an unrelenting wave of regulatory requirements, and as the post-crisis regulatory agenda nears completion with the finalization of Basel III, banks need to continually assess the overall impact on their business models and whether certain activities remain viable. In addition, new regulations are important regarding the implementation of the Action Plan on financing sustainable growth (European Commission, 2018) and the resulting consequences of the development and implementation of standards for the exchange of information on ESG (in force from 2022). These consequences are the following: (1) regulation of the European Parliament and of the council on disclosure of information on sustainable investments and sustainable development risks and on amending Directive (EU) 2016/2341; (2) regulation of the European Parliament and of the council amending Regulation (EU) 2016/1011 as regards low-carbon benchmarks and positive carbon impact benchmarks; (3) regulation of the European Parliament and of the council on the establishment of a framework to facilitate sustainable investment. In addition, regulations on taxonomy, EU green bond standards, and disclosure of climate indicators and ESG factors are becoming important for banks.

It is worth mentioning the research by Jones and Upward (2014), who analyze all the elements in a social, environmental, and financial context. This approach may be important for banks to incorporate the assumptions of Jones and Upward (2014) in banks' business models. The downside of this approach is the poor governance risk analysis. The analysis of the approaches to ESG risk proposed in the literature shows that the environmental factor and environmental risk should be considered in business models by accounting for all ESG risks from the point of view of sustainable development. This postulate is formulated by Cardeal et al. (2020). However, in order to better understand the impact of environmental risk on the bank's operations, in particular the development of their products and the impact on stakeholders and customers, it becomes necessary to conduct an in-depth analysis of the impact of the environmental factor on the business behavior of customers and stakeholders of banks. This approach will allow banks to better refine not only the offer, but above all, to determine the impact of this risk on their financial situation as well as the value they build.

The analysis of the literature on the subject leads to the conclusion that it is worth expanding the "environment" risk E "layer from the point of view of the principles" formulated by Schoormann et al. (2016) regarding the analysis of factors affecting the environment the environmental, as there is an increase in environmental risk. Schoormann et al. (2016) indicates, on the basis of his literature analysis, three groups of factors important for the environmental risk "E" that should be analyzed by banks: (1) pollution control, clean production, eco-efficiency, life cycle thinking, closed-loop production, waste management, recycling, noise control, using renewable energy, environmental monitoring, and nature protection (the importance of this factor is indicated by Henriksen et al., 2012, Nilsson-Andersen et al., 2012, Duarte et al., 2013, Abuzeniab and Thompson, 2014); (2) regarding processes and activities of companies, sensitive areas have been defined: using natural resources, supplier selection, reserve logistics, delivery options (considering emissions, waste, noise, energy, and heat), reducing waste, reusing products, reducing CO_2 impacts, applying deposits to ensure taking back, and pollution prevention (the importance of this factor is highlighted by El-Gayar et al., 2006, Duarte et al., 2013, Hvass, 2013, Dewan et al., 2013); (3) aim of the action: determine principles regarding environmental awareness, sustainable consumption, sharing, motivation, and coaching (the importance of this factor is indicated by Watson et al., 2010, Boehm et al., 2011, Hvass, 2013, Schoormann et al., 2016).

The indicated factors should be integrated so that the business models ensure the bank's stability. Despite the fact that the "E" risk does not have a direct impact on the bank's business, it is necessary to consider this risk in addition to the "S—social" and "G—governance" factors of the ESG risk. Environmental risk affects the environment in which bank customers operate and affects banks' stakeholders as well as access to resources and the climate. The environment indirectly influences man as well, so the people and planet factors correlate with the profit factor, which is important for banks. Therefore, when constructing their business models, banks should pay attention to the "E" risk and link it with value-building and the offer addressed to clients. Practice and principles show that there is both a need and a necessity for links between environmental risks and opportunities to financial impacts, innovation, reputation, and access to capital and markets.

The bank should pay attention to the natural environment, society, and corporate governance, but in shaping its business models, it should pay attention to the risk of "double standards." ESG is an important factor to account for when making business decisions in many companies around the world, but the reputation of the bank itself as an institution implementing green standards is also important. It is getting harder and harder to identify the secondary environmental risk resulting from the introduced changes. Banks should develop internal standards for the identification of the secondary environmental risk based on potential environmental threats and check critical points. On the basis of practice, the following critical points can be identified that may be a starting point for the secondary environmental risk identification procedures:

- Spreading the idea of morality and cleanliness by people/companies/institutions, which then breaks the environmental standards of sustainable development;
- Analysis of environmental reports in terms of violation of environmental regulations;

- Checking whether the stakeholders conduct pseudo-ecological marketing (greenwashing)—that is, unjustified claims of companies that their activities are environmentally friendly—or not;
- Checking whether the desire for profit is related to the will to break environmental declarations or not;
- Checking whether the stakeholders who declare that they are running a green business are in countries where the green order does not apply or not;
- Despite the guidelines, banks should start implementing sustainability reporting for all clients, although EU taxonomy regulations—to a limited extent—for SME entities will enter in 2026.

Central banks, as well as international institutions (such as UE Commission or UE Central Bank), should take into account the problem of the risk of "double standards" in relation to the environment in changes to the applicable law and in reporting, in particular, in taxonomy. These indicated actions will allow building environmentally friendly banking business models, taking into account ESG factors, while at the same time being clean from the risk of "double standards."

7.3 Archetypes of bank business models

Actions for sustainable development as well as strong climate changes require not only changes in banks' business models. They enforce a holistic approach to tackle the challenges of a sustainable future: responses to environmental changes will necessarily need to be in parallel with economic and social change and take into account the ESG risk in building new bank value.

Bocken et al. (2014), in the most comprehensive and cross-sectional way, developed categorization of sustainable business model archetypes to describe groupings of mechanisms and solutions. The categorization of sustainable business model archetypes seeks to create new development paths or a capacity to innovate. The approach of Bocken et al. (2014, Bocken and Short 2015) is based on the literature (Stubbs and Cocklin, 2008; Bocken et al., 2013), and postulates the need to take a value network or systemic perspective, which means going toward creating new systems and generating value across the value network. For banks, it is important to understand which archetype(s) is/are well received by customers or stakeholders because this contributes to the economic factor that can motivate businesses to practice sustainability and respect for environmental risk.

Considering that the archetypes aim to categorize and explain business model innovations for sustainability, it is necessary to consider them by two key elements—two ideas. Banks know that eco-innovations, eco-efficiency, and corporate social responsibility are based on innovation for the environment and sustainable development and taking into account the holistic connections of the services/banking industry—banks' stakeholders and customers. Eco-innovations, eco-efficiency, and corporate social responsibility in banks are also based on the approach to ESG risk, including environmental risk "E." Therefore, in the preface literature, it is shown that banking is necessarily a key industry to transform to achieve environmental transformation (Bocken et al., 2014; Nilsson-Andersen and Andersen, 2012; Yip and Bocken, 2018). Table 7.1 shows two key ideas as determinants of the environmental transformation on the basis of which the archetypes of banks' business models should be formulated.

TABLE 7.1 Key ideas determining the steps toward environmental transformation in archetypes of banks' business models

Ideas, which determine the transformation	*Authors*	*Key characteristics*
Sustainable innovation	Richardson (2008); Girotra and Netessine (2013); Coulter et al. (2013); Edgeman and Eskildsen (2013); Bocken and Short (2015); Schaltegger et al. (2016)	(1) Balance both the competing and complementary interests of key stakeholder segments; (2) Business sustainability should manifest as economic viability and contribute to both societal and environmental sustainability; (3) Innovations seek to create significant positive benefits or significantly reduce negative impacts for the environment and on the quality of society's life in the environment; (4) Concept of value—create value network; create, deliver, and capture value.
Sustainable for services/ banking industry	Sheehan (2006); Gummesson (2008); Bocken et al. (2013); Alexander (2014)	(1) Growing significance of services, which is created not just by the supplier and the customer but also by a network of activities involving a host of stakeholders; (2) Value creation should extend to different stakeholders, not only the value to shareholders; (3) Integration of ecological limits, social equity, and economic justice into corporate strategies with core business areas of banks (including credit, investing, underwriting, advising); (4) Put sustainability objective on an equal footing with maximization of shareholder value and client satisfaction; (5) Actively strive to finance transactions that promote sustainability

Source: Own elaboration.

The starting point for the formulation of the archetypes of sustainable business models was the Weill research (Weill et al., 2005), in which the following thematic archetypes were formulated: (1) an entrepreneur creates and sells financial assets; (2) a manufacturer creates and sells physical assets; (3) an inventor creates and then sells intangible assets such as patents and copyrights; (4) a human creator creates and sells human assets; (5) financial trader buys and sells financial assets without significantly transforming (or designing) them; (6) wholesaler/retailer buys and sells physical assets; (7) an intellectual property (IP) trader buys and sells intangible assets; (8) human distributor buys and sells human assets; (9). a financial landlord lets others use cash (or other financial assets) under certain (often time-limited) conditions; (10) a physical landlord sells the right to use a physical asset; (11) an intellectual landlord licenses or otherwise gets paid for limited use of intangible assets; (12) a contractor sells a service provided primarily by people; (13) a financial broker matches buyers and sellers of financial assets; (14) physical broker matches buyers and sellers of physical assets; (15) an intellectual property (IP) broker matches buyers and sellers of intangible assets; (16) a human resources (HR) broker matches buyers and sellers of human services.

The archetypes presented here gave the basis for discussion and determination of banking business models and then their development toward sustainable bank business models, taking into account two key ideas as determinants of the environmental transformation. The research by Bocken et al. (2014) was selected as a starting point for a comprehensive framework to bring together innovations from research and practice to provide banking services for clients on the way to the environmental transformation of their businesses. In Figure 7.1, they were classified according to the degree of generality and the impact on the sphere of transformation as well as accounting for the generic classification—namely, technological, social, and organizational innovation. This approach was suggested by the research of Boons and Lüdeke-Freund (2013), which shows the main innovation types of the environment.

The approach to building archetypes must also account for the reorientation of the goals indicated when building business models (three main goals of change, formulated by Nosratabadi et al. 2020) and, in addition to measurable goals, non-measurable goals, including risk (Karkowska, 2020). Research indicates that factors such as the diversification process based on different sources of noninterest income and nontraditional activities that account for environmental activities have positive effects on bank sustainability (Karkowska, 2020; Yip and Bocken, 2018). Therefore, in their business models, banks should analyze the indicated nonfinancial factors (including ESG risk, in particular, environmental risk), as well as increase the impact on bank customers by changing the scope of services toward sustainability and financing stimulating environmental changes.

The development of climate action, as well as the evolution of sustainable development goals and accounting for the environmental risk factor "E," has also forced the need to verify the archetypes. The literature on the subject shows that they need to be analyzed when accounting for "customer traction in relation to these

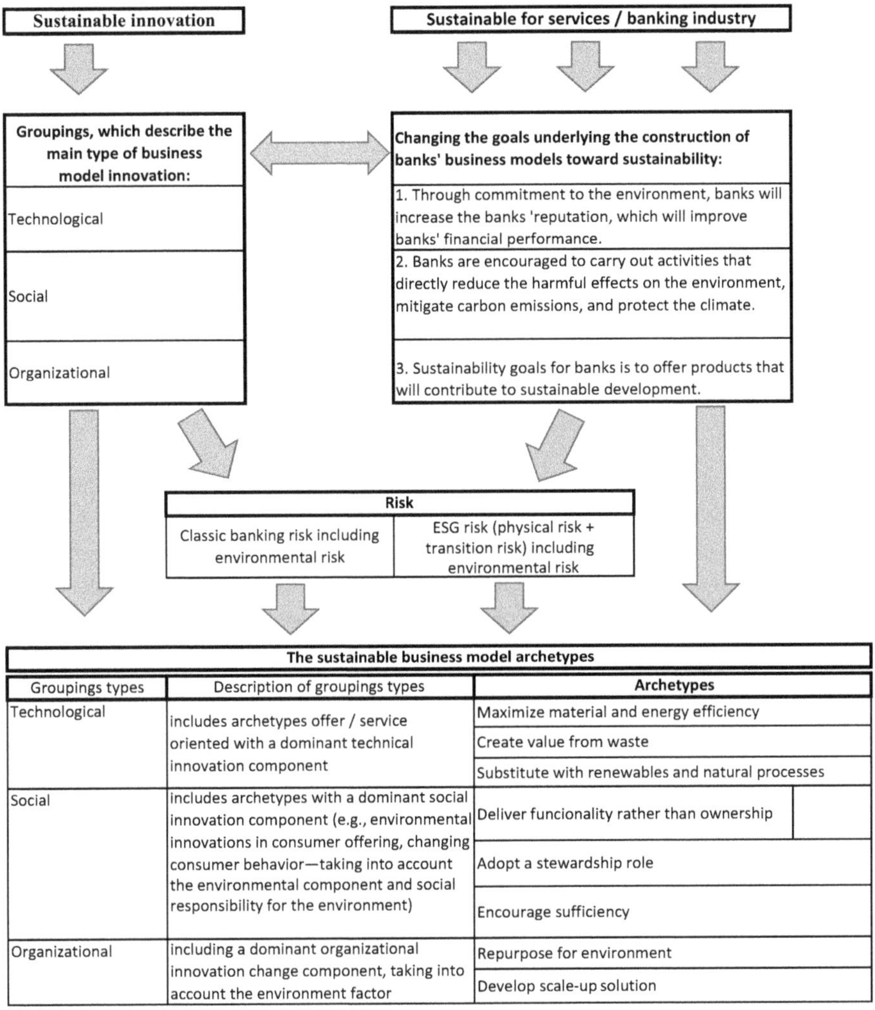

FIGURE 7.1 Classification of sustainable business model archetypes, taking into account the degree of generality.

Source: Own elaboration based on: Boons and Lüdeke-Freund (2013), Bocken et al. (2014), Nosratabadi et al. (2020), Karkowska (2020).

new 'financial archetypes.'" This modification was carried out by Yip and Bocken (2018). They validated and tested the customer receptiveness for the archetypes. According to their research results, the customers of banks welcome more "substitutes with digital processes," "adopt a stewardship role," and "encourage sufficiency" archetypes. Figure 7.2 presents a new archetype matrix.

Two archetypes have been negatively validated. They are marked in the picture with a red "x" In addition, it has been shown that archetype modifications are necessary: "Substitute with renewables and natural process" has been modified

Groupings types	Archetypes (2014)	Decision made	Archetypes after validation and testing (2018)
Technological	Maximize material and energy efficiency	Useful	Maximize material and energy efficiency
	Create value from waste	Canceled	
	Substitute with renewables and natural processes	Modified	Substitute with digital processes (modified)
Social	Deliver funcionality rather than ownership	Canceled	Inclusive value creation (new)
	Adopt a stewardship role	Useful	Adopt a stewardship role
	Encourage sufficiency	Useful	Encourage sufficiency
Organizational	Repurpose for environment	Useful	Repurpose for environment
	Develop scale-up solution	Modified	Resilience in loan granting (new/modified)
			Sustainable financial products (new/modified)

FIGURE 7.2 New archetype matrix.

Source: Own elaboration based on: Yip and Bocken (2018) and Nosratabadi et al., 2020.

to "Substitute with digital processes," and "Develop scale up solution" has been modified to two archetypes: resilience in loan granting and sustainable financial products. In their activities, banks force environmental reorientation through innovation, change of thinking, and environmental protection. Their business model based on green finance accounts for environmental values and sustainability factors and eliminates the ESG risk.

7.4 The mechanism of building lasting value in the banks' business models

Banks today are challenged to contribute to sustainable development on the individual, not only by financing innovation related to reorientation toward sustainability. Sustainability management in banks refers to approaches dealing with social, environmental, and economic issues in an integrated manner to transform the way they contribute in their 'clients' and 'stakeholders' businesses toward sustainability and within the limits of the ecosystem (Starik and Kanashiro, 2013; Schaltegger et al., 2012; Boons and Lüdeke-Freund, 2013). It appears that the "technological fix toward sustainability"—is insufficient to create the required transformation of bank customers and stakeholders and industries and societies. Therefore, banks must deviate from the traditionally projected value in their business models. Rana et al. (2013), Yang et al. (2013, 2016; Yang, 2015), and Bocken et al. (2014) responded to understanding opportunities for value creation in business models. They describe and define multiple forms of value (e.g., value absence, value surplus, value destroyed, value missed); also, in their research, they propose a framework for business model innovation for sustainability by explicitly considering value destroyed and value missed within the business model. Previous research on value creation in business models a qualitative framework to facilitate systematic exploration of the different forms of value for each stakeholder (Figure 7.3) and provides the basis for linking business model archetypes with various types of value for customers and banks' stakeholders.

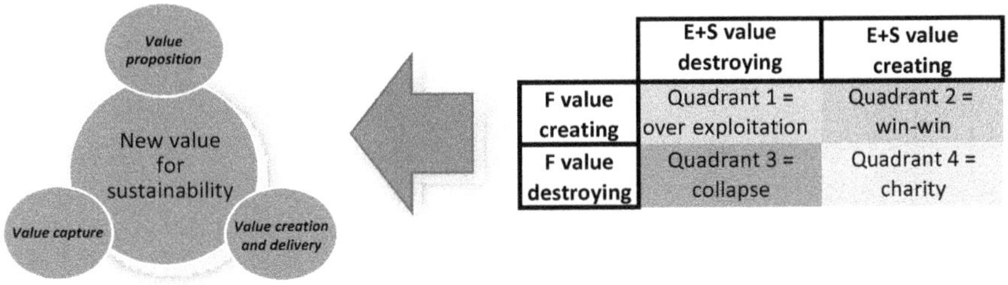

FIGURE 7.3 Relationship between the value creation matrix and the concept of new value in business models.

Source: Own elaboration based on: Rana et al. (2013), Yang et al. (2013, 2016), Bocken et al. (2014), Evans et al. (2017), Schoenmaker (2021).

In Figure 7.3, the relationship between the value creation matrix, based on the use of integrated value, and the concept of value in business models is shown. The integrated value consist of the sum of value: financial value (FV), social value (SV), and ecological value (EV), developed toward the achievement of the environmental goals of sustainable development. The integrated value influences the shaping of the new value for sustainability, which is created in banking business models.

The idea behind the integrated concept of value is that a socially responsible bank would build value in all three areas: financial, social, and environmental (Mayer, 2018; Schoenmaker and Schramade, 2019; Edmans, 2020; Schoenmaker, 2021). The integrated concept of value for sustainable banks, using sustainable business models, requires combining the environment with the social factor as a utility for society, ensuring the reduction of "E—environmental" risk. The banks would then be in quadrant 2 of the value matrix (Figure 7.3). To achieve this, environmental (E—environmentally and ecologically useful), social (S—useful for society) and financial (F—building financial value of banks for their stakeholders) value will need to become positive for most banks. Banks now in quadrant 1 will have to move to quadrant 2 to remain in business or face collapse (quadrant 3). The objective is quadrant 2. The same applies for banks in quadrant 4 (charity). These banks will have to become profitable if they want to scale up and achieve more societal and environmental impact. Transition pathways to move to quadrant 2 are needed for quadrants 1 and 4 (Kurznack et al., 2021; Schoenmaker, 2021).

Value-building for banks' business models is implemented in various ways. The value will be dropped depending on the archetype the business model represents and the kind of value being analyzed. In Table 7.2, value in sustainable business models of banks is presented, taking into account the archetypes and kind of value: (value proposition), the way value is built; (value creation and delivery), the way value is delivered; (value capture), the methods of its disclosure. Regarding banks, four key drivers of value creation are proposed (Gilding et al., 2002; Stankeviciene and Nikonorova, 2014; Ziolo et al., 2021): margin improvement, risk reduction, growth enhancement, and capital efficiency.

TABLE 7.2 Value-building for sustainable business models' archetypes

Archetypes	*Kind of value*	*Key characteristics*
Maximizing material and energy efficiency	Value proposition	Targeting product financing and services that consume less energy and generate less waste with similar functionality.
	Value creation and delivery	Focus on an offer of services implying innovation in internal processes.
	Value capture	Costs are reduced through increased operational efficiency, leading to increased profits. This results in a better position for the bank's profitability.
	Value added compared to conventional models	Fragmentary approach to the environment is replaced by comprehensive environmental efficiency improvement strategies.
Substitute with digital processes	Value proposition	Reducing the negative impact on the environment by using electronic means/carriers in business activities, a dedicated offer for financing to stakeholders and customers.
	Value creation and delivery	Innovation in banks' service delivery design enhances the speed, convenience, cost, and accuracy of service delivery to customers and stakeholders, offer of financing services and banking products for customers and stakeholders.
	Value capture	Increase in revenues created by the possibility of using digitalization, a decrease in costs related to the reduction of costs generated by the human factor.
	Value added compared to conventional models	Digitization provides banks with innovation and easy and quick contact with the customer without the need to maintain traditional bank branches. Digitization forces pro-environmental changes in banks' customers and stakeholders.
Inclusive value creation	Value proposition	Inclusive environmental value is created through innovative product and service that is dedicated to previously unserved markets or high-risk customers.
	Value creation and delivery	Process innovation is used to reduce environmental risk and all ESG risk.
	Value capture	Increase of market share and increased customer loyalty when customers become more profitable in the future. Environmental and social benefits are also captured.
	Value added compared to conventional models	Banks dedicate their services to segments of sustainable business clients and strengthen the loyalty of clients working for environmental protection.

Adopt a stewardship role	Value proposition	Building long-term relationships with stakeholders and customers as an important element of building value; strengthening customer relationships with environmental activities.
	Value creation and delivery	Implementation of benefit and commission systems; making sure that all actions and activities are aimed at ensuring stakeholder satisfaction. The value chain is geared toward social and environmental benefits.
	Value capture	Environmental stewardship strategies can generate brand value, increased market share, potential cost savings, and opportunities resulting from customer loyalty and secure future business. Stakeholders' well-being generates long-term business benefits; social benefits are also included.
	Value added compared to conventional models	Banks tend to adopt a shared value approach to leverage and benefit their core business, counting on the improvement of their situation in the future and an increase in profitability on these relationships in the long term.
Encourage sufficiency	Value proposition	Solutions reducing mis-selling of financial products and moral hazard in lending, aimed at pro-ecological activities. The focus is on the customer relationship and pro-environmental bonuses system.
	Value creation and delivery	Changes in payroll systems, linking remuneration to environmental activities and promoting pro-environmental attitudes, increasing the sales corresponding to the demand.
	Value capture	Customer satisfaction and loyalty can increase and provide more business revenue.
	Value added compared to conventional models	Banks give up the approach of "selling more" by replacing it with premier services/products to match the exact needs of customers financing environmental change.
Repurpose toward environment and society	Value proposition	Creating environmental and society benefits through specializing the product offer dedicated to customer needs and, in particular, environmental reorientation.
	Value creation and delivery	The sustainable business criterion and, in particular, the environmental criterion, is the customer selection criterion; banks specialize in servicing businesses and goals related to environmental reorientation and count on sustainable economies of scale.
	Value capture	Banking services reserved for the segment of sustainable business and disadvantaged clients based on positive screening and not only on environmental and social benchmarks.
	Value added compared to conventional models	High specialization toward sustainability and the exclusion of unsustainable customer segments.

(*Continued*)

TABLE 7.2 (Continued)

Archetypes	*Kind of value*	*Key characteristics*
Resilience in loan granting	Value proposition	Financial factors and factors of ESG risk are incorporated in credit and loan decisions, allowing for negative screening of projects that do not meet the criteria compatible with sustainable development and high ESG factors.
	Value creation and delivery	The impact of ESG risk on the cost of capital; this factor reduces the risk of the so-called "bad debts."
	Value capture	Customer reorientation with low or toward zero ESG risk can directly reduce financial resources for companies with adverse sustainability impacts.
	Value added compared to conventional models	Banks use a more comprehensive system to screen out unsustainable borrowers who are characterized by a high ESG risk.
Sustainable financial product	Value proposition	Asset-side and liability-side products and services for sustainability are created for savers/investors and borrowers, respectively.
	Value creation and delivery	Product and services innovation opens up new markets in sustainable finance and supports sustainable development and environment.
	Value capture	Product innovation enables participation in sustainable development that can provide a platform for both savers and borrowers to obtain a financial return on sustainable business, obtain a better market position, or enter a new market segment that brings measurable financial benefits.
	Value added compared to conventional models	Banks focus on the new market demand for sustainable business by providing clients with new platforms and financial products and platforms, use sustainable service distribution channels, and strengthen products and services for environmental change.

Source: Yip and Bocken (2018); Ziolo et al. (2021).

To sum up, the presented typology of bank business models allows one to indicate that we can talk about green (environmental) business models, social models, governance models, or the so-called mixed/hybrid models using a mix of ESG factors to build sustainable value in banks business models (Zhelyazkova and Kitanov, 2015; Ziolo et al., 2021). The literature on the subject indicates that for evolution in creating business models towards a green bank business model. We can talk about sustainable, green value or environmental value in banks' business models, which is a component of the green bank business model.

7.5 Tools supporting building banking business models and environmental risk

The literature on the subject points to the Cambridge Value Mapping Tool and the Sustainable Value Analysis Tool as important tools, which provide a structured way of helping banks identify opportunities for building sustainable banking business models and environmental risk "E."

The process of sustainable business model creation consists of five steps, and Figure 7.4 presents the idea (Bocken et al., 2014; Vladimirova, 2019):

1. Step 1: Defining the unit of analysis. The unit of analysis is typically a new value opportunity for the bank, which is connected with sustainability and the environment factor. This could be a product, service, a new idea of cooperation related to environmental transformation, a new sustainable business idea or sustainability innovation. Key stakeholders of the unit of analysis require considerations and definitions. These can be the environment, society, employees, partners, intermediaries, investors, borrowers, or other customers than borrowers.
2. Step 2: Selection of key stakeholders of the unit of analysis. The key stakeholders should be placed in each segment of the tool (Figure 7.4). This arrangement is to facilitate the generation of ideas with specific stakeholders related to the new value opportunity.
3. Step 3: Brainstorming then carried out to populate each stakeholder segment with the various forms of value generated for that stakeholder. This starts with identifying positive benefits that stakeholders might receive, followed by identifying contributions that stakeholders need to provide in order to realize the new value opportunity.
4. Step 4: Preparing a list of weakness factors, which is related to the possibility of the value destroyed or missed or negative outcomes for any of the stakeholders.
5. Step 5: Proposing from a balanced value proposition for each stakeholder identified in the process.

The Value Mapping Tool process for sustainable business modelling typically consists of four simple actions (brainstorms) (Bocken et al., 2014):

1. Action 1: What is the purpose of the bank business? Why is the business here in the first place? What is the product or service offered? Is it possible to combine business and environmental activities?

2. Action 2: What value is created for different types of stakeholders? Is sustainability and environmental value possible, and how does it position itself in relation to other factors? What is the impact of ESG risk factors? What positive value is created, and what negative value do the stakeholders mitigate?
3. Action 3: What is the value destroyed or missed or negative outcomes for any of the stakeholders? What is the significance of ESG risk factors? Is the business missing an opportunity to capture value or wasting value in its existing operations? Is the business missing an opportunity to capture value due to the ESG risk incurred? Is bank capture value dependent on the environmental factor? Does the bank lose capture value due to environmental risk?
4. Action 4: The focus is on turning negatives into positives. Do they require establishing whether new positive value can be created by a cooperation network for stakeholders through the introduction of activities and collaborations? What can banks learn from competitors, suppliers, customers, or even

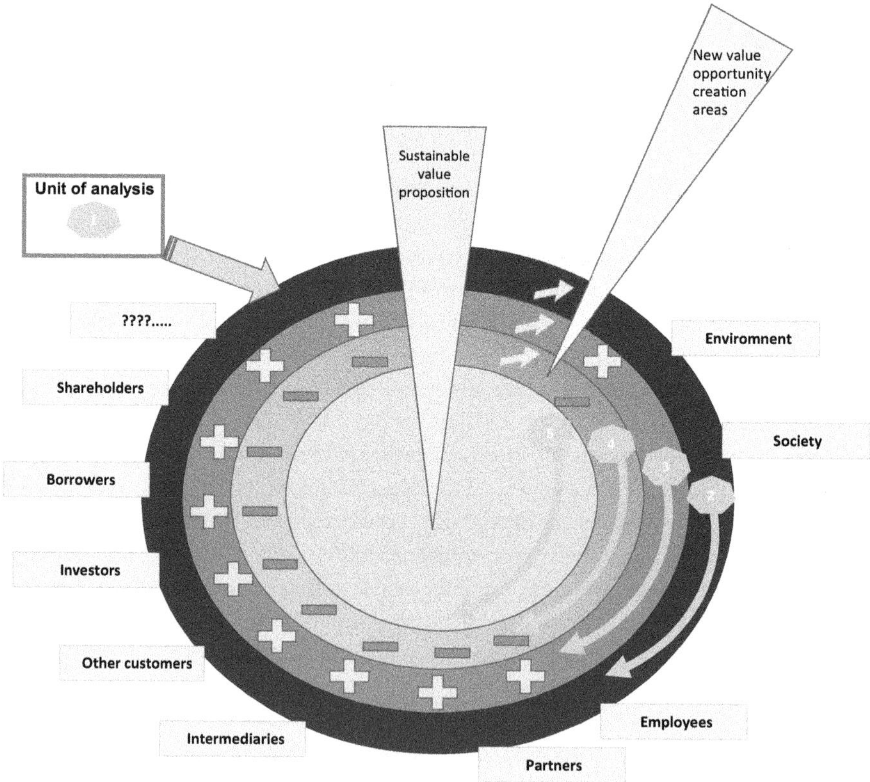

FIGURE 7.4 Process of sustainable business model creation.

Source: Own elaboration based on: Bocken et al. (2014); Yip and Bocken (2018); Evans et al. (2017); Vladimirova (2019).

other industries? What does the bank get from working toward sustainable financing and supporting environmental transformation? What can influence the bank's ESG risk?

It must be remembered that core values impact all the choices made in the area of "the unit of analysis" (Stec and Zwolinski, 2018) and are determined by the conducted brainstorms (actions).

The Sustainable Value Analysis Tool's purpose is to identify opportunities for sustainable value creation. This tool combines life cycle thinking and value forms analysis. The tool distinguishes the following types of values: VP—the Value Proposition, which defines the benefits delivered to stakeholders (e.g., the bank's product and service); VD—the Value Destroyed, which defines the negative value outcomes of the current model (e.g., depletion of nonrenewables, environmental damage, climate threats, negative social impacts); VM—the Value Missed, which is the value currently squandered, lost, captured too late, or inadequately captured by the current model (e.g., underutilized assets and funding sources, lost resources, waste streams, failure to capture value); VO—the Value Opportunity, which implies new opportunities for additional value creation in an environmentally friendly manner and positively influencing sustainability and capture through new activities, products, services, and relationships; VA—the Value Absence, which is the value required but not yet created (e.g., the additional labor required during operational periods in a bank); VS—the Value Surplus, which is the redundant value that is larger than the requirement. In order to achieve a more sustainable value proposition, the VD, VM, VA, and VS need to be analyzed in a life cycle so as to identify the value opportunities of improving contribution to sustainable development and improving the state of the environment (Yang, 2015; Yang et al., 2016). The idea of analyzing multiple forms of value is presented in Figure 7.5.

The tool provides the bank with a scheme to systematically look for each form of value uncaptured in the perspective of the life cycle—that is, the beginning of life (BoL), middle of life (MoL), and end of life (EoL) of the product. For this purpose, a matrix is used that in addition to the life cycle of a banking product or service takes into account ESG risk factors along with the determination of and potential profitability of sustainable value elements. The life cycle stages depend on specific products, services, and processes taking place in a banking enterprise. A specific matrix is described by Xij elements, in which X represents the segment of life cycle; i represents the value elements; j represents the specific life cycle stage in its segment (Yang et al., 2013). An example of a matrix is illustrated in Table 7.3.

The process of using the Value Analysis Tool consists of six steps. Yang et al. (2013) defined them as follows: (1) set the sustainability goal of the business; (2) clarify the current business model; (3) define the entire life cycle; (4) identify the VP, VD, VM, VS, and VA stage by stage throughout the life cycle with the consideration of sustainability; (5) identify the VO based on the identified VD, VM, VS, and VA; (6) implement the identified value opportunities. The tool can elicit value

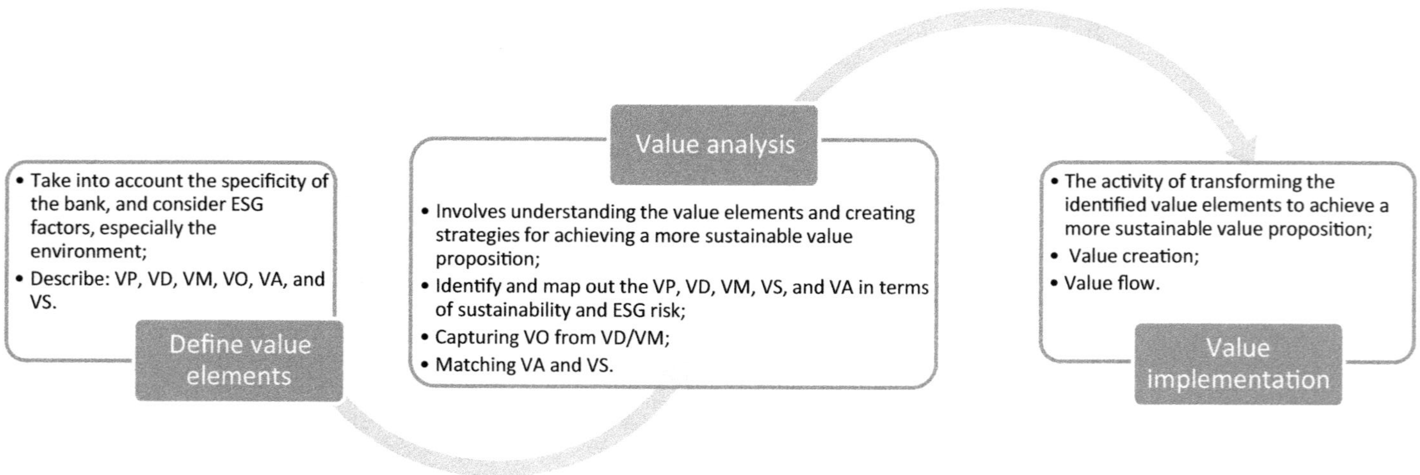

FIGURE 7.5 The idea of a process approach to analysis of multiple forms of value.

Source: Own elaboration based on: Yang (2015); Yang et al. (2016), Evans et al. (2017).

TABLE 7.3 Matrix of Sustainable Value Analysis Tool

Sustainable value elements			*Beginning of life (BOL)*					*Middle of life (MOL)*					*End of life (EOL)*					
			Design	*Procurment*	*Products, services, and others*	*Assembly*	. . .	*Distribution*	*Use*	*Maintenance*	*Others service*	. . .	*Remanufacture/ redefinition*	*Disassembly/ lean*	*Reconstruction/ redefinition*	*Cannibalization*	*Disposal*	. . .
i	j		1	2	3	4	n	1	2	3	4	n	1	2	3	4	5	n
VP	1	ECON																
		ENV																
		SOC																
		GOV																
VD	2	ECON																
		ENV																
		SOC																
		GOV																
VW	3	ECON																
		ENV																
		SOC																
		GOV																
VS	4	ECON																
		ENV																
		SOC																
		GOV																
VA	5	ECON																
		ENV																
		SOC																
		GOV																
VO	6	ECON																
		ENV																
		SOC																
		GOV																

Source: Own elaboration based on: Yang (2015), Yang et al. (2016), Evans et al. (2017).

uncaptured across life cycle banking products and services and uncover new value opportunities through a structured and visual approach and, in particular, can support ESG risk management, which carries additional value in itself.

7.6 Good and bad practices of banks in the context of implementing their business models and the problem of environmental risk

This section elaborates to present good and bad practices related to the implementation of banks' business models toward sustainability and ESG risk. Talking about bad practice is difficult, but it should be pointed out that every organization learns from mistakes. Thus, maybe a bad practice will not be identified, but a problem, a critical situation that can be avoided by building your business models, will be identified. Table 7.4 presents the critical moments, errors that have been identified as problems in the construction and operation of banking business models toward sustainability and innovation. Table 7.4 takes into account elements of the business model BMC according to the Osterwalder and Pigneur concept for banking institutions.

Taking into account the fact that sustainable banking is a global trend to transform the banking sector and develop new sustainable business models, apart from the critical element of building banking business models, it is necessary to present good practices and positive trends in shaping the business model innovation toward sustainability.

Transforming the business and technology of a corporate bank toward sustainable business models is slow, costly, and complex. This activity requires planning your own activities as well as effective interaction with customers and stakeholders. When implementing sustainable business models without taking into account all the intentions, and needs of customers and stakeholders, this is the first mistake. Then sustainable business models fail because there is a problem with the value offered. This aspect should also be considered as a critical element and considered as bad practice.

Accounting for the fact that sustainable banking is a global trend to transform the banking sector and develop new sustainable business models, apart from the critical elements of building banking business models, it is necessary to present good practices and positive trends in shaping the business model innovation toward sustainability. Table 7.5 presents good practices and positive trends in shaping the business model innovation toward sustainability.

It should be emphasized that environmental declarations of banks, which form the basis of their business models, are good practices. Such good practices are used in particular by ING Bank and Triodos Bank. These banks provide support for their clients in making decisions in the field of sustainability activities in order to improve the quality of life and counteract climate change. Therefore, they recognize that their responsibility is to actively participate in counteracting climate change.

TABLE 7.4 Critical elements in the construction and operation of the banking business model toward sustainability and innovation

Business areas	*Canvas*	*Description of the canvas (banks' business model element)*
Offer	**Value proposition**	The problem, or even the mismatch, between the product offer and customer needs is the degree to which the needs of customers and stakeholders are met after the transformation of the business model toward sustainability; another problem in this area is insufficient or misinterpreted information by customers regarding what value it will have for the customer's "new offer toward sustainability."
Customers	**Segments**	Mis-defining the profile of your ideal client, as well as individual customer segments with own characteristics; this situation may result in the loss of important customers.
	Relationships	Failure to consider important customer relationships, which causes loss of customers, lack of adequate products, problems with distribution channels, financial problems.
	Channels	Communication errors, insufficient communication with clients and stakeholders; this can upset the cost model and profitability.
Infrastructure	**Key resources**	Mis-definition of resources may result in improper functioning of the business model.
	Key actions	Failure to cover all activities, failure to account for all types of risks, including environmental risk, which may affect the degree of achievement of business and environmental goals.
	Key partners	Failure to cover all suppliers and associates, on whom the smooth functioning of the bank depends, in the network of relationships
Financial situation	**Revenue streams**	Incorrect estimation or failure to achieve the financial and environmental goals related to servicing each of the segments, financial flow plans, and generating profits; reputational breach
	Cost structures	Incorrectly estimated fixed and variable costs of the business model adopted, incorrectly estimated activities causing increased costs, no environmental effects despite high expenditure.

Source: Own elaboration based on: Qastharin (2016); Ziolo et al. (2021); Oliver Wyman (2022).

TABLE 7.5 Good practices and positive trends in shaping the business model innovation toward sustainability

An example of good practice	*Country (region) in which it occurs*	*Implications for ESG risk and the environment*
Responsibility for issues related to sustainable development and environmental activities has been assigned to bank boards and management bodies, and the process of supervision over the implementation of the sustainability concept has been detailed.	Europe, Australia, and North America	On average, 66% of the banks currently comply with the sustainability criteria.
The banks have set goals for their activities in the field of sustainable development.	Europe, Australia, and South America	1. 24% of them have set zero emission targets in line with the targets set under the Paris Agreement. 2. 33% of the banks introduced clear assessment criteria for their internal sustainability initiatives as well as for financial activities in this area.
It uses different criteria and approaches to assess exposure to climate change risk.	Europe, Australia, and North America	1. As many as 70% of banks build models for the analysis of various scenarios and stress tests, but the so-called data gap remains a major challenge for climate change risk assessment. 2. Only 19% of the banks analyze the weight of climate risk using credit or market risk indicators.
Banks have implemented sustainability reporting standards, focusing mainly on climate goals (taxonomy TCFD).	Europe, Australia, and North America	92% of banks have already adjusted their sustainability reporting to TCFD standards.
Strengthening ESG risk management and its strong positioning among banking risks.	France, Great Britain	The highest results in ESG risk management.
Disclosure of ESG information.	North America	Preparatory activities for the introduction of the reporting standard under TCFD. Integration of ESG risks with the risk management structure.
Implementing measures to foster a governance for sustainability.	Europe	Between 50% and 69% of banks' measures to foster governance for sustainability, in France and Great Britain up to 89%.

Source: Own elaboration based on: Mazars (2021), Responsible bank practices, benchmark studies, www.mazars.com/content/download/1070302/55653782/version//file/Mazars-Responsible-banking-practices-benchmark-study-2021.pdf (accessed: 30.04.2022).

7.7 Case of ING Bank

ING's declaration indicates the following changes in business models (ING, 2022):

1. Withdrawal from financing projects, coal-based production, including power plants;
2. Activities related to the negative impact on protected areas;
3. Activities related to a negative impact on animal welfare;
4. Activities related to the cultivation and production of tobacco products, palm oil production, and trade in palm oil;
5. Activities related to the negative impact on forestry.

Thereby, the customer canvas and offer have been changed toward sustainability and toward limiting climate change. The bank emphasizes that it will help industries, sectors, and private individuals in their green transformation and in running their businesses in a sustainable manner. Thus, it declares a special value, which is climate neutrality. The bank's activity is based on the pursuit of a circular economy, reducing paper documentation, and eliminating plastic. ING Bank declares to monitor activities for the benefit of the environment on an ongoing basis and also conducts environmental education as a value. The bank definitely strives for integrated value within the business models it has defined Schoenmaker (2021).

7.8 Case of Triodos Bank

It declares its value as integrated in the mission "to make money work for positive social, environmental, mental and cultural change," but also emphasizes that it has human dignity at its core. The bank strongly adheres to its values, which are the basis of innovation in business models. Their value is based on running "purposeful banking, banking on values or value-based banking." The bank focuses on the three Ps, "people, planet, and prosperity," at its very core. Products and services need to be designed and developed to meet the needs of people and safeguard, at the same time, the environment and society in its broadest sense. The "Offer" area of canvas focuses on products and services that bring you closer to four goals:

1. Reduction of property-based emissions;
2. Invest in green power;
3. Growth of natural resources to sequester carbon and support biodiversity;
4. Reduce carbon intensity in our whole portfolio and community and build a movement around it.

The bank also declares sustainable and ESG industry initiatives are merely a good start. Investments: from an exclusion strategy to a positive selection process, actions and supporting actions in accordance with the principle "Stop regulating the solution, start tackling the problem instead."

Both good practices show actions, but also a new value, which, apart from traditionally designated profits, is connected with actions for the benefit of the environment and society. The best practices aim to make it easier for other banks to build their innovative banking models toward sustainability.

7.9 Conclusion

In recent years, many bank activities that need to run while accounting for environmental factors have changed (reports and analyses of Mazars, 2021 or good practices of ING Bank and Triodos Bank). Banks are moving away from their traditional business models, seeing the need for innovation, but also for new values toward sustainability. Business models based on environmental innovations mean not only prestige and new integrated value but are also perceived as an opportunity to make ethical choices for the environment. The role of banks as financial intermediaries means that the challenges posed by ESG factors imply the need for an innovative approach and adaptation measures. As shown in the Mazars report (2021), European banks are leaders in changing business models, followed by North America, but it is not without significance that the faces of Latin American, Chinese, and Asian banks are also changing.

Despite the ever-growing stock of new challenges, including expected regulatory changes, banks approach ESG risks and change toward sustainability and environmental activities in a structured manner. Initiatives that banks are already taking and should be taking include, but are not limited to the following: (1) building new innovative business models toward sustainability, and in particular, in their canvassing, should modify the areas of offers, customers, and value; (2) defining the new integrated value as defined by Schoenmaker (2021); (3) defining their degree of integration of sustainability into business (over 50% in North and South America, Asia, and Australia and over 70% in the EU); (4) selecting sustainability risks to be communicated (e.g., in EU Disclosure Regulation), which may be different in each region of the world, and this is an important element of the business model; (5) adapting the business model to the required and accepted costs, skills, and technical capacities; (6) assessing the impact of ESG factors on pricing (integrated value) and evaluating the same for stakeholders. The identified challenges include the reconstruction of banking business models toward sustainability.

Not without significance in the discussion on environmental risk is the product offer (as indicated by the good practices of banks with sustainable business models). Until now, banks' business models toward sustainability have been based on simple product solutions, as indicated by Yip and Bocken (2018). At present, it is necessary, as indicated earlier and as shown by the Schoenmaker (2021) research, to create integrated value archetypes of business models. Banks are a learning organization. Therefore, good practice, in terms of developed business model archetypes towards sustainability and a new look at integrated value requires, will help to create new business models for new conditions towards supporting green business.

References

Abuzeinab, A. A. M., and Thompson, W. (2014). *Green Business Models in the UK Construction Sector: Empirical Study*. Proceedings of the 2014 Industrial and Systems Engineering Research Conference, San Antonio.

Alexander, K. (2014). *Stability and Sustainability in Banking Reform: Are Environmental Risks Missing in Basel III*. Cambridge and Geneva: CISL & UNEPFI.

Bocken, N. M. P., Rana, P., and Short, S. W. (2014). Using the Value Mapping Tool for Sustainable Business Thinking. *Sustainable Design and Manufacturing* sdm14–012: 333–349.

Bocken, N. M. P., and Short, S. W. (2015). Towards a Sufficiency-Driven Business Model: Experiences and Opportunities. *Environmental Innovation and Societal Transitions* 18: 41–61.

Bocken, N. M. P., Short, S. W., Rana, P., and Evans, S. (2013). A Value Mapping Tool for Sustainable Business Modelling. *Corporate Governance* 13(5): 482–497.

Bocken, N. M. P., Short, S. W., Rana, P., and Evans, S. (2014). A Literature and Practice Review to Develop Sustainable Business Model Archetypes. *Journal of Cleaner Production* 65: 42–56.

Boehm, M., Freundlieb, M., Stolze, C. Thomas, O., and Teuteberg, F. (2011). *Towards an Integrated Approach for Resource-Efficiency in Server Rooms and Data Centers*. Proceedings of the European Conference on Information Systems (ECIS). Paper 100. https://www.scopus.com/inward/record.uri?eid=2-s2.0-84870642770&partnerID=40&md5=e96be45818c4af8df4c31f511c398562

Boons, F., and Lüdeke-Freund, F. (2013). Business Models for Sustainable Innovation: State of – the art and Steps Towards a Research Agenda. *Journal of Cleaner Production* 45: 9–19.

Breitenstein, M., Nguyen, K., and Walther, T. (2021). Environmental Hazards and Risk Management in the Financial Sector: A Systematic Literature Review. *Journal of Economic Surveys* 35(2): 512–538.

Cardeal, G., Höse, K., Ribeiro, I., and Götze, U. (2020). Sustainable Business Models–Canvas for Sustainability, Evaluation Method, and Their Application to Additive Manufacturing in Aircraft Maintenance. *Sustainability* 12: 9130.

Coulter, A., Roberts, S., and Dixon, A. (2013). Delivering Better Services for People with Long-Term Conditions: Building the House of Care. *The King's Fund*. http://zelfzorgondersteund.nl/wp-content/uploads/2014/11/delivering-betterservices-for-people-with-long-term-conditions-1.pdf

Dewan, M. N. A., Biswas, N. R., Chowdhury, Md. M. H., and Quaddus, M. A. (2013). *An AHP-QFD Integrated Approach to Meet Three Dimensional Environmental Value Requirements in Sustainable E-Business Modelling*. Proceedings of the Pacific Asia Conference on Information Systems (PACIS). Paper 92. Jeju Island, Korea: PACIS.

Drei, A., Le Guenedal, T., Lepetit, F., Mortier, V., Roncalli, T., and Sekine, T. (2019). ESG Investing in Recent Years: New Insights from Old Challenges. *SSRN Electronic Journal*. http://dx.doi.org/10.2139/ssrn.3683469

Duarte, S., and Cruz-Machado, V. (2013). Lean and Green: A Business Model Framework. In *Proceedings of the Sixth International Conference on Management Science and Engineering Management*. London: Springer, pp. 751–759.

ECB. (2021). *The State of Climate and Environmental Risk Management in the Banking Sector: Report on the Supervisory Review of Banks' Approaches to Manage Climate and Environmental Risks*. Frankfurt: European Central Bank. November.

Edgeman, R., and Eskildsen, J. (2013). *Socio-Ecological Innovation: Strategic Integration of Innovation for Sustainability and Sustainable Innovation*. Proceedings of the International

Conference on Intellectual Capital, Knowledge Management & Organizational Learning. Bogotá, Colombia, pp. 114–122.

Edmans, A. (2020). Company Purpose and Profit Need Not Be in Conflict If We 'Grow the Pie'. *Economic Affairs*, 40 (2): 287–294. https://doi.org/10.1111/ecaf.12395

El-Gayar, O., and Fritz, B. D. (2006). Environmental Management Information Systems (EMIS) for Sustainable Development: A Conceptual Overview. *Communications of the Association for Information Systems* 17(1): 34, 756–784.

European Commision. (2018). *Renewed Sustainable Finance Strategy and Implementation of the Action Plan on Financing Sustainable Growth*. https://finance.ec.europa.eu/publications/renewed-sustainable-finance-strategy-and-implementation-action-plan-financing-sustainable-growth_en (accessed: 25.06.2022).

Evans, S., Fernando, L., and Yang, M. (2017). Sustainable Value Creation—From Concept Towards Implementation. In *Sustainable Manufacturing. Sustainable Production, Life Cycle Engineering and Management*, R. Stark, G. Seliger, and J. Bonvoisin (eds.). Cham: Springer.

Fisk, P. (2010). *People Planet Profit: How to Embrace Sustainability for Innovation and Business Growth*. London: Kogan Page Publishers.

Freeman, R. E. (1984). *Strategic Management: A Stakeholder Approach*. Boston, MA: Pitman.

Gilding, P., Hogarth, M., and Reed, D. (2002). *Single Bottom Line Sustainability: How a Values Centred Approach to Corporate Sustainability Can Pay Off for Shareholders and Society*. Sydney, Australia: Ecos Corporation.

Girotra, K., and Netessine, S. (2013). OM Forum—Business Model Innovation for Sustainability. *Manufacturing & Service Operations Management* 15(4): 523–700.

Gummesson, E. (2008). Extending the Service-Dominant Logic: From Customer Centricity to Balanced Centricity. *Journal of the Academy of Marketing Science* 36(1): 15–17.

Henriksen, K., Bjerre, M., Almasi, A. M., and Damgaard-Grann, E. (2012). *Green Business Model Innovation: Conceptualization Report*. Oslo: Nordic Innovation Publication.

Hvass, K. K. (2013). *Exploring Business Model Innovation for Closed Loop Fashion*. Proceedings of the Sustainable Innovation 2013–18th International Conference, Istanbul, pp. 111–117.

ING. (2022). *Ecological Declaration 2021 Capital Group of ING Bank Śląski S.A.* www.ing.pl/o-banku/esg/esg-srodowisko/polityka-srodowiskowa (accessed: 30.05.2022).

Jones, P., and Upward, A. (2014). *Caring for the Future: The Systemic Design of Flourishing Enterprises*. Proceedings of the RSD3, Third Symposium of Relating Systems Thinking to Design, Oslo, Norway, 15–17 October 2014.

Karkowska, R. (2020). Business Model as a Concept of Sustainability in the Banking Sector. *Sustainability* 12: 111. https://doi.org/10.3390/su12010111

KPMG. (2021). *ESG in Banks Effective Strategies to Use Opportunities and Mitigate Risks*. https://assets.kpmg/content/dam/kpmg/xx/pdf/2021/05/esg-risks-in-banks.pdf (accessed: 24.04.2022).

Kurznack, L., Schoenmaker, D., and Schramade, W. (2021). A Model of Long-Term Value Creation. *Journal of Sustainable Finance & Investment*. May 03. https://doi.org/10.1080/20430795.2021.1920231

Malone, T. W., Weill, P., Lai, R. K., and D'Urso, V. T., Herman, G., Apel, T. G., and Woerner, S. (2006). *Do Some Business Models Perform Better than Others?* MIT Sloan Research Paper No. 4615-06. May. http://dx.doi.org/10.2139/ssrn.920667. Available at SSRN: https://ssrn.com/abstract=920667

Marrewijk, M., and Were, M. (2003). Multiple Levels of Corporate Sustainability. *Journal of Business Ethics* 44(2/3): 107–119.

Mason, K., and Spring, M. (2011). The Sites and Practices of Business Models. *Industrial Marketing Management* 40: 1032–1041.

Mayer, C. (2018). The Future of the Corporation: Towards Humane Business. *Journal of the British Academy* 6(s1): 1–16. https://doi.org/10.5871/jba/006s1.001

Mazars. (2021). *Responsible Bank Practices, Benchmark Studies*. www.mazars.com/content/download/1070302/55653782/version//file/Mazars-Responsible-banking-practices-benchmark-study-2021.pdf (accessed: 30.04.2022).

Nilsson-Andersen, P., and Andersen, J. B. (2012). *Green Business Model Innovation in the Tourism and Experience Economy-Cases from Austria, Portugal, Denmark, Finland, Mexico, Norway, Sweden, Iceland, Russia and South Korea*. Oslo: Nordic Council of Ministers & Nordic Innovation Publication.

Nosratabadi, S., Pinter, G., Mosavi, A., and Semperger, S. (2020). Sustainable Banking; Evaluation of the European Business Models. *Sustainability* 12: 2314. https://doi.org/10.3390/su12062314

Oliver, Wyman. (2022). *Time To Start Again: How Greenfield Can Transform Corporate Banking*. www.oliverwyman.com/our-expertise/insights/2019/sep/greenfield-corporate-banking (accessed: 20.05.2022).

Osterwalder, A., Ondrus, J., and Pigneur, Y. (2005). *Skype's Disruptive Potential in the Telecom Market: A Systematic Comparison of Business Models*. HEC LAUSANNE Working Paper, May 2005. http://assets.fiercemarkets.net/public/smartgridnews/05-skype.pdf (accessed: 18.05.2022).

Qastharin, A. R. (2016). Business Model Canvas for Social Enterprise. *Journal of Business and Economics* 7(4): 627–637.

Powell, J. R., and Vo, D. H. (2020). A Comprehensive Stability Indicator for Banks. *Risks* 8: 13.

Rana, P., Short, S. W., Bocken, N., and Evans, S. (2013). Towards a Sustainable Business form: A Business Modelling Process and Tools. In *Sustainable Consumption Research and Action Initiative (SCORAI) Conference: The Future of Consumerism and Well-Being in a World of Ecological Constraints, 12–14 June*. Worcester: Clark University.

Richardson, J. (2008). *The Business Model: An Integrative Framework for Strategy Execution. Strategic Change* 17(56): 133–144.

Schaltegger, S., Lüdeke-Freund, F. and Hansen, E. (2016). Business Models for Sustainability: A Co-Evolutionary Analysis of Sustainable Entrepreneurship, Innovation, and Transformation. *Organization & Environment* 29(3): 264–289.

Schaltegger, S., Viere, T., and Zvezdov, D. (2012). Tapping Environmental Accounting Potentials of Beerbrewing: Information Needs for Successful Cleaner Production. *Journal of Cleaner Production* 29: 1–10.

Schaltegger, S., Hansen, E. G., and Lüdeke-Freund, F. (2016). Business Models for Sustainability: Origins, Present Research, and Future Avenues. *Organization & Environment* 29(1): 3–10.

Schoenmaker, D. (2021). A New Integrated-Value Assessment Method Forcorporate Investment. *Policy Contribution* 19/21: 1–8.

Schoenmaker, D., and Schramade, W. (2019). *Principles of Sustainable Finance*. Oxford: Oxford University Press. Available at SSRN: https://ssrn.com/abstract=3282699

Schoormann, T., Behrens, D., Kolek, E., and Knackstedt, R. (2016). *Sustainability in Business Models—A Literature-Review-Based Design-Science-Oriented Research Agenda*. Proceedings of the European Conference on Information Systems (ECIS) 2016, Istanbul, Turkey, 12–15 June 2016.

Schutten, W. (2016). *Sustainable Banking Business Models*. https://essay.utwente.nl/70548/1/Schutten_MA_BMS.pdf (accessed: 20.05.2022).

Sebbag, N., and Denaye, D. (2017). *Banks' Business Models: Enhanced Monitoring by the ECB*. Avantage Reply, pp. 1–4, January, Amsterdam, Roma, Torino, Brussels, London, Berlin, Luxembourg, Frankfurt am Main, Hamburg, Paris, München.

Sheehan, J. (2006). Understanding Service Sector Innovation. *Communications of the ACM* 49(7): 42–47.

Starik, M., and Kanashiro, P. (2013). Toward a Theory of Sustainability Management: Uncovering and Integrating the Nearly Obvious. *Organization & Environment* 26(1): 7–30. https://doi.org/10.1177/1086026612474958

Stankeviciene, J., and Nikonorova, M. (2014). Sustainable Value Creation in Commercial Banks during Financial Crisis, Contemporary Issues in Business, Management and Education 2013. *Procedia—Social and Behavioral Sciences* 110: 1197–1208.

Stec, T., and Zwolinski, P. (2018). Using Values Management for Shifting Companies to Circular Economy. *Procedia CIRP* 69: 805–809.

Stubbs, W., and Cocklin, C. (2008). Conceptualizing a Sustainability Business Model. *Organization & Environment* 21(2): 103–127.

Vladimirova, D. (2019). Building Sustainable Value Propositions for Multiple Stakeholders: A Practical Tool. *Journal of Business Models* 7(1): 1–8.

Watson, R. T., Boudreau, M.-C., and Chen, A. J. (2010). Information Systems and Environmentally Sustainable Development: Energy Informatics and New Directions for the IS Community. *Management Information Systems (MIS) Quarterly* 34(1): 4.

Weber, O., Hoque, A., and Islam, M. A. (2015). Incorporating Environmental Criteria into Credit Risk Management in Bangladeshi Banks. *Journal of Sustainable Finance & Investment* 5(1–2): 1–15.

Yang, M. (2015). *Sustainable Value Creation for Product-Service Systems (PSS)*. Cambridge, MA: University of Cambridge.

Yang, M., Evans, S., Vladimirova, D., and Rana, P. (2016). Value Uncaptured Perspective for Sustainable Business Model Innovation. *Journal of Cleaner Production* 140(3): 1794–1804. https://dx.doi.org/10.1016/j.jclepro.2016.07.102.

Yang, M., Rana, P., and Evans, S. (2013). *Product Service System (PSS) Life Cycle Value Analysis for Sustainability*. Proceedings of the 6th conference on Design and Manufacture for Sustainable Development (ISBN: 978-1-84919-709-0). Hangzhou, China.

Yip, A. W. H., and Bocken, N. M. P. (2018). Sustainable Business Model Archetypes for the Banking Industry. *Journal of Cleaner Production* 174: 150–169.

Zhelyazkova, V., and Kitanov, Y. (2015). Green Banking – Definition, Scope and Proposed Business Model. *Ecology & Safety, Journal of International Scientific Publications* 9: 309–315.

Ziolo, M., Filipiak, B. Z., and Tundys, B. (2021). Sustainability in Bank and Corporate Business Models. The Link between ESG Risk Assessment and Corporate Sustainability. Palgrave Macmillan. https://doi.org/10.1007/978-3-030-72098-8

8

ENVIRONMENTAL RISK VERSUS DEFAULT RISK IN BANKING

Krzysztof Kluza and Magdalena Zioło

8.1 Introduction

The relationship between environmental risk and financial risk is recognized (Bank of England, 2019). Climate-related and environmental risk is one of the factors initiating changes in the banking sector (ERA, 2016). These changes mainly relate to regulations and risk management systems and particularly to the inclusion of environmental risk and, more broadly, ESG risk, in the risk assessment and decision-making processes in terms of assessing their impacts on financial stability (ECB, 2020). Environmental risk may not only affect the size of a bank's revenues and costs but also the valuation of its assets and liabilities and finally its profits/losses (N, 2020). According to the FSR (2022), in the European Union, loans to polluting firms still represent around two-thirds of the credit exposures of banks, and environmental risk has a comprehensive impact on the financial situations of banks and their financial risk (Calice and Miguel, 2021).

Banks play a key role in ensuring the sustainability, and especially the financing, of the energy transformation sector (FSR, 2022), as well as even broader economic system transformation (Kemp-Benedict, 2018); hence, the assessment of the impact of environmental risk on the bank default risk is justified. The second issue concerns reputation risk, which is related to environmental risk and which has an impact on financial risk. Banks, bearing in mind reputation risk, must decide what policies to pursue with clients from the so-called dirty businesses, and they may exclude these companies from cooperation or propose less favorable cooperation terms (including the cost of access to financing) that are related to the higher risk that they bear. Usually, however, the pressure from stakeholders concerns the refusal of banks to cooperate with dirty businesses in favor of entering into environmentally friendly projects, which builds positive renown for the bank and minimizes the reputation risk.

DOI: 10.4324/9781003310099-8

Researchers have diagnosed positive relationships between sustainability and financial performance in the literature (Friede et al., 2015). However, such analyses mainly concern the nonfinancial corporate sector (Ferrell et al., 2016). Scholtens and van't Klooster (2019) show that banks with high sustainability scores (i.e., those who perform relatively well) have lower default risk as well as lower contributions to financial system risk. Research related to sustainability and bank risk is still lacking, and the research results are inconclusive (some neutral and positive impacts) (Boutin-Dufresne and Savaria, 2004; Bouslah et al., 2018). Moreover, we still lack in-depth research on the impact of sustainability on the default risk of banks (Scholtens and van't Klooster, 2019). Such research is highly desirable due to the impact of ESG risk, and particularly environmental risk, on financial markets, institutions, and default risk. According to Scholtens and van't Klooster (2019), both banks and financial authorities should "extend the scope of their risk analysis and management and explicitly account for information about how banks interact with sustainability."

The aim of the chapter is to present the knowledge of environmental risk in the context of its impact on the bank's default risk and to analyze the models in which environmental risk has been accounted for in the context of its impact on the bank's financial stability and the bank's financial risk. The chapter is organized as follows: Section 8.1 introduces the chapter; in Section 8.2 theoretical aspects and the research gap are presented. Section 8.3 presents approaches to evaluate the environmental risk impact on the bank's default risk, and Section 8.4 concludes the chapter.

8.2 Theoretical framework and the research gap

A review of the traditional research results on default risk indicates that the dominant trend in this type of analysis is usually the study of factors that influence default risk in different research environments (e.g., under the conditions of specific regulations). An example of such a study is an analysis of the default risk in microfinance institutions under the Basel III framework (Durango-Gutiérrez et al., 2021). According to the research results, the main variables that are related to default risk are the loan amount, number of payments in arrears, guarantees provided, assessment of the credit analyst, male gender of the borrower, and level and trend of the general stock exchange index. Because environmental risk has become one of the impactful risks according to Global Risks Reports, researchers have extended the analysis of bank default risks and have begun to analyze the impact of environmental sustainability. Researchers have identified climate change as a source of systemic risk, with potentially severe consequences for financial institutions and financial markets alike (FSR, 2022). The research on the impact of sustainability on the bank's risk is heterogeneous, and several main trends can be distinguished, such as Table 8.1: the sustainability impact on costs and equity in banking (Ciciretti et al., 2014); social performance, financial indicators, and sustainability (Ciciretti et al., 2014; Chih et al., 2010); the bank's engagement in sustainability and its

TABLE 8.1 Sustainability versus bank risk

Research problem	*Research results*	*Authors*
Sustainability impact on cost and equity in banking	Banks were more likely to be rewarded with lower cost of capital for both debt and equity.	Ciciretti et al., 2014
Social performance versus financial performance	In terms of causality, social and financial outcomes can be co-decided; larger companies are more CSR oriented, and financial performance and CSR are not related.	Ciciretti et al., 2014; Chih et al., 2010
Banks' engagement in sustainability and financial performance	Banks that engage in CSR activities are able to improve their financial performance.	Shen et al., 2016
Role of Islamic banking in ensuring financial sustainability	The study highlights the positive relationship between CSR disclosure and financial performance as well as the positive and very significant relationship between the size of the Sharia Governing Board (SSB) and the CSR disclosure rate. The article assumes a significant positive relationship between the complex CSR Disclosure Index measure and financial results. The results show no statistically significant relationship between each dimension of the CSR Disclosure Index and current financial KPIs, except for "Mission and Vision" and "Products and Services."	Mallin et al., 2014; Platonova et al., 2016
Link between environmental performance and operational efficiency	The study concludes that reducing environmental costs has a more immediate and substantial effect on the performance of financial services companies in well-developed financial markets than in less-developed financial markets.	Jo et al., 2015

Source: Scholtens, B., and van't Klooster, S. (2019), *Sustainability and Bank Risk*, Palgrave Communications, https://doi.org/10.1057/s41599-019-0315-9.

financial performance (Shen, 2016); the role of Islamic banking in ensuring financial sustainability (Mallin et al., 2014; Platonova et al., 2016); and the link between environmental performance and operational efficiency (Jo et al., 2015).

Nowadays, researchers cannot ignore the role of regulations nor the environmental sustainability context. Feridun and Güngör (2020) tackled the problem of regulatory and supervisory practices with respect to the prudential risks from climate change in the banking sector. The authors state that a research gap exists in the regulatory and supervisory approaches with respect to the prudential risks from climate change in the banking sector. The role of regulations is important and especially in the transition process toward a more sustainable economy. Governments play a key role in this process; however, their involvement may create extra costs or even losses for the banking industry (BIS, 2021). The transmission of climate-related risk into the banking sector involves two main channels: macro- and microeconomic transmission channels. As a result of the macroeconomic transmission channel, banks may suffer from economic costs and financial losses due to the increasing severity and frequency of the physical-climate risk drivers. Microeconomic channels are linked to transition risks because of the economic transition to GHG neutrality and its aftermath, such as changes in government policies, technological developments, or investor and consumer sentiment (BIS, 2021).

In the regression results of Scholtens and van't Klooster (2019), sustainability is negatively associated with bank risk. Banks[1] with high sustainability scores have substantially less default risk. The general research results are in line with the statement that better sustainability is associated with lower default risk, and systemic-risk contribution enhances the understanding of what constitutes bank risk.

A comprehensive overview of the environmental risk analyses by financial institutions is presented in the technical document of the Network for Greening the Financial System (ERA, 2020). In the document, the authors summarize the preliminary findings of other studies that are related to the financial impact on the transition risk (Table 8.2), and they present and analyze models and tools for assessing different types of risks, models used by different types of financial institutions, and other methodologies).

The exposure to environmental risk depends on several factors, including the sector and place of business. In the case of the enterprise sector, the companies classified as "dirty business" (i.e., companies from the fuel, chemical, agricultural, and mining sectors) bear the highest risk (Table 8.3). In turn, the issue of location is related to the level of development of a given country and thus to legislative advancement in ensuring "sustainability" (Figure 8.1). Currently, Europe remains a leader in the commitment to and the legal framework around protecting the climate and, in particular, ensuring climate neutrality.

An additional factor is the comparative advantage and involvement of individual industries in the creation of the GDP and the challenges that countries face in terms of, inter alia, coal mining in the context of climate change. The specificity of a given country and its location (e.g., in zones at risk of floods or extreme weather events) determines the type of risk that it has to face and prevent.

TABLE 8.2 Financial impact on transition risk

Study	*Preliminary findings*
A study by Tsinghua University Sun, T. Y., and Ma, J. (2020), Quantifying the Impact of Physical Risks on Default Probability of Bank Loans. NGFS Occasional Paper on Case Studies of ERA Methodologies.	The nonperforming loan ratio of representative coal-fired power companies could exceed 20% by 2030 (currently less than 3%). Responsible factors are the expected decline in clean energy costs, pressure to lower the price of coal-fired power plants, rising carbon prices, a decline in demand and an increase in financing costs for green and carbon-intensive companies.
A study by HSBC Global Research Robins, N., Mehta, K., and Spedding, P. (2013), Oil & Carbon Revisited: Value at Risk from Unburnable Reserves. HSBC Global Research.	Nonflammable fossil fuels could result in more than 40%–60% decline in the EBITDA of business valuations for some major resource-focused global companies including Shell, BP, Total and Statoil.
Mercure, J. F., Pollitt, H., Viñuales, J. E., Edwards, N. R., Holden, P. B., Chewpreecha, U., Salas, P., Sognnaes, I., Lam, A., and Knobloch, F. (2018), Macroeconomic Impact of Stranded Fossil Fuel Assets. *Nature Climate Change* 8(7): 588–593; NGFs, A Call for Action: Climate Change as a Source of Financial Risk, www.ngfs.net/sites/default/files/medias/documents/synthese_ngfs-2019_-_17042019_0.pdf	Loss potential ranging from USD 1 trillion to 4 trillion for the energy sector itself or up to USD 20 trillion in a broader view of the economy.
Allen, M. R., Barros, V. R., Broome, J., Cramer, W., Christ, R., Church, J. A., Clarke, L., Dahe, Q., Dasgupta, P., and Dubash, N. K. (2014), IPCC Fifth Assessment Synthesis Report: Climate Change 2014 Synthesis Report, www.ipcc.ch/report/ar5/syr/.	The mitigation costs of limiting warming to 2°C, including consumption losses due to risks of food and water security, loss of livelihoods and income, breakdown of infrastructure networks and critical services and the like, would be between 1% and 4% of global aggregate consumption by 2030.
Battiston, S., Mandel, A., Monasterolo, I., Schütze, F., and Visentin, G. (2017) A Climate Stress-Test of the Financial System. *Nature Climate Change* 7(4): 283–288.	The value at risk amounts to about 1% of the banks' regulatory capital, while losses vary between 8% and over 30% of capital across banks under "severe" scenarios.

Source: Own elaboration based on: ERA (2020), Overview of Environmental Risk Analysis by Financial Institutions, *Network for Greening the Financial System Technical Document*, September 2020, p. 11.

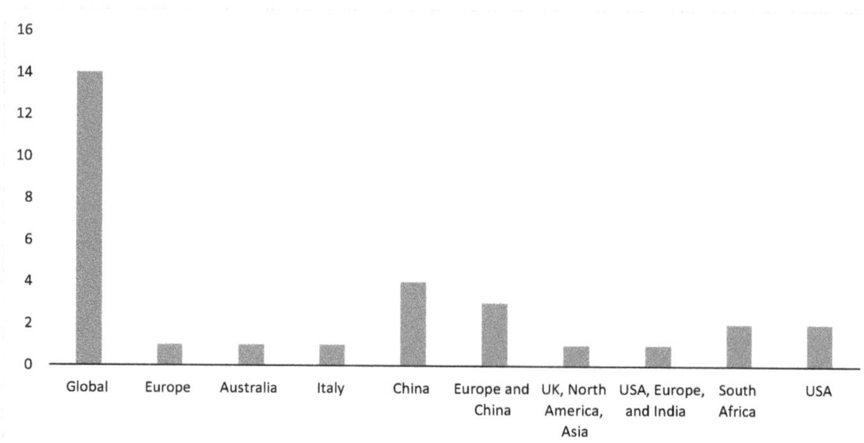

FIGURE 8.1 Countries according to environmental risk methodology mentioned the most in case studies.

Source: Own elaboration based on: ERA (2020), Overview of Environmental Risk Analysis by Financial Institutions, *Network for Greening the Financial System Technical Document*, September 2020, p. 51 (Appendix 2).

TABLE 8.3 Companies' sectors exposed most to environmental risk

Multisectors		*Real estate*	
Coal and related infrastructure	Oil and gas	Thermal power, cement	Thermal power, oil
	Agriculture	Power, steel	Fossil fuel and other carbon-sensitive sectors
Coal and related sector and infrastructure	Power, mining and beverage	Power, fuel, and transport infrastructure	Power and others
	Real estate, infrastructure	Energy, building materials, chemicals, mining, automobile, logistics	Utility and others

Source: Own elaboration based on: ERA (2020), Overview of Environmental Risk Analysis by Financial Institutions, *Network for Greening the Financial System Technical Document*, September 2020, p. 51 (Appendix 2).

The dominant risk that poses challenges to almost all countries in the world is the climate transition risk (Figure 8.2).

Related to the climate risk is the analysis of the banking risk that accompanies it. As the review of case studies shows, it is most often the credit risk (Figure 8.3).

There is a variety of models for assessing environmental risk, many methodologies for scenario analysis, and alternative methodologies used by financial

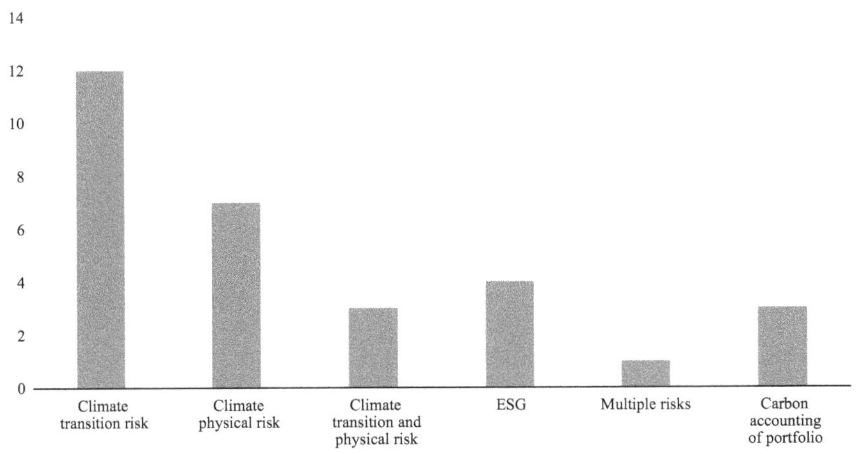

FIGURE 8.2 Type of environmental risk companies and countries face the most.

Source: Own elaboration based on: ERA (2020), Overview of Environmental Risk Analysis by Financial Institutions, *Network for Greening the Financial System Technical Document*, September 2020, p. 51 (Appendix 2).

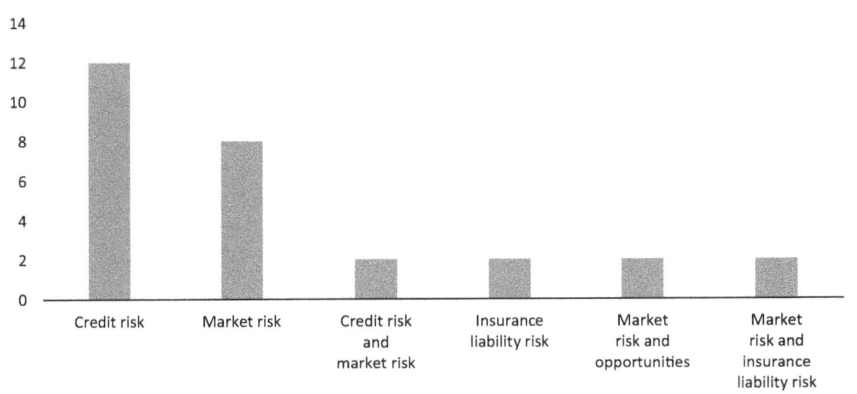

FIGURE 8.3 Type of bank risk impacted the most by environmental risk.

Source: Own elaboration based on: ERA (2020), Overview of Environmental Risk Analysis by Financial Institutions, *Network for Greening the Financial System Technical Document*, September 2020, p. 51 (Appendix 2).

institutions for nonfinancial risk. Every model has its limitations and benefits; however, the model selection is determined by the type of risk the model is linked to. CAT model and ESG scoring model based on analysis of case studies carried out by ERA (2020) are the most popular ones (Table 8.4).

TABLE 8.4 Types of models used for environmental risk assessment/scenarios

ESG scoring, factor pricing model		*CAT model*		*GHG accounting, compliance assessment*	
	IAMs, Merton model, CAT model	Own "late and sudden scenarios" model, valuation model, PD mode	Macroeconometric model, stochastic financial model	Extended CAMP model, carbon-factor regression model	Input-output model
ESG scoring, ESG integration into rating	IAMs, CAT models, Merton model, DCF model	Energy sector model, financial statement projection models	Macroeconometric model, IAMs, valuation model	PD model, LGD model, rating analysis	Total economic value model, financial ratios
Bottom-up approach, life cycle GHG accounting	Energy sector model, valuation model	Macroeconometric model, CAT model, valuation model	Weighted multifactor model	CAT model, PD model, LGD model	PD model
ESG scoring, ESG index construction	CAT model, valuation model	IAMs, valuation model	Energy sector model/ IAMs, PD model	IAMs, PD model, pricing model	IAMs and PD model

Source: Own elaboration based on: ERA (2020), Overview of Environmental Risk Analysis by Financial Institutions, *Network for Greening the Financial System Technical Document*, September 2020, p. 51 (Appendix 2).

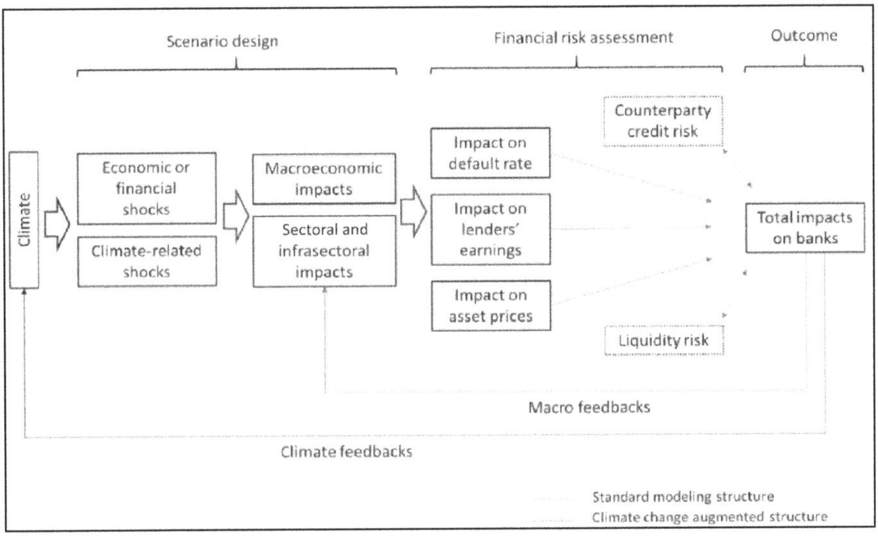

FIGURE 8.4 Structure of climate-augmented stress test.

Note: See also Moody's (2021), p. 18, for alternative modelling concept.

Source: Allen et al. (2020, p. 10).

8.3 Environmental risk impact on the bank's default risk

There are two basic methods of assessing the impact of environmental risks on the banks' risk profiles. The first one is based on modelling future scenarios related to climate change and evaluating their impact on banks' financial performance (see Figure 8.4). This approach typically means incorporating climate-related physical and transition risks in long-term macroeconomic scenarios and verifying both the particular scenario impact against the banks' risk profiles at the starting point and evaluating the differences between the scenarios in order to identify more preferred policies.

Transition risks mean the impact of specific activities of regulators or legislators conducted in order to promote pro-environmental behavior and technologies or ban unstainable ones for corporates and households. Such activities may include, for example, the introduction of CO_2 taxation on certain fuels. Transition risks also encompass possible long-term changes in technologies used (including some breakthrough innovations) as well as structural changes in supply and demand for commodities, products, and services. As a result, transition risks may exert a significant impact on all sectors of the economy by affecting the profitability of corporates and the value of financial assets.

Physical risks are the possible outcomes associated with climate changes such as global increase of temperatures. In turn, they may increase the frequency of local natural disasters such as floods, droughts, and heat waves and could also result in a rise in the global sea level. Physical risks may also cause business interruption, either directly, due to some losses to properties, or indirectly, by distorting global and regional supply chains or forcing businesses to relocate. As several analyses show, they are more significant for insurers than for banks.

Similarly, the approach employed by rating agencies also covers physical and transition risks and their impact on credit risk and market risk (the revaluation of portfolios at fair value and the counterparty risk) as well as sovereign risks. However, regarding financial metrics, rating agencies in their analyses typically focus on the current-year risk profile of the bank and its possible change within two years, as the goal of bank credit rating is to assess its risk for existing and soon-to-be lenders and shareholders (S&P, 2021a). Thus, the modeled horizon is much shorter, but the analysis is more extensive and, on a single entity level, encompassing also bank liquidity risk as well as several nonfinancial risks such as operational risks, business and strategic risks and even reputational risks. The framework for assessing the bank risk profile with indication, where ESG factors exert their influence, is depicted in Figure 8.5.

In both these approaches, it is important to identify sensitive sectors and geographic locations to transition and physical risks, as the impact of these risks will not be distributed uniformly across economies.

The results of the analyses carried out under these approaches will be described later in this section. From the systemic side, testing of the financial sector in terms of the impact of climate risks was initiated in 2017. The first such significant exercise was carried out by the Dutch central bank. Another exercise was carried out by the French ACPR and then by the Bank of England. A deepened methodology comparison of these stress tests is presented in Baudino and Svoronos (2021).

In 2022, the climate risk stress test for banks was carried out for the first time by the European Central Bank. The methodology of this test is described in ECB (2021). However, the results of the ECB's test have not been available at the date of this publication.

It is also worth mentioning the top-down climate-risk assessment conducted in 2021 by the European Central Bank—see Alogoskoufis et al. (2021). It examined the impact on default probabilities in several industrial sectors as well as banking sector average metrics under different environmental transition scenarios. However, this analysis compared the risk impact of different scenarios with respect to the orderly transition scenario only, so it did not evaluate changes in banks' risk profiles from the perspective of their current financial standing. So although it delivered several insightful pieces of information on the relative costs of risk for banks of different transition paths, it did not measure absolute risk changes for the banking sector. Thus, it will not be described in more detail in this section.

The pioneering exercise of testing the impact of environmental risks on the banking sector as well as insurers and pension funds was undertaken in 2017 by the Dutch central bank (DNB). The analysis embraced a five-year modelling horizon with the assumption of static balance sheets of the examined institutions. The Dutch analysis did not include physical risks, solely focusing on transition risks.

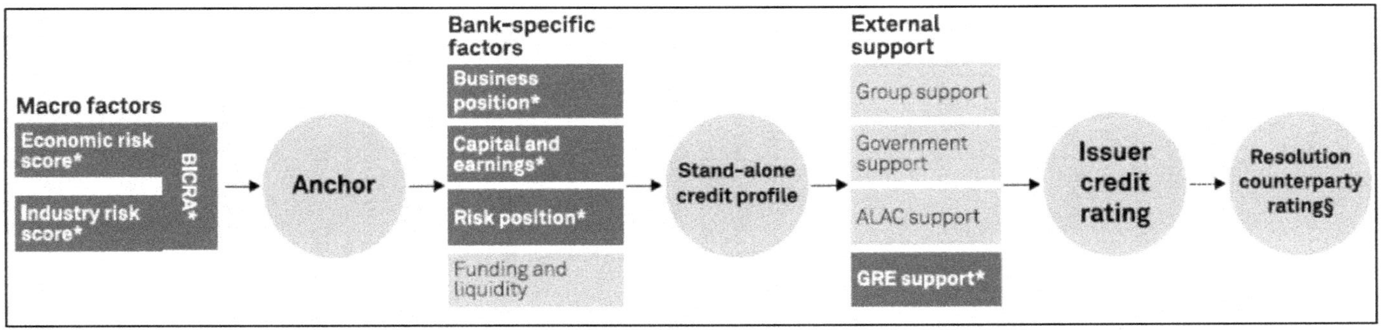

FIGURE 8.5 S&P Bank Criteria Framework with indication of influence of ESG credit factors.

*Categories most likely to include consideration for environmental, social, and governance credit factors are marked in blue.

BICRA = Banking industry country risk assessment; GRE = Government-related entity.

Source: S&P (2021b).

The transition variables comprised changes in energy technologies and climate policies.

The tests were granular to the level of 56 industries. Mining and petrochemical, utilities, basic industry and transport were identified as carbon-intensive industries. These industries accounted for 13% of total bank credit exposure. The stress tests were based on four scenarios:

- Policy shock—a disorderly transition scenario caused by a delayed policy action on the increase of carbon emission prices.
- Confidence shock—corporates and households postpone, respectively, investments and consumption due to uncertainty regarding policy measures and technology.
- Technology shock—the share of renewable energy in the energy mix doubles in five years due to technological progress.
- Double shock—the scenario where the policy shock and technology shock happen conjointly.

The impact of the Dutch pilot for banks is also significant, especially under the most severe scenario. In the worst case scenario, there would be both a sharp and global rise in carbon prices due to strong and abrupt policy measures and a doubling of the share of renewables in the energy mix within five years as a result of technological breakthroughs. These combined shocks could result in overall losses of 1%–3% of banks' total stressed assets, with this representing a decrease by two percentage points to four percentage points of the Common Equity Tier 1 ratio of Dutch banks, from its initial level of 15.6%. As the report concludes, despite such asset losses, the impact on supervisory ratios seems manageable (Vermeulen et al., 2018, p. 46). The impact of individual scenarios on bank financials is presented in Table 8.5. The probabilities of default were not projected.

TABLE 8.5 Scenario impact on bank assets and bank supervisory ratio (CET-1)

	Policy shock	*Technology shock*	*Double shock*	*Confidence shock*
Asset losses in % of total stressed assets*	2.1%	1.1%	2.6%	1.7%
Of which interest rate effect**	0.9%	0.2%	1.1%	~0%
Decrease in CET-1 ratio in % points	3.4%	1.8%	4.3%	2.8%

* A joint impact consisting of impact on carbon-intensive industries and other industries as well as interest rate effect. These are five-year cumulative losses.

** Interest rate effect is mainly due to holdings in government bonds with a long residual maturity and therefore a high duration.

Source: Own elaboration based on: Vermeulen et al. (2018).

However, even the most severe outcome of 2.6% losses of bank assets cumulated over a five-year horizon translates into 0.4% of the annual GDP. Although this value is not negligible, it is far lower than the typical cost of losses incurred due to financial crises in the past. Such crises used to cost typically between 3% and 10% of the annual GDP (see IMF, 1998; Kluza & Kluza, 2021). Thus, the impact of climate stress tests on banks' financial standing ranges from mild to moderate, depending on the scenario, and it is manageable from the perspective of supervisory ratio requirements.

Another one of the first exercises carried out to verify the impact of climate risks on the financial sector was undertaken by the French supervisory authority (ACPR) in the fourth quarter of 2020. It covered both French banks and insurance companies. The conducted stress tests differed from the typical former testing approach as they encompassed a 30-year horizon covering the 2020–2050 period in order to adequately integrate the effects of climate change in contrast to the usual 3–5 year time spans for stress tests. Bearing in mind that climate risk is highly location specific and sector specific, the scenario analysis was conducted for 55 sectors and for each geographical area (see ACPR 2021).

The scenarios examined were based on the guidelines published by the Network for Greening the Financial System (NGFS)—see Allen et al. (2020). The transition variables comprised changes in energy technologies and climate policies and physical variables, and the physical variables comprised temperature increases between 1.4°C and 2.6°C.

They assumed the following environmental policies and circumstances to take place:

- Orderly transition (the basic scenario), corresponding to the French National Low Carbon Strategy;
- Sudden transition, which combined a sharp increase in the price of carbon emissions, and less favorable changes in productivity than in the basic scenario, commencing after 2025;
- Delayed transition, which resulted in the implementation of more proactive measures and a very high increase in the price of carbon emissions after 2030.

The stress tests revealed an overall moderate exposure of French banks and insurers to climate risks, with a significantly lower impact on banks and nonsensitive sectors, which accounted for 90.3% of the banks' total corporate portfolio. Specifically, the exposure to the transition risk was evaluated (see Table 8.6). However, this conclusion was subject to the model assumptions such as the speed and the economic impact of climate change.

Noticeably, there are several "sensitive" sectors that will be affected the most—for example, crop and animal production, mining and quarrying, manufacturing of coke and refined petroleum products (see full list in Table 8.6). There, a significant part of credit losses will be concentrated, as their cost of risk is supposed to triple over the analyzed time period in the sudden scenario, compared to a 40% increase

TABLE 8.6 Cost of credit risk by sector categories and scenarios (in bps)—due to the transition risk

in bps	*Orderly scenario—2025*	*Orderly scenario—2050*	*Sudden scenario—2050*
Sensitive sectors*	12.4	30.8	37.3
Other sectors of interest**	19.0	23.3	27.8
Other sectors	19.4	24.1	26.8
Not allocated***	39.1	36.4	37.0
Total	**21.6**	**26.3**	**29.5**

Source: ACPR (2021).

* Crop and animal production; hunting and related service activities; mining and quarrying; manufacture of coke and refined petroleum products; manufacture of chemicals and chemical products; manufacture of other nonmetallic mineral products; manufacture of basic metals; sewerage; waste collection, treatment, and disposal activities; materials recovery; remediation activities and other waste management services.

** Manufacture of food products, beverages and tobacco products; manufacture of rubber and plastic products; manufacture of fabricated metal products, except machinery and equipment; manufacture of motor vehicles, trailers, and semitrailers; electricity, gas, steam, and air conditioning supply; construction; wholesale and retail trade and repair of motor vehicles and motorcycles; wholesale trade, except of motor vehicles and motorcycles; retail trade, except of motor vehicles and motorcycles; land transport and transport via pipelines; air transport; accommodation and food service activities; administrative and support services activities.

*** Corporate exposures not assigned to a NACE code (often SMEs/VSEs) were grouped in a common segment.

for the all-sector average. As a result, nonsensitive sectors are mildly affected by climate risks.

In general, the cost of risk deviation from the orderly transition scenario stems from the corporate portfolio. It amounted to 11.6% increase between the orderly transition scenario and the sudden transition scenario, which produces 75% of the whole inter-scenario difference. The risk assessment of the retail portfolio is mainly evaluated via macroeconomic variables such as unemployment rate and GDP change. As these variables do not vary much within different scenarios, the difference in the cost of risk on the retail portfolio amounts to 0.5% between scenarios. Table 8.6 shows the cost of risk by sectors with respect to their sensitivity to the transition risk.

The scenarios presented above translated into increasing probabilities of default for entities in given sectors. In 2019, the probabilities of default amounted to approximately 1.0%, ranging from 0.5% in the motor vehicles and trailers sector to approximately 1.8% in land transport and fabricated metal products sectors. In 2050, under the sudden scenario, they are predicted to rise to approximately 1.7%, ranging from 0.9% in the electricity and gas sector to approximately 2.6% in sewerage and waste collection and crop and animal production sectors.

Physical risks, not surprisingly, appeared to be not negligible for insurers, but for banks, they were relatively unimportant. For insurers, the models revealed that a twofold to fivefold increase in the loss ratio for claims related to natural disasters could emerge in the most affected regions. This would cause an increase in insurance premiums by 130%–200% over 30 years to cover such losses. It is important to note that the partial insignificance of physical risks for banks was due to some methodological difficulties encountered. Physical risks were expected to be considered via indirect (second-round) effects such as the impact on portfolios secured by immovable properties (retail and corporate) as well as the impact of climate events on business disruption, supply chain disruptions, and so on. Due to the lack of proper data, they were, in fact, not assessed.

In 2021, the Bank of England carried out its first Climate Biennial Exploratory Scenario, which aimed to explore the financial risks posed by climate change for the largest UK banks and insurers. Similarly to the ACPR exercise, it analyzed a 30-year horizon up to 2050. It examined the impact of both physical risk and transition risk. The transition variables comprised energy technologies, climate policies, and consumer preferences, and the physical variables reflected global and regional temperature pathways.

Three scenarios were analyzed, which were compared further with a "counterfactual" scenario that assumed no climate risks:

Early action—climate policy is ambitious from the beginning, with a gradual intensification of carbon taxes and other relevant policies. Global carbon dioxide emissions are reduced to net zero by 2050.

Late action—policies aimed at achieving a net-zero economy are delayed by a decade. Subsequent policy measures are more sudden and disorderly.

No additional action—this scenario primarily explores physical risks from climate change that would materialize if governments fail to enact policy responses to global warming. It is a deliberately severe scenario.

Different scenarios showed that if banks do not respond effectively, climate risks could cause a material burden on their profitability. Projections indicated an average annual loss of profits of around 10%–15%. Such losses, although controllable would make not only individual banks but the whole financial system as well more vulnerable to other future shocks. The impairment losses projected by climate stress tests are presented in Table 8.7.

Similarly to the Dutch and French stress tests, sensitive sectors were identified, in which banks projected the highest loss rates. These were mining (including extraction of petroleum and natural gas), manufacturing, transport, and wholesale and retail trade. For these sectors, projected cumulative impairment rates amounted to 35%, more than twice the aggregate projected impairment rate on the whole corporate portfolio (BoE, 2022, p. 44).

Although, the impairment losses projected by the Climate Biennial Exploratory Scenario were higher than in the case of stress tests conducted by Dutch and French monetary and supervisory authorities (see Tables 8.6–8.8, respectively), they were still assumed to be manageable without extraordinary state support. As the report

TABLE 8.7 Climate-related losses in corporate portfolio (cumulative 30-year impairment losses on bank lending)

	Early action scenario 2050	*Late action scenario 2050*	*No additional action scenario 2050*
Total impairment losses (billion GBP)	200	225	175
Of which: additional losses over "counterfactual" scenario (billion GBP)	85	110	60
Additional losses per annum as % of initial lending portfolio*	0.76%	0.99%	0.54%

Source: Own analysis based on: BoE (2021) and BoE (2022).

* Calculated under assumption that the analyzed banks accounted for 70% of UK banks lending to UK businesses (BoE, 2022, p. 19).

states: "Based on banks' and insurers' projections in this exercise, the overall costs to these firms from the transition to net zero should be bearable without substantial impacts on firms' capital positions" (BoE, 2022, p. 12). Possible business responses, especially under the no-additional-action scenario, involved a significant reduction in access to lending and insurance for sectors and households that were most exposed to physical risks. However, these rational strategies for protecting banks' financial standing would in fact deprive some market participants of financing and insurance, showing that banks' risk profile could be protected, but typically, this happens at the cost of their customers. Thus, the CBES exercise showed that the transition to net-zero targets would have a material impact on several sectors that banks were exposed to in future, forcing the individual market players in those sectors to change their business models.

The above stress testing exercises assessed the impact of environmental factors on bank risk based on modelling future scenarios, in particular in a long-term horizon, under assumed specific climatic and regulatory changes. Evaluating how banks' current financial standing and operational model are influenced by environmental factors and to what extent these factors deteriorate the current risk profiles of banks is a complementary approach to the above stress tests. The impact of environmental factors on banks' risks may be transmitted via different channels, as presented in Figure 8.5. As Chodnicka-Jaworska (2021) shows, ratings agencies, in general, have recently started to stronger price the ESG risk factors in their rating scores.

Environmental factors are incorporated mainly in the risk position segment of ratings analysis, including their impact on an institution's risk appetite and other material risks, which are not addressed within the capital and earnings assessment, as they are difficult to quantify in the expected RAC ratio due to their longer-term

TABLE 8.8 Definitions of environmental credit indicators by S&P Global

Environmental credit indicator	*Influence on credit rating analysis*	*Definition*
E-1	Positive	Environmental factors are, on a net basis, a positive consideration in credit rating analysis, affecting at least one analytical component.
E-2	Neutral	Environmental factors are, on a net basis, a neutral consideration in credit rating analysis.
E-3	Moderately negative	Environmental factors are, on a net basis, a moderately negative consideration in credit rating analysis, affecting at least one analytical component.
E-4	Negative	Environmental factors are, on a net basis, a negative consideration in credit rating analysis, affecting more than one analytical component or one severely.
E-5	Very negative	Environmental factors are, on a net basis, a very negative consideration in credit rating analysis, affecting several analytical components or one very severely.

Source: S&P (2021c).

Note: "Affecting" means leading to a different outcome for an analytical component or lower/higher headroom for an analytical component.

nature (S&P, 2021a), (Fitch, 2021). They are also included in macroeconomic circumstances, affecting general country risk rating, as very often, transition risks are triggered by some regulatory initiatives and government policy responses. In addition, the environmental perspective is embedded in industry risk analysis, mainly due to possible sectoral concentrations of physical and transition risks. These could be significant bank credit exposures to industries primarily engaged in extracting and manufacturing fossil fuels, industries manufacturing environmentally damaging physical commodities, and investments in or ownership of assets with below-average energy efficiency—see Fitch (2022), S&P (2021a), S&P (2022).

The combined impact of the above environmental risk factors is measured by environmental credit indicators. An example of the rating scale definitions of environmental credit indicators elaborated by S&P Global is presented in Table 8.8. The environmental factors evaluated for each institution, both sector/region specific and entity specific, are, among others, climate transition risk, physical risk, greenhouse gas emissions, waste and pollution (S&P, 2021c); for more details, see exemplary ESG ratings of banks available at the S&P Global website (www.spglobal.com/ratings/en/products-benefits/public-reports/esg-evaluations).

Table 8.9 shows the results of recent ratings of banks with respect to ESG factors conducted by S&P Global (S&P, 2022). The rating scores indicate that currently environmental risks do not have any material impact on bank risk profiles, the same

TABLE 8.9 Distribution of S&P Global ESG credit indicators for EMEA banks (Europe, Middle East, Africa)

ESG credit indicator	*Environmental*	*Social*	*Governance*
Positive (1)	0%	3%	0%
Neutral (2)	96%	96%	85%
Moderately negative (3)	0%	0.4%	14%
Negative (4)	4%	0.4%	15%
Very negative (5)	0%	0%	0.4%

Source: Own elaboration based on: S&P (2022).

Note: The survey encompassed 260 banks.

as social factors (96% of banks received E-2 and S-2 credit indicators). Nowadays, from this perspective, governance is the single most important ESG factor, although also with a limited influence on bank risk, especially in the European Union.

Similar results of evaluating the impact of ESG factors on the bank risk profile were obtained by FitchRatings with their analyses carried out at the end of 2021. Of the 950 banks rated by Fitch, ESG risk factors turned out to be either minimal or irrelevant to credit ratings for 83% of them. The environmental relevance score for each rated bank was either minimal or irrelevant (no medium or high-relevance scores). As in S&P (2022) results, governance factors had some influence on bank risk scores (17% of "moderate" scores), and, in 2% of cases, social factors also did (see Fitch, 2022).

In the view of both mentioned ratings agencies, the environmental factors do not currently affect bank ratings. However, they agree that climate-related risks are likely to become a more important credit consideration for banks, especially since climate change and the energy transition are of growing importance for policy-makers. This will be more important for banks operating in countries where the transition toward a low-carbon economy has to be shorter or in geographic areas more exposed to extreme weather events and other climate-related physical risks. Such future circumstances will materially affect bank credit ratings in a negative way—Fitch (2022) and S&P (2022).

8.4 Conclusions

In the short term, it can be seen that the impact of environmental factors on banks' credit risk is small or even neutral; see ACPR (2021), Fitch (2022), S&P (2022), Vermeulen et al. (2018). This is due to both the still limited materialization of physical and transition risks and the modification of risk strategies by banks, which, as financial intermediaries, they managed to identify some in advance and properly value them in their risk models or limited their risk appetite for selected sectors. In addition, banks are largely immune to direct physical risks, which are key threats to industrial structures. Such risks are usually connected with the location of facilities.

Banks, as the service providers, are only tied in a limited extent, compared to their total scale of operations, to a specific geographic location. Moreover, the development of cloud computing and decentralized data centers has further decreased in a significant way their exposure to physical risks. However, market risk may be a problem here for banks, since the duration of existing long-term contracts or maturity of financial instruments at time of their conclusion or issuance did not adequately consider environmental factors.

It is noteworthy that the above risks are considerably higher for insurers and pension funds, both due to the physical risks (for insurers) and market risks related to the revaluation of bond portfolios and related financial instruments (for insurers and pension funds) as well as changes in equity prices (for pension funds).

In the long-term horizon, lasting more than five years, environmental risks may start to materialize stronger in banks. From such a perspective, the following trends are very likely:

- A general decline in the profitability of projects and industries (the effect of climate-related regulatory actions, intensified Pareto taxation, and other public interventions), whose impact won't be fully transferable to customers.
- High concentration of environmental risks in a sizeable number of sectors and geographic locations.
- The emergence of catastrophic risks, not accounted for in risk models.
- Growing consumer demand for ESG-compliant and climate transition–supportive business models in the financial sector.

In order to achieve sustainable development, banks will have to define, finance, and implement an adequate business strategy with respect to both internal and external stakeholders. From the credit risk management perspective, it will be crucial to design new strategies for carbon-sensitive sectors. However, even with relatively passive adjustments conducted by banks, the environmental risk impact on banks will still be moderate, as, according to models, some climate costs that initially fall on banks, and insurers, may ultimately be passed on to their customers (BoE, 2022).

The above conclusions are subject to limitations caused both by the quality of data used in climate impact testing and the high uncertainty related to the future shape of economic and environmental trends. One recurrent theme across conducted stress tests was a lack of data on many key factors that participating banks need to understand to manage climate risks. For example, in the Climate Biennial Exploratory Scenario this resulted in vast (up to 10-fold) differences of climate risk impact on loan impairment rates between individual banks (BoE, 2022, p. 12). Similarly, modelling results may yield vastly different outcomes depending on the assumptions used. Future risk profiles of banks may just as well be more positive (e.g., due to some breakthrough innovations in renewable energy sources) or more negative (e.g., due to profound migrations, caused by severe climate changes, and their social, economic and political consequences).

Acknowledgment

Research project OPUS13 no 2017/25/B/HS4/02172 supported by the National Science Centre Poland (NCN).

Note

1 Banks situated in Euro countries in the period January 2002 until 2016. Research relies on Thomson Reuters DataStream to obtain information about corporate social responsibility from their ASSET4 database. Banks without such ratings were excluded and not analyzed.

References

ACPR. (2021). *A First Assessment of Financial Risks Stemming from Climate Change: The Main Results of the 2020 Climate Pilot Exercise*. Autorité de Contrôle Prudentiel et de Résolution No. 122–2021. Paris: Banque de France.

Allen, T., Dees, S., Caicedo Graciano, C. M., Chouard, V., Clerc, L., de Gaye, A., . . . Vernet, L. (2020). *Climate-Related Scenarios for Financial Stability Assessment: An Application to France*. Working Paper No. 774. Paris: Banque de France. July.

Alogoskoufis, S., Dunz, N., Emambakhsh, T., Hennig, T., Kaijser, M., Kouratzoglou, C., . . . Salleo, C. (2021). *ECB Economy-Wide Climate Stress Test: Methodology and Results*. ECB Occasional Paper No. 281. Frankfurt: European Central Bank.

Bank of England, B. (2019). *Climate Change: What are the Risks to Financial Stability?* Discussion Paper. www.bankofengland.co.uk/knowledgebank/ climate-change-what-are-the-risks-to-financial-stability

Baudino, P., and Svoronos, J. P. (2021). *Stress-Testing Banks for Climate Change: A Comparison of Practices*. Basel, Switzerland: Bank for International Settlements, Financial Stability Institute.

BIS. (2021). *Climate-Related Risk Drivers and Their Transmission Channels*. Basel, Switzerland: Basel Committee on Banking Supervision, Bank for International Settlements.

BoE. (2021). Money and Credit—December 2020, Bank of England, Published on 01 February 2021.

BoE. (2022). Results of the 2021 Climate Biennial Exploratory Scenario, Bank of England, Published on 24 May 2022.

Bouslah, K., Kryzanowski, L., and M'Zali, B. (2018). Social Performance and Firm Risk: Impact of the Financial Crisis. *Journal of Business Ethics* 149: 643–669.

Boutin-Dufresne, F., and Savaria, P. (2004). Corporate Social Responsibility and Financial Risk. *The Journal of Investing* 13: 57–66.

Calice, P., and Miguel, F. (2021). *Climate-Related and Environmental Risks for the Banking Sector in Latin America and the Caribbean: A Preliminary Assessment*. Policy Research Working Paper No. 9694. Washington, DC: World Bank. https://openknowledge.worldbank.org/handle/10986/35764

Chih, H. L., Chih, H. H., and Chen, T. Y. (2010). On the Determinants of Corporate Social Responsibility: International Evidence on the Financial Industry. *Journal of Business Ethics* 93: 115–135.

Chodnicka-Jaworska, P. (2021). ESG as a Measure of Credit Ratings. *Risks* 9(12): 226.

Ciciretti, R., Kobeissi, N., and Zhu, Y. (2014). Corporate Social Responsibility and Financial Performance: An Analysis of Bank Community Responsibility. *International Journal of Banking, Accounting and Finance* 5: 342–373.

Durango-Gutiérrez, Maria, Lara-Rubio, Juan, and Navarro-Galera, Andrés. (2021). Analysis of Default Risk in Microfinance Institutions Under the Basel III Framework. *International Journal of Finance & Economics*. https://doi.org/10.1002/ijfe.2475

ECB. (2020). *Guide on Climate-Related and Environmental Risks, Supervisory Expectations Relating to Risk Management and Disclosure*. Frankfurt: European Central Bank. November.

ECB. (2021). *Climate Risk Stress Test*. Frankfurt: European Central Bank. October.

ERA. (2016). *Environmental Risk Analysis by Financial Institutions—A Review of Global Practice. An Input Paper for the G20 Green Finance Study Group*. Cambridge, UK: University of Cambridge, Institute of Sustainability Leadership, Centre for Sustainable Finance.

NGFS. (2020). *Overview of Environmental Risk Analysis by Financial Institutions, Network for Greening the Financial System Technical Document*. Network for Greening the Financial System, Central Banks and Supervisors, Banque de France, Eurosysteme, NGFS Secretariat. September. www.ngfs.net/sites/default/files/media/2020/09/23/overview_of_environmental_risk_analysis_by_financial_institutions.pdf (accessed: 19.09.2022).

Feridun, M., and Güngör, H. (2020). Climate-Related Prudential Risks in the Banking Sector: A Review of the Emerging Regulatory and Supervisory Practices. *Sustainability* 12: 5325. https://doi.org/10.3390/su12135325

Ferrell, A., Liang, H., and Renneboog, L. (2016). Socially Responsible Firms. *Journal of Financial Economics* 122: 585–606.

Fitch. (2021). *Bank Rating Criteria*. New York: Fitch Ratings. November 12.

Fitch. (2022). *Where ESG Matters for Bank Ratings*. New York: Fitch Ratings. March 14.

Friede, G., Busch, T., and Bassen, A. (2015). ESG and Financial Performance: Aggregated Evidence from More than 2000 Empirical Studies. *Journal of Sustainable Finance & Investment* 5: 210–233.

FSR. (2022). *Financial Stability Review*. Frankfurt: European Central Bank, Supplement B. May.

IMF. (1998). *World Economic Outlook. Financial Crises: Causes and Indicators*. Washington: International Monetary Fund. May.

Jo, H., Kim, H., and Park, K. (2015). Corporate Environmental Responsibility and Firm Performance in the Financial Services Sector. *Journal of Business Ethics* 131: 257–284.

Kemp-Benedict, E. (2018). Investing in a Green Transition. *Ecological Economics* 153: 218–236.

Kluza, K., and Kluza, S. (2021). Finanse Publiczne a stabilność systemu finansowego. In *Finanse publiczne*, M. Ziolo (ed.). Polska Akademia Nauk, pp. 97–122. ISBN 978-83-66847-18-7

Mallin, C., Hisham, F., and Kean, O. W. (2014). Corporate Social Responsibility and Financial Performance in Islamic Banks. *Journal of Economic Behavior and Organization* 103: S21–S38.

Moody's. (2021). *Bank of England's CBES Climate Stress Test*. Philadelphia, PA: Moody's Analytics. August 3.

Platonova, E., Asutay, M., Dixon, R., and Mohammad, S. (2016). The Impact of Corporate Social Responsibility Disclosure on Financial Performance: Evidence from the GCC Islamic Banking Sector. *Journal of Business Ethics*. https://doi.org/10.1007/s10551-016-3229-0

S&P. (2021a). *Financial Institutions Rating Methodology*. New York: S&P Global Ratings. December 9.

S&P. (2021b). *S&P Global's Approach to ESG In Banks' Analysis*. New York: S&P Global Ratings. June 16.

S&P. (2021c). *ESG Credit Indicator Definitions and Application*. New York: S&P Global Ratings. October 13.

S&P. (2022). *How We Rate Financial Institutions*. New York: S&P Global Ratings. February 2.

Scholtens, B., and van't Klooster, S. (2019). Sustainability and Bank Risk. *Palgrave Communications*. https://doi.org/10.1057/s41599-019-0315-9

Shen, C. H., Wu, M. W., Chen, T. H., and Fang, H. (2016). To Engage or not to Engage in Corporate Social Responsibility: Empirical Evidence from Global Banking Sector. *Economic Model* 55: 207–225.

Vermeulen, R., Schets, E., Lohuis, M., Kölbl, B., Jansen, D. J., and Heeringa, W. (2018). An Energy Transition Risk Stress Test for the Financial System of the Netherlands. *Occasional Studies* 16–17. October.

BIBLIOGRAPHY

Abad, P., Benito, S., and López, C. (2014). A Comprehensive review of Value at Risk Methodologies. *The Spanish Review of Financial Economics* 12: 15–32. https://doi.org/10.1016/j.srfe.2013.06.001

Abuzeinab, A. A. M., and Thompson, W. (2014). *Green Business Models in the UK Construction Sector: Empirical Study*. Proceedings of the 2014 Industrial and Systems Engineering Research Conference. https://dora.dmu.ac.uk/bitstream/handle/2086/12669/Camera%20ready%203185301.doc?sequence=1 (accessed: 24.05.2022).

Acemoglu, Daron, Asu Ozdaglar, and Alireza Tahbaz-Salehi. (2016). Networks, Shocks, and Systemic Risk. In *The Oxford Handbook of the Economics of Networks,* Y. Bramoullé, A. Galeotti, and B. Rogers (eds.). Oxford, UK: Oxford University Press.

ACPR. (2021). *A First Assessment of Financial Risks Stemming from Climate Change: The Main Results of the 2020 Climate Pilot Exercise*. Autorité de Contrôle Prudentiel et de Résolution, No. 122–2021. Paris: Banque de France.

ALD. (2022a). *ALD Reliability and Safety Tools*. https://aldservice.com/Reliability-products/ald-reliability-and-safety-tools-overview.html (accessed: 24.05.2022).

ALD. (2022b). *ALD Software Architecture*. www.aldsoftware.com/download/ald/White Papers/ALD_Software_Architecture.pdf (accessed: 24.05.2022).

Alexander, K. (2014). *Stability and Sustainability in Banking Reform: Are Environmental Risks Missing in Basel III*. Cambridge and Geneva: CISL & UNEPFI.

Allen, T., Dees, S., Caicedo Graciano, C. M., Chouard, V., Clerc, L., de Gaye, A., . . . Vernet, L. (2020). *Climate-Related Scenarios for Financial Stability Assessment: An Application to France*. Working Paper No. 774, Banque de France. July.

Allianz ESG Integration Framework. (2019). https://www.allianz.com/content/dam/onemarketing/azcom/Allianz_com/sustainability/documents/Allianz_ESG_Integration_Framework.pdf (accessed:18.09.2022).

Alogoskoufis, S., Dunz, N., Emambakhsh, T., Hennig, T., Kaijser, M., Kouratzoglou, C., . . . Salleo, C. (2021). *ECB Economy-Wide Climate Stress Test: Methodology and Results*. ECB Occasional Paper No. 281. Frankfurt: European Central Bank.

Aven, Terje. (2003). *Foundation of Risk Analysis*. West Sussex, England: John Wiley & Sons.

Bakeli, Tarik Hafidi, and Alaoui, Adil. (2020). *Fault Tree Analysis (FTA) Based Approach for Construction Projects Safety Risk Management*. Proceedings of the 5th NA International

Conference on Industrial Engineering and Operations Management Detroit, MI, USA, 10–14, August. www.ieomsociety.org/detroit2020/papers/434.pdf (accessed: 30.05.2022).

Bank of England, B. (2019). *Climate Change: What Are the Risks to Financial Stability?* Discussion Paper. www.bankofengland.co.uk/knowledgebank/ climate-change-what-are-the-risks-to-financial-stability.

Barabási, Albert-László, and Bonabeau, Eric. (2003). Scale-Free Networks. *Scientific American* 288(5): 60–69.

Barnhill, Theodore Jr, and Marcos, Souto. (2009). *Systemic Bank Risk in Brazil: A Comprehensive Simulation of Correlated Market, Credit, Sovereign, and Interbank Risks.* International Monetary Fund. www.elibrary.imf.org/downloadpdf/books/071/20952-9781484368589-en/ch008.pdf (accessed: 22.05.2022).

Battiston, S., Caldarelli, Guido, D'Errico, Marco, and Gurciullo, Stefano. (2016a). *Leveraging the Network: A Stress-Test Framework Based on DebtRank.* February 22. https://ssrn.com/abstract=2571218 or http://dx.doi.org/10.2139/ssrn.2571218

Battiston, S., Glattfelder, J. B., Garlaschelli, D., Lillo, F., and Caldarelli, G. (2010). The Structure of Financial Networks. In *Network Science*, London: Springer, pp. 131–163.

Battiston, S., et al. (2016b). The Price of Complexity in Financial Networks. *Proceedings of the National Academy of Sciences* 113(36): 10031–10036.

Baudino, P., and Svoronos, J. P. (2021). *Stress-Testing Banks for Climate Change: A Comparison of Practices.* Basel, Switzerland: Bank for International Settlements, Financial Stability Institute.

BCBS. *Principles for the Effective Management and Supervision of Climate-Related Financial Risks.* www.bis.org/bcbs/publ/d532.pdf (accessed: 25.06.2022).

Bell, D. E., Raiffa, H., and Tversky, A. (1988). Descriptive, Normative, and Prescriptive Interactions in Decision Making. In *Decision Making*, D. E. Bell, H. Raiffa, and A. Tversky (eds.). New York: Cambridge University Press, pp. 9–30.

Bellman, R. E., and Zadeh, L. A. (1970). Decision-Making in a Fuzzy Environment. *Management Science* 17(4): B-141.

Benedikter, R. (2011). *European Answers to the Financial Crisis: Social Banking and Social Finance.* Stanford, Spice: Freeman Spogli Institute for International Studies. www.researchgate.net/publication/248388817_Social_Banking_and_Social_Finance.

Bernstein, A., Gustafson, M. T., and Lewis, R. (2019). Disaster on the Horizon: The Price Effect of Sea Level Rise. *Journal of Financial Economics* 134(2): 253–272.

Bian, Xun, Lin, Zhenguo, and Liu, Yingchun. (2018). House Price, Loan-to-Value Ratio and Credit Risk. *Journal of Banking & Finance* 92: 1–12. https://doi.org/10.1016/j.jbankfin.2018.04.006

BIS. (2021). *Climate-Related Risk Drivers and Their Transmission Channels.* Basel, Switzerland: Basel Committee on Banking Supervision, Bank for International Settlements.

Blacconiere, W., and Dennis, P. (1993). Environmental Disclosures, Regulatory Costs, and Changes in Firm Value. *Journal of Accounting and Economics*. December.

Bocken, N. M. P., Rana, P., and Short, S. W. (2014b). Using the Value Mapping Tool for Sustainable Business Thinking. *Sustainable Design and Manufacturing* sdm14–012: 333–349.

Bocken, N. M. P., and Short, S. W. (2015). Towards a Sufficiency-Driven Business Model: Experiences and Opportunities. *Environmental Innovation and Societal Transitions* 18: 41–61.

Bocken, N. M. P., Short, S. W., Rana, P., and Evans, S. (2013). A Value Mapping Tool for Sustainable Business Modelling. *Corporate Governance* 13(5): 482–497.

Bocken, N. M. P., Short, S. W., Rana, P., and Evans, S. (2014). A Literature and Practice Review to Develop Sustainable Business Model Archetypes. *Journal of Cleaner Production* 65: 42–56.

BoE. (2021). Money and Credit—December 2020, Bank of England, Published on 01 February 2021.

BoE. (2022). Results of the 2021 Climate Biennial Exploratory Scenario, Bank of England, Published on 24 May 2022.

Boehm, M., Freundlieb, M., Stolze, C., Thomas, O., and Teuteberg, F. (2011). *Towards an Integrated Approach for Resource-Efficiency in Server Rooms and Data Centers.* Proceedings of the European Conference on Information Systems (ECIS). Paper 100.

Bolton, P., and Kacperczyk, M. (2021). Global Pricing of Carbon-Transition Risk. *VoxEU.org*, 24 March.

Boons, F., and Lüdeke-Freund, F. (2013). Business Models for Sustainable Innovation: State-of-the-Art and Steps Towards a Research Agenda. *Journal of Cleaner Production* 45: 9–19.

Borys, G. (2000). *Ryzyko ekologiczne w działalności banku.* Warszawa: Biblioteka Menedżera i Bankowca.

Borysiewicz, Mieczysław, Andrzej, Furtek, and Sławomir, Potempski. (2000). *Poradnik Metod ocen ryzyka związanego z niebezpiecznymi instalacjami procesowymi.* Otwock and Świerk: Instytut Energii Atomowej.

Bouslah, K., Kryzanowski, L., and M'Zali, B. (2018). Social Performance and Firm Risk: Impact of the Financial Crisis. *Journal of Business Ethics* 149: 643–669.

Boutin-Dufresne, F., and Savaria, P. (2004). Corporate Social Responsibility and Financial Risk. *The Journal of Investing* 13: 57–66.

Brown, M. T. (1990). *Working Ethics: Strategies for Decision Making and Organizational Responsibility.* San Francisco, CA: Jossey-Bass Publishers. ISBN 1555422802.

Breitenstein, M., Nguyen, K., and Walther, T. (2021). Environmental Hazards and Risk Management in the Financial Sector: A Systematic Literature Review. *Journal of Economic Surveys* 35(2): 512–538.

Calice, P., and Miguel, F. (2021). *Climate-Related and Environmental Risks for the Banking Sector in Latin America and the Caribbean: A Preliminary Assessment.* Policy Research Working Paper No. 9694. Washington, DC: World Bank. https://openknowledge.worldbank.org/handle/10986/35764

Cambridge Centre for Sustainable Finance. (2016). *Environmental Risk Analysis by Financial Institutions: A Review of Global Practice.* Cambridge, UK: Cambridge Institute for Sustainability Leadership.

Cardeal, G., Höse, K., Ribeiro, I., and Götze, U. (2020). Sustainable Business Models–Canvas for Sustainability, Evaluation Method, and Their Application to Additive Manufacturing in Aircraft Maintenance. *Sustainability* 12: 9130.

CCSF. (2016). *Environmental Risk Analysis by Financial Institutions—A Review of Global Practice. An Input Paper for the G20 Green Finance Study Group.* Cambridge Institute for Sustainability Leadership. www.cisl.cam.ac.uk/system/files/documents/environmental-risk-analysis.pdf (accessed: 20.05.2022).

Cegan, J. C., Filion, A. M., Keisler, J. M., and Linkov, I. (2017). Trends and Applications of Multi-Criteria Decision Analysis in Environmental Sciences: Literature Review. *Environment Systems and Decisions* 37(2): 123–133.

Chavarria, Esteban, Cifuentes, Arturo, Hawas, and Francisco, Javier. (2014). *A Numerical Simulation Approach to Study Systemic Risk in Banking Systems.* https://dx.doi.org/10.2139/ssrn.2539020

Chih, H. L., Chih, H. H., and Chen, T. Y. (2010). On the Determinants of Corporate Social Responsibility: International Evidence on the Financial Industry. *Journal of Business Ethics* 93: 115–135.

Chodnicka-Jaworska, P. (2021). ESG as a Measure of Credit Ratings. *Risks* 9(12): 226.

Chu, Wang, and Feng, Yanli. (2009). *Fault Tree Based Architectural Analysis for E-Business Systems.* Proceedings of the Second Symposium International Computer Science and Computational Technology (ISCSCT '09), Huangshan, China, 26–28 December, 052–057. http://citeseerx.ist.psu.edu/viewdoc/download?doi=10.1.1.404.828&rep=rep1&type=pdf (accessed: 15.05.2022).

Ciciretti, R., Kobeissi, N., and Zhu, Y. (2014). Corporate Social Responsibility and Financial Performance: An Analysis of Bank Community Responsibility. *International Journal of Banking, Accounting and Finance* 5: 342–373.

Communication from the Commission to the European Parliament, the Council, the European Economic and Social Committee and the Committee of the Regions. *Action Plan: Financing Sustainable Growth.* https://eur-lex.europa.eu/legal-content/EN/TXT/?uri=CELEX%3A52018DC0097.

Communication from the Commission to the European Parliament, the Council, the European Economic and Social Committee and the Committee of the Regions. *EU Taxonomy, Corporate Sustainability Reporting, Sustainability Preferences and Fiduciary Duties: Directing Finance Towards the European Green Deal.* https://eur-lex.europa.eu/legal-content/EN/TXT/PDF/?uri=CELEX:52021DC0188&from=EN

Communication from the Commission to the European Parliament, the Council, the European Economic and Social Committee and the Committee of the Regions. *The European Green Deal.* https://eur-lex.europa.eu/legal-content/EN/TXT/?qid=1576150542719&uri=COM%3A2019%3A640%3AFIN.

Communication from the Commission to the European Parliament, the Council, the European Economic and Social Committee and the Committee of the Regions. *Strategy for Financing the Transition to a Sustainable Economy.* https://eur-lex.europa.eu/legal-content/EN/TXT/?uri=CELEX:52021DC0390.

Coulter, A., Roberts, S., and Dixon, A. (2013). Delivering Better Services for People with Long-Term Conditions: Building the House of Care. *The King's Fund.* http://zelfzorgondersteund.nl/wp-content/uploads/2014/11/delivering-betterservices-for-people-with-long-term-conditions-1.pdf.

D&B. (2022). *D&B Finance Analytics.* May 30. www.dnb.com/products/finance-credit-risk/dnb-finance-analytics.html\.

Davis, K. How Technology Is Shaping the Future of Operational Risk Management. *Risk & Compliance Journal.* https://deloitte.wsj.com/articles/how-technology-is-shaping-the-future-of-operational-risk-management-1528171333 (accessed: 24.04.2022).

De Bandt, O., and Hartmann, P. (2000). *Systemic Risk: A Survey.* CEPR Discussion Paper No. 2634.

Dean, Marco. (2020a). Multi-Criteria Analysis. In *Advances in Transport Policy and Planning*, Vol. 6, Niek Mouter (ed.). Academic Press, pp. 165–224. https://doi.org/10.1016/bs.atpp.2020.07.001

Dean, Marco. (2020b). Participatory Multi-Criteria Analysis Methodologies: Comprehensive, Inclusive, Transparent and User-Friendly? An Application to the Case of the London Gateway Port. *Research in Transportation Economics* 88(C), 100887.

Dean, Marco, and Hickman, R. (2018). Comparing Cost-Benefit Analysis and Participatory Multicriteria Analysis Methodologies. In *Decision-Making for Sustainable Transport and Mobility: Multi Actor Multi Criteria Analysis*, G. Baudry and C. Macharis (eds.). Cheltenham, UK: Edward Elgar Publishing, pp. 100–119.

Degryse, H., Goncharenko, R., Theunisz, C., and Vadasz, T. (2021). *When Green Meets Green.* CEPR Discussion Paper, DP16536, Working Paper Research No 392. Brussels: National Bank of Belgium.

Deloitte. (2018). *The Future of Non-Financial Risk in Financial Services: Building an Effective Non-Financial Risk Management Program.* https://www2.deloitte.com/content/dam/Deloitte/sg/Documents/risk/sea-ra-future-non-financial-risk.pdf (accessed: 18.09.2022).

Deloitte. (2021). *FSOC Report on Climate-related Financial Risks.* www.2deloitte.com (accessed:18.09.2022).

Dewan, M. N. A., Biswas, N. R., Chowdhury, Md. M. H., and Quaddus, M. A. (2013). *An AHP-QFD Integrated Approach to Meet Three Dimensional Environmental Value Requirements in Sustainable E-Business Modelling.* Proceedings of the Pacific Asia Conference on Information Systems (PACIS). Paper 92.

Dodgson, J. S., Spackman, M., Pearman, A., and Phillips, L. D. (2009). *Multi-Criteria Analysis: A Manual.* London: Department for Communities and Local Government. ISBN 9781409810230.

Directive 2004/35/CE of the European Parliament and of the Council of 21 April 2004 on Environmental Liability with Regard to the Prevention and Remedying of Environmental Damage. https://eur-lex.europa.eu/legal-content/EN/TXT/?uri=celex%3A32004L0035.

Drei, A., Le Guenedal, T., Lepetit, F., Mortier, V., Roncalli, T., and Sekine, T. (2019). ESG Investing in Recent Years: New Insights from Old Challenges. *SSRN Electronic Journal.* http://dx.doi.org/10.2139/ssrn.3683469

Duarte, S., and Cruz-Machado, V. (2013). Lean and Green: A Business Model Framework. In *Proceedings of the Sixth International Conference on Management Science and Engineering Management.* London: Springer, pp. 751–759.

Durango-Gutiérrez, Maria, Lara-Rubio, Juan, and Navarro-Galera, Andrés. (2021). Analysis of Default Risk in Microfinance Institutions Under the Basel III Framework. *International Journal of Finance & Economics.* http://dx.doi.org/10.1002/ijfe.2475

EBA. *Final Draft Implementing Technical Standards on Prudential Disclosures on ESG Risks in Accordance with Article 449a CRR.* www.eba.europa.eu/sites/default/documents/files/document_library/Publications/Draft%20Technical%20Standards/2022/1026171/EBA%20draft%20ITS%20on%20Pillar%203%20disclosures%20on%20ESG%20risks.pdf (accessed: 25.06.2022).

EBA. *Guidelines on Loan Origination and Monitoring.* www.eba.europa.eu/sites/default/documents/files/document_library/Publications/Guidelines/2020/Guidelines%20on%20loan%20origination%20and%20monitoring/884283/EBA%20GL%202020%2006%20Final%20Report%20on%20GL%20on%20loan%20origination%20and%20monitoring.pdf (accessed: 25.06.2022).

EBA. (2021a). *EBA Report on Management and Supervision of ESG Risks for Credit Institutions and Investment Firms.* EBA/REP/2021.18. Paris, France: European Banking Authority. https://www.eba.europa.eu/sites/default/documents/files/document_library/Publications/Reports/2021/1015656/EBA%20Report%20on%20ESG%20risks%20management%20and%20supervision.pdf (accessed: 19.09.2022).

EBA. (2021b). *Report on Environmental, Social and Governance (ESG) Risks Management and Supervision.* June 23. www.eba.europa.eu/sites/default/documents/files/document_library/Publications/Reports/2021/1015656/EBA%20Report%20on%20ESG%20risks%20management%20and%20supervision.pdf (accessed: 25.06.2022).

EBA. (2022b). *The role of environmental risks in the prudential framework, Discussion Paper.* EBA/DP/2022/02. https://www.eba.europa.eu/sites/default/documents/files/document_library/Publications/Discussions/2022/Discussion%20paper%20on%20the%20role%20of%20environmental%20risk%20in%20the%20prudential%20framework/1031947/Discussion%20paper%20on%20role%20of%20ESG%20risks%20in%20prudential%20framework.pdf (accessed: 20.09.2022).

EBA.ESMA. *Guidelines on the Assessment of the Suitability of Members of the Management Body and Key Function Holders.* www.eba.europa.eu/sites/default/documents/files/document_library/Publications/Guidelines/2021/EBA-GL-2021-06%20Joint%20GLs%20on%20the%20assessment%20of%20suitability%20%28fit%26propoer%29/1022127/Final%20report%20on%20joint%20EBA%20and%20ESMA%20GL%20on%20the%20assessment%20of%20suitability.pdf (accessed: 25.06.2022).

ECB. (2020). *Guide on Climate-Related and Environmental Risks, Supervisory Expectations Relating to Risk Management and Disclosure*, p. 10. Frankfurt: European Central Bank. November.

ECB. (2020a). *Guide on Climate-Related and Environmental Risks, Supervisory Expectations Relating to Risk Management and Disclosure.* November. www.bankingsupervision.europa.eu/ecb/pub/pdf/ssm.202011finalguideonclimate-relatedandenvironmentalrisks~58213f6564.en.pdf (accessed: 25.06.2022).

ECB. (2020b). *Guide on Climate-Related and Environmental Risks, Supervisory Expectations Relating to Risk Management and Disclosure.* Frankfurt: European Central Bank. November.

ECB. (2020c). *Guide on Climate-Related and Environmental Risks, Supervisory Expectations Relating to Risk Management and Disclosure.* Frankfurt: European Central Bank. November. www.bankingsupervision.europa.eu/ecb/pub/pdf/ssm.202011finalguideonclimate-relatedandenvironmentalrisks~58213f6564.en.pdf (accessed: 10.06.2022).

ECB. (2021a). *Climate Risk Stress Test.* Frankfurt: European Central Bank. October.

ECB. (2021b). *Guide on Climate-Related and Environmental Risks, Supervisory Expectations Relating to Risk Management and Disclosure.* Frankfurt: European Central Bank. November.

ECB. (2021c). *The State of Climate and Environmental Risk Management in the Banking Sector: Report on the Supervisory Review of Banks' Approaches to Manage Climate and Environmental Risks.* Frankfurt: European Central Bank. November.

ECB. (2021d). *The State of Climate and Environmental Risk Management in the Banking Sector: Report on the Supervisory Review of Banks' Approaches to Manage Climate and Environmental Risks.* Frankfurt: European Central Bank. November. www.bankingsupervision.europa.eu/ecb/pub/pdf/ssm.202111guideonclimate-relatedandenvironmentalrisks~4b25454055.en.pdf (accessed: 11.06.2022).

ECB. (2021e). www.bankingsupervision.europa.eu/banking/priorities/html/ssm.supervisory_priorities2022~0f890c6b70.en.html (accessed: 24.04.2022).

Edgeman, R., and Eskildsen, J. (2013). *Socio-Ecological Innovation: Strategic Integration of Innovation for Sustainability and Sustainable Innovation.* Proceedings of the International Conference on Intellectual Capital, Knowledge Management & Organizational Learning. Bogotá, Colombia, pp. 114–122.

Edmans, A. (2020). Company Purpose and Profit Need Not Be in Conflict If We 'Grow the Pie'. *Economic Affairs*, 40(2): 287–294. https://doi.org/10.1111/ecaf.12395

El-Gayar, O., and Fritz, B. D. (2006). Environmental Management Information Systems (EMIS) for Sustainable Development: A Conceptual Overview. *Communications of the Association for Information Systems* 17(1): 34, 756–784.

Enhancing Environmental Risk Assessment in Financial Decision-Making. (2017). https://g20sfwg.org/wp-content/uploads/2021/07/Enhancing_Environmental_Risk_Assessment_in_Financial_Decision-making.pdf (accessed: 7.06.2022).

Environment Foundation. (1996). *Banking, the Environment and Sustainable Development.* Pozyskano z. www.environmentfoundation.net/consultations/1996-sustainable-banking.htm.

Equator Principles. (2006). *Final Version.* www.banktrack.org (accessed:18.09.2022).

ERA. (2016). *Environmental Risk Analysis by Financial Institutions—A Review of Global Practice. An Input Paper for the G20 Green Finance Study Group.* Cambridge, UK: University of Cambridge, Institute of Sustainability Leadership, Centre for Sustainable Finance.

EPA. (2021). The *NRC Risk Assessment Paradigm*. United States Environmental Protection Agency, USA. www.epa.gov/fera/nrc-risk-assessment-paradigm (accessed: 27.06.2022).

ESAS. (2021). *Final Report on Draft Regulatory Technical Standards with Regard to the Content and Presentation of Disclosures Pursuant to Article 8(4), 9(6) and 11(5) of Regulation (EU) 2019/2088*. October 22. www.esma.europa.eu/sites/default/files/library/jc_2021_50_-_final_report_on_taxonomy-related_product_disclosure_rts.pdf (accessed: 25.06.2022).

European Commission. (2018). *Renewed Sustainable Finance Strategy and Implementation of the Action Plan on Financing Sustainable Growth*. https://finance.ec.europa.eu/publications/renewed-sustainable-finance-strategy-and-implementation-action-plan-financing-sustainable-growth_en (accessed: 25.06.2022).

Evans, S., Fernando, L., and Yang, M. (2017). Sustainable Value Creation—From Concept Towards Implementation. In *Sustainable Manufacturing. Sustainable Production, Life Cycle Engineering and Management*, R. Stark, G. Seliger, and J. Bonvoisin (eds.). Cham: Springer.

Fatica, S., Panzica, R., and Rancan, M. (2019). *The Pricing of Green Bonds: Are Financial Institutions Special?* JRC Working Papers in Economics and Finance.

Feridun, M., and Güngör, H. (2020). Climate-Related Prudential Risks in the Banking Sector: A Review of the Emerging Regulatory and Supervisory Practices. *Sustainability* 12: 5325. https://doi.org/10.3390/su12135325

Ferrell, A., Liang, H., and Renneboog, L. (2016). Socially Responsible Firms. *Journal of Financial Economics* 122: 585–606.

Fisk, P. (2010). *People Planet Profit: How to Embrace Sustainability for Innovation and Business Growth*. London: Kogan Page Publishers.

Fitch. (2020). *ESG in Credit 2020*. White Paper. New York. www.your.fitch.group (accessed: 18.09.2022).

Fitch. (2021). *Bank Rating Criteria*. New York: Fitch Ratings. November 12.

Fitch. (2022a). *Where ESG Matters for Bank Ratings*. New York: Fitch Ratings. March 14.

Fitch. (2022b). www.fitchratings.com/research/banks/where-esg-matters-for-bank-ratings-14-03-2022 (accessed: 20.04.2022).

Forbes. (2020). www.forbes.com/sites/betsyatkins/2020/06/08/demystifying-esgits-history-current-status/?sh=3e2064ed2cdd (accessed: 24.04.2022).

Freeman, R. E. (1984). *Strategic Management: A Stakeholder Approach*. Boston, MA: Pitman.

Friede, G., Busch, T., and Bassen, A. (2015). ESG and Financial Performance: Aggregated Evidence from More Than 2000 Empirical Studies. *Journal of Sustainable Finance & Investment* 5: 210–233.

FSR. (2022) FSR. (2021). *Financial Stability Review*. Frankfurt: European Central Bank, Supplement B, May.

Gatfaoui, Hayette. (2004). *From Fault Tree to Credit Risk Assessment: A Case Study*. EERI Research Paper Series 5. https://econwpa.ub.uni-muenchen.de/econ-wp/em/papers/0509/0509002.pdf (accessed: 15.05.2022).

GFSG. (2017). *G20 Green Finance Synthesis Report 2017*. Indonesia: G20 Green Finance Study Group.

Gilding, P., Hogarth, M., and Reed, D. (2002). *Single Bottom Line Sustainability: How a Values Centred Approach to Corporate Sustainability Can Pay Off for Shareholders and Society*. Sydney, Australia: Ecos Corporation.

Girotra, K., and Netessine, S. (2013). OM Forum—Business Model Innovation for Sustainability. *Manufacturing & Service Operations Management* 15(4): 523–700.

Gleeson, James P., Hurd, T. R., Melnik, Sergey, and Hackett, Adam. (2013). Systemic Risk in Banking Networks Without Monte Carlo Simulation. In *Advances in Network Analysis and Its Applications*, R. Kranakis (eds.). Berlin, Heidelberg: Springer, pp. 27–56. https://dx.doi.org/10.1007/978-3-642-30904-5_2

Global Risks Report. (2021). 16th Edition. Geneva, Switzerland: World Economic Forum. https://www.weforum.org/reports/the-global-risks-report-2021/ (accessed: 18.09.2022).

Global Risks Report. (2022). https://www.weforum.org/reports/global-risks-report-2022/ (accessed:18.09.2022)

Goldar, B. N. (2007). Impact of Corporate Environmental Performance or Profitability and Market Value: A Case Study of Indian Firms. *Institute of Economic Growth* 5(1): 13–25.

Gordon, Dan. (2014). Using Incident Response Trees as a Tool for Risk Management of Online Financial Services. *Risk Analysis* 34(9). https://dx.doi.org/10.1111/risa.12195

Grippa, P., Schmittmann, J., and Suntheim, F. (2019). Climate Change and Financial Risk, Finance & Development. *IMF*, Vol. 56, No F. 4. December. www.imf.org/external/pubs/ft/fandd/2019/12/climate-change-central-banks-and-financial-risk-grippa.htm (accessed: 30.04.2022).

Gummesson, E. (2008). Extending the Service-Dominant Logic: From Customer Centricity to Balanced Centricity. *Journal of the Academy of Marketing Science* 36(1): 15–17.

Gupta, S. (2003). *Do Stock Market Penalise Environment-Unfriendly Behaviour? Evidence from India*. Working Paper Series No. 116. Delhi School of Economics.

Gurjar, Bhola Ram, and Mohan, Manju. (2002). Environmental Risk Analysis: Problems and Perspectives in Different Countries. *RISK: Health, Safety & Environment* 13(1): 3. https://scholars.unh.edu/risk/vol13/iss1/3/ (accessed: 15.05.2022).

Hamilton, J. T. (1995). Pollution as News: Media and Stock Markets Reactions to the Toxics Release Inventory Data. *Journal of Environmental Economics and Management* 28.

Hao, Xiaoling. (2013). *Operational Risk Control of Commercial Banks Based on Bayesian Network*. Proceedings of the 2013 the International Conference on Education Technology and Information System (ICETIS 2013), Sanya, China, 21–22. June. https://doi.org/10.2991/icetis-13.2013.209

Hart, S. (1995). Does It Pay to Be Green? An Empirical Examination of the Relationship Between Emissions Reduction and Firm Performance. *Business Strategy and the Environment*, September.

Hausenblas, Václav, Kubicová, Ivana, and Lešanovská, Jitka. (2012). *Contagion Risk in the Czech Financial System: A Network Analysis and Simulation Approach*. CNB Working Paper Series 14. www.cnb.cz/export/sites/cnb/en/economic-research/.galleries/research_publications/cnb_wp/cnbwp_2012_14.pdf (accessed: 12.05.2022).

Heim, G., and Zenklusen, O. (2005). *Sustainable Finance: Strategy Options for Development Financing Institutions*. Zurich: EcoFact.

Hein, Olivier, Schwind, Michael, and König, Wolfgang. (2006). Scale-Free Networks. *Wirtsch. Inform* 48: 267–275. https://doi.org/10.1007/s11576-006-0058-2

Henriksen, K., Bjerre, M., Almasi, A. M., and Damgaard-Grann, E. (2012). *Green Business Model Innovation: Conceptualization Report*. Oslo: Nordic Innovation Publication.

Henriques de Gusmão, Ana Paula, Mendonça Silva, Maisa, Poleto, Thiago, Camara e Silva, Lucio, and Cabral Seixas Costa, Ana Paula. (2018). Cybersecurity Risk Analysis Model Using Fault Tree Analysis and Fuzzy Decision Theory. *International Journal of Information Management* 43: 248–260. https://doi.org/10.1016/j.ijinfomgt.2018.08.008

Hillson, David. (2020). Quantitative Risk Analysis: Strengths and Weaknesses. *Multibriefs.com*, December 03. http://exclusive.multibriefs.com/content/quantitative-risk-analysis-strengths-and-weaknesses/business-management-services-risk-management (accessed: 15.05.2022).

Holska, A. (2016). Teorie podejmowania decyzji, [w] *Zarządzanie, organizacje i organizowanie–przegląd perspektyw teoretycznych*, K. Klincewicz (red.). Warszawa: Wydawnictwo Naukowe Wydziału Zarządzania Uniwersytetu Warszawskiego.

Hong, Eun-Soo, Lee, In-Mo, Shin, Hee-Soon, Nam, Seok-Woo, and Kong Jung-Sik. (2009). Quantitative Risk Evaluation based on Event Tree Analysis Technique: Application to the Design of Shield TBM. *Tunnelling and Underground Space Technology* 24: 269–277. https://dx.doi.org/10.1016/j.tust.2008.09.004

Hongoh, Valerie, Hoen, A. G., Aenishaenslin, C. et al. (2011). Spatially Explicit Multi-Criteria Decision Analysis for Managing Vector-Borne Diseases. *International Journal of Health Geographics* 10: 70. https://doi.org/10.1186/1476-072X-10-70

Hvass, K. K. (2013). *Exploring Business Model Innovation for Closed Loop Fashion*. Proceedings of the Sustainable Innovation 2013–18th International Conference, pp. 111–117.

IFC. *Review Environmental and Social Regulatory Framework*. First for Sustainability. Financial Institutions: Resources, Solutions and Tools. https://firstforsustainability.org/risk-management/managing-environmental-and-social-risk-2_2/implementing-an-esms/review-environmental-and-social-regulatory-framework/ (accessed: 20.09.2022).

IMF. (1998). *World Economic Outlook. Financial Crises: Causes and Indicators*. Washington: International Monetary Fund, May.

ING. (2022). *Ecological Declaration 2021 Capital Group of ING Bank Śląski S.A.* www.ing.pl/o-banku/esg/esg-srodowisko/polityka-srodowiskowa (accessed: 30.05.2022).

Isograph. (2022). *Reliability Workbench*. www.isograph.com/software/reliability-workbench/ (accessed: 24.05.2022).

IUCN–UNEP–WWF. (1980). *World Conservation Strategy: Living Resource Conservation for Sustainable Development*. www.iucn.org/content/world-conservation-strategy-living-resource-conservation-sustainable-development.

Jacobs, Michael Jr. (2021). Validation of Corporate Probability of Default Models Considering Alternative Use Cases. *International Journal of Financial Studies* 9(4): 63. https://doi.org/10.3390/ijfs9040063

Jeucken, M. (2004). *Sustainability in Finance. Banking on the Planet*. Delft: Eburon, pp. 15–17.

Jeucken, M., and Bouma, J. (1999). The Changing Environment of Banks. In *GMI Theme Issue: Sustainable Banking: The Greening of Finance*, No. 27. Greener Management International, pp. 20–35.

Jo, H., Kim, H., and Park, K. (2015). Corporate Environmental Responsibility and Firm Performance in the Financial Services Sector. *Journal of Business Ethics* 131: 257–284.

Johnson, H. (2008). *Risks in Banking, Chapter 3*. Washington Bankers Association. www.wabankers.com (accessed: 18.09.2022).

Jones, P., and Upward, A. (2014). *Caring for the Future: The Systemic Design of Flourishing Enterprises*. Proceedings of the RSD3, Third Symposium of Relating Systems Thinking to Design, Oslo, Norway, 15–17 October 2014.

Jones, M., and Ranasinghe, D. (2020). *Reuters News, Central Banks Flexing Their Green Muscle for Climate Fight*. https://www.zawya.com/en/business/central-banks-flexing-their-green-muscle-for-climate-fight-r33fgqvo (accessed:18.09.2022).

Kabir, Sohag. (2017). An Overview of Fault Tree Analysis and Its Application in Model Based Dependability Analysis. *Expert Systems with Applications* 77: 114–135. http://dx.doi.org/10.1016/j.eswa.2017.01.058

Karkowska, R. (2020). Business Model as a Concept of Sustainability in the Banking Sector. *Sustainability* 12: 111. https://doi.org/10.3390/su12010111

Keith-Roach, M. (2016). Legislation and Best Practice in the Emerging European Rare Earth Element Industry. In *Rare Earths Industry. Technological, Economic, and Environmental*

Implications, I. Borges De Lima (ed.), Elsevier, pp. 279–291. https://www.researchgate.net/publication/299390404_Environmental_Legislation_and_Best_Practice_in_the_Emerging_European_Rare_Earth_Element_Industry (accessed: 20.09.2022).

Kemp-Benedict, E. (2018). Investing in a Green Transition. *Ecological Economics* 153: 218–236.

Kiker, G. A., Bridges, T. S., Varghese, A., Seager, T. P., and Linkov, I. (2005). Application of Multicriteria Decision Analysis in Environmental Decision Making. *Integrated Environmental Assessment and Management: An International Journal* 1(2): 95–108.

Kim, Myong-Hee, Jin, Eun-Ji, Park, and Man-Gon. (2013). Fault Tree Analysis and Fault Modes and Effect Analysis for Security Evaluation of IC Card Payment Systems. *Journal of Korea Multimedia Society* 16(1): 87–99. http://dx.doi.org/10.9717/kmms.2013.16.1.087

Kim, So Young, Kim, Myong Hee, and Park, Man-Gon. (2015). Fault Tree Analysis and Failure Mode Effects Analysis for Software Security Improvements in Mobile Banking Information Systems. *Journal of Korea Multimedia Society* 18(11): 1342–1350. http://dx.doi.org/10.9717/kmms.2015.18.11.1342

Kinsley, Amy C., et al. (2020). Multilayer and Multiplex Networks: An Introduction to Their Use in Veterinary Epidemiology. *Frontiers in Veterinary Science* 7: 596.

Klaassen, P., and Blijlevens, S. (2022). *EBA's Binding Standards on Pillar 3 Disclosures on ESG Risks*. https://zanders.eu/en/latest-insights/ebas-binding-standards-on-pillar-3-disclosures-on-esg-risks/ (accessed: 25.04.2022).

Kluza, K., and Kluza, S. (2021). Finanse Publiczne a Stabilność Systemu Finansowego. In *Finanse publiczne*, M. Ziolo (ed.). Polska Akademia Nauk, pp. 97–122. ISBN 978-83-66847-18-7.

KNF. (2022). *Dane miesięczne sektora bankowego—kwiecień*. www.knf.gov.pl/publikacje_i_opracowania/dane_statystyczne/bankowy?articleId=56224&p_id=18.

KPMG. (2021). *ESG in Banks Effective Strategies to Use Opportunities and Mitigate Risks*. https://home.kpmg/xx/en/home/insights/2021/05/esg-risks-in-banks.html (accessed: 24.04.2022).

Krawczyk, Ewa. (2006). Zastosowanie modelu ryzyka Value at Risk (VaR) opartego na metodzie Monte Carlo do rynku nieruchomości. *Zeszyty Naukowe SGGW—Ekonomika i Organizacja Gospodarki Żywnościowej* 58: 117–133. https://sj.wne.sggw.pl/pdf/EIOGZ_2006_n58_s117.pdf (accessed: 20.05.2022).

Krogulec E., Sawicka K., Zabłocki S., Falkowska E. (2018). Ocena ryzyka środowiskowego w zakresie zanieczyszczenia wód podziemnych i gruntów w rejonie robót górniczych. *Górnictwo Odkrywkowe. No. 2/2018*. Instytut Górnictwa Odkrywkowego. Wrocław. pp. 51–52.

Kulińska-Sadłocha, E. (2009). Banki a zmiany klimatyczne. In *Finanse 2009—Teoria i praktyka. Bankowość*, W. K. Brzozowska and S. Flejterski (red.). Szczecin: Wydawnictwo Uniwersytetu Szczecińskiego.

Kumar, Santhosh, and Fragkos, Grigorios. (2020). Quantitative Vs Qualitative Cyber Risk Management Approach. *digital14.com*, November 30. www.digital14.com/insights/blogs/cyber-risk-management (accessed: 16.05.2022).

Kurznack, L., Schoenmaker, D., and Schramade, W. (2021). A Model of Long-Term Value Creation. *Journal of Sustainable Finance & Investment*. May 03. https://doi.org/10.1080/20430795.2021.1920231

Kyriba. (2022). *The Kyriba Enterprise Liquidity Management Platform*. www.kyriba.com/resource/optimize-liquidity-reduce-risk-unlock-growth/ (accessed: 30.05.2022).

Kyritsis, Costas, Rekleitis, Panagiotis, and Trivelas, Panagiotis. (2015). Simulation for the Stability and DEA Risk Analysis of Greek Banks Within a Prolonged Duration of the Debt Crisis. *Procedia Economics and Finance* 33: 376–387. https://dx.doi.org/10.1016/S2212-5671(15)01722-0

Lacasse, Suzanne. (2008) Event Tree Analysis of Åknes Rock Slide Hazard. In *Proceedings of the 4th Canadian Conference on Geohazards: From Causes to Management*, J. Locat, D. Perret, D. Turmel, D. Demers, et S. Leroueil (eds.). Presse de l'Université, Canadian Geotechnical Society, Engineering Geology Division, Canada, p. 594.

Langfield, Sam, and Soramäki, Kimmo. (2016). Interbank Exposure Networks. *Computational Economics* 47: 3–17. https://doi.org/10.1007/s10614-014-9443-x

Leinonen, Harry (eds.). (2005). Liquidity, Risks and Speed in Payment and Settlement Systems—A Simulation Approach. *Bank of Finland Studies* E31. https://helda.helsinki.fi/bof/bitstream/handle/123456789/9355/118263.pdf?sequence=1&isAllowed=y (accessed: 22.05.2022).

LimbleCMMS. (2021). *What Is Fault Tree Analysis and How to Perform It*. https://limblecmms.com/blog/fault-tree-analysis/ (accessed: 10.05.2022).

Lin, Li. (2014). Optimal Loan-to-Value Ratio and the Efficiency Gains of Default. *Annals of Finance* 10: 47–69. https://doi.org/10.1007/s10436-013-0232-7

Linkov, I., Satterstrom, F. K., Kiker, G., Batchelor, C., Bridges, T., and Ferguson, E. (2006). From Comparative Risk Assessment to Multi-Criteria Decision Analysis and Adaptive Management: Recent Developments and Applications. *Environment International* 32(8): 1072–1093. https://dx.doi.org/10.1016/j.envint.2006.06.013

Luu, D. T., and Lux, T. (2018). *Multilayer Overlaps and Correlations in the Bank-Firm Credit Network of Spain*. Economics Working Paper No. 2018–04. Kiel: Kiel University, Department of Economics.

Lux, Thomas. (2016). A Model of the Topology of the Bank–Firm Credit Network and Its Role as Channel of Contagion. *Journal of Economic Dynamics and Control* 66: 36–53.

Macroption. (2022). *Value At Risk (VAR) Limitations and Disadvantages*. www.macroption.com/value-at-risk-var-limitations-disadvantages/#so-many-problems-should-you-still-use-var (accessed: 23.05.2022).

Maggi, Filippo, Natale, Alfonso, Pepanides, Theodore, Risso, Enrico, and Schröck, Gerhard. (2017). IFRS 9: A Silent Revolution in Banks' Business Models. *Mckinsey.com*, April 13. www.mckinsey.com/business-functions/risk-and-resilience/our-insights/ifrs-9-a-silent-revolution-in-banks-business-models (accessed: 18.05.2022).

Mallin, C., Hisham, F., and Kean, O. W. (2014). Corporate Social Responsibility and Financial Performance in Islamic Banks. *Journal of Economic Behavior and Organization* 103: S21–S38.

Manganelli, Simone, and Engle, Robert F. (2001). *Value at Risk Models in Finance*. ECB Working Paper No. 75. www.ecb.europa.eu/pub/pdf/scpwps/ecbwp075.pdf (accessed: 12.05.2022).

Marrewijk, M., and Were, M. (2003). Multiple Levels of Corporate Sustainability. *Journal of Business Ethics* 44(2/3): 107–119.

Martinez, R., Monaco, M., Goldblum, C., and Hales, D. (2021). *Embedding Climate Risk into Banks' Credit Risk Management. Practical Considerations*. Deloitte. https://www2.deloitte.com/xe/en/insights/industry/financial-services/climate-change-credit-risk-management.html.

Martinez-Jaramillo, Serafin, Kabadjova, Biliana, Bravo-Benitez, Bernardo, and Solorzano-Margain, Juan. (2012). *Systemic Risk Analysis by Means of Network Theory: An Empirical Study of the Mexican Banking System*. Technical Report (Working Paper). Mexico City, Mexico: Banco de México. https://www.researchgate.net/publication/320170380_Systemic_risk_analysis_by_means_of_network_theory_an_empirical_study_of_the_Mexican_banking_system (accessed:18.09.2022).

Mason, K., and Spring, M. (2011). The Sites and Practices of Business Models. *Industrial Marketing Management* 40: 1032–1041.

Mayer, C. (2018). The Future of the Corporation: Towards Humane Business. *Journal of the British Academy* 6(s1): 1–16. https://doi.org/10.5871/jba/006s1.001

Mazars. (2021). *Responsible Bank Practices, Benchmark Studies*. www.mazars.com/content/download/1070302/55653782/version//file/Mazars-Responsible-banking-practices-benchmark-study-2021.pdf (accessed: 30.04.2022).

McIntosh, A., and Pontius, J. (2017). *Science and the Global Environment. Case Studies Integrating Science Global Environment*. Elsevier, USA.

McKinsey, Quartely. (2022). *Five Ways that ESG Creates Value*, 2019. www.mckinsey.com/business-functions/strategy-and-corporate-finance/our-insights/five-ways-that-esg-creates-value (accessed: 24.04.2022).

McLennan, M. (2021). *The Global Risks Report 2021*, 16th Edition. Cologny, Switzerland: World Economic Forum.

Michalak, M. (2017). Zasada przezorności w Unii Europejskiej—hamulec postępu czy najbardziej racjonalna droga? *Studia Prawnoustrojowe* 37, Uniwersytet Warmińsko-Mazurski, s. 45–56.

Mitic, Peter. (2020). Systemic Shock Propagation in a Complex System. *Soft Computing* 24: 13667–13685. https://doi.org/10.1007/s00500-019-04466-6

MKŚ. *Konwencje międzynarodowe*. Warszawa: Ministerstwo Klimatu i Środowiska. www.gov.pl/web/klimat/konwencje-miedzynarodowe (accessed: 18.05.2022).

Molnar, Eva, Fodor, Istvan, Svigruha, Reka, and Pirger Zsolt. (2021). Issues, Challenges, Directives, and Limitations Concerning the Improvement of Environmental Risk Assessment of Pharmaceutically Active Compounds. *Ecotoxicology and Environmental Safety* 216: 112212. https://doi.org/10.1016/j.ecoenv.2021.112212

Monetary Authority of Singapore. (2020). *Guidelines on Environmental Risk Management (Banks)*. September. www.mas.gov.sg/-/media/MAS/Regulations-and-Financial-Stability/Regulations-Guidance-and-Licensing/Commercial-Banks/Regulations-Guidance-and-Licensing/Guidelines/Guidelines-on-Environmental-Risk—Banks/Guidelines-on-Environmental-Risk-Management-for-Banks.pdf (accessed: 5.06.2022).

Montagna, Mattia, and Kok, Christoffer. (2016). *Multi-Layered Interbank Model for Assessing Systemic Risk*. ECB Working Paper No. 1944. August 26. https://ssrn.com/abstract=2830546 or http://dx.doi.org/10.2139/ssrn.2830546

Montagna, Mattia, and Lux, Thomas. (2013). *Hubs and Resilience: Towards More Realistic Models of the Interbank Markets*. Kiel Working Papers 1826. Kiel, Germany: Kiel Institute for the World Economy.

Moody's. (2021). *Bank of England's CBES Climate Stress Test*. Philadelphia, PA: Moody's Analytics. August 3.

MSCI ESG Metric. (2020). https://www.msci.com/our-solutions/esg-investing/esg-ratings (accessed:18.09.2022).

MSZ. *Internetowa Baza Traktatowa*. Warszawa: Ministerstwo Klimatu i Środowiska. https://traktaty.msz.gov.pl/umowa-3 (accessed: 18.05.2022).

Murex. (2022). *MX.3*. www.murex.com/en (accessed: 30.05.2022).

Murray-Smith, R., and Taylor, D. (2018). Policy, Regulations, and Risk Assessment. In *Environmental Contaminants, Health Care and Environmental Contamination*, Alistair B. A. Boxall and Rai S. Kookana (eds.). Elsevier, USA pp. 239–260.

NGFS. (2020). *Overview of Environmental Risk Analysis by Financial Institutions, Network for Greening the Financial System Technical Document*. Network for Greening the Financial System, Central Banks and Supervisors, Banque de France, Eurosysteme, NGFS Secretariat. September. www.ngfs.net/sites/default/files/media/2020/09/23/overview_of_environmental_risk_analysis_by_financial_institutions.pdf (accessed: 19.09.2022).

Nilsson-Andersen, P., and Andersen, J. B. (2012). *Green Business Model Innovation in the Tourism and Experience Economy-Cases from Austria, Portugal, Denmark, Finland, Mexico, Norway, Sweden, Iceland, Russia and South Korea*. Oslo: Nordic Council of Ministers & Nordic Innovation Publication.

Nosratabadi, S., Pinter, G., Mosavi, A., and Semperger, S. (2020). Sustainable Banking; Evaluation of the European Business Models. *Sustainability* 12: 2314. https://doi.org/10.3390/su12062314

Nowak, Z. (2001). *Zarządzanie środowiskiem*. Gliwice: Wydawnictwo Politechniki Śląskiej.

NRC Risk Assessment Paradigm. www.epa.gov/fera/nrc-risk-assessment-paradigm (accessed: 27.06.2022).

Oliver, Wyman. (2022). *Time To Start Again: How Greenfield Can Transform Corporate Banking*. www.oliverwyman.com/our-expertise/insights/2019/sep/greenfield-corporate-banking (accessed: 20.05.2022).

Onaran, Y. (2021). ESG Risks Top the List of Near-Term Concerns for Bank Executives. *Bloomberg News*, February 02. www.bloomberg.com/professional/blog/esg-risks-top-the-list-of-near-term-concerns-for-bank-executives/ (accessed: 30.04.2022).

Osterwalder, A., Ondrus, J., and Pigneur, Y. (2005). *Skype's Disruptive Potential in the Telecom Market: A Systematic Comparison of Business Models*. HEC LAUSANNE Working Paper, May 2005. (accessed: 18.05.2022).

Pisano, U., Martinuzzi, A., and Bruckner, B. (2012). *The Financial Sector and Sustainable Development: Logics, Principles and Actors*. ESDN Quarterly Report No 27. Pozyskano z. December. www.sd-network.eu/quarterly%20reports/report%20files/pdf/2012-December-The_Financial_Sector_and_Sustainable_Development.pdf.

Platonova, E., Asutay, M., Dixon, R., and Mohammad, S. (2016). The Impact of Corporate Social Responsibility Disclosure on Financial Performance: Evidence from the GCC Islamic Banking Sector. *Journal of Business Ethics*. https://doi.org/10.1007/s10551-016-3229-0

Poppensieker, Thomas, Schneider, Roland, Schneider, Sebastian, and Stackebrandt, Lennart. (2018). Basel III: The Final Regulatory Standard. *Mckinsey.com*, April 18. www.mckinsey.com/business-functions/risk-and-resilience/our-insights/basel-iii-the-final-regulatory-standard (accessed: 18.05.2022).

Powell, J. R., and Vo, D. H. (2020). A Comprehensive Stability Indicator for Banks. *Risks* 8: 13.

Pracodawcy, R. P. https://pracodawcyrp.pl/upload/files/2019/11/karta-odpowiedzialnosci-ekologicznej-polskiego-biznesu-v2.pdf (accessed: 27.06.2022).

Press Room Team. (2019). *A Role for Financial and Monetary Policies in Climate Change Mitigation*. https://internationalworldofbusiness.com/a-role-for-financial-and-monetary-policies-in-climate-change-mitigation/ (accessed: 30.04.2022).

Proposal for a Directive of the European Parliament and of the Council amending Directive 2013/34/EU, Directive 2004/109/EC, Directive 2006/43/EC and Regulation (EU) No 537/2014, as Regards Corporate Sustainability Reporting. https://eur-lex.europa.eu/legal-content/EN/TXT/?uri=CELEX%3A52021PC0189.

Przybojewska, I. (2018). Wykładnia rozszerzająca prawa ochrony środowiska jako szczególnej gałęzi prawa. *Studia prawnicze KUL* 2(74): 67–69.

Qastharin, A. R. (2016). Business Model Canvas for Social Enterprise. *Journal of Business and Economics* 7(4): 627–637.

Rana, P., Short, S. W., Bocken, N., and Evans, S. (2013). Towards a Sustainable Business Form: A Business Modelling Process and Tools. In *Sustainable Consumption Research and Action Initiative (SCORAI) Conference: The Future of Consumerism and Well-Being in a World of Ecological Constraints, 12–14 June*. Worcester, USA: Clark University.

Redziak, Z. (2013). *Podstawy teorii podejmowania decyzji*. Warszawa: Wydawnictwo Akademii Obrony Narodowej.

Relyence. (2022). *The Relyence Product Line Up*. https://relyence.com/products/ (accessed: 24.05.2022).

Renn, Ortwin. (1985). Risk Analysis: Scope and Limitations. In *Regulating Industrial Risk: Science, Hazards and Public Protection*, H. J. Otway and M. Peltu (eds.). London: Butterworths, pp. 111–127. https://elib.uni-stuttgart.de/bitstream/11682/7340/1/ren80.pdf (accessed: 20.05.2022).

Ribeiro, R. A. (1996). Fuzzy Multiple Attribute Decision Making: A Review and New Preference Elicitation Techniques. *Fuzzy Sets and Systems* 78(2): 155–181.

Richardson, J. (2008). The Business Model: An Integrative Framework for Strategy Execution. *Strategic Change* 17(56): 133–144.

Robu, Brîndușa Mihaela, Căliman, Florentina Anca, Bețianu, Camelia, and Gavrilescu, Maria. (2007). Methods and Procedures for Environmental Risk Assessment. *Environmental Engineering and Management Journal* 6(6): 573–592. www.researchgate.net/publication/322921157_Methods_and_procedures_for_environmental_risk_assessment (accessed: 6.05.2022).

Rogall, H. (2010). *Ekonomia zrównoważonego rozwoju*. Poznań: Wydawnictwo Zysk i S-Ka, pp. 219–223.

Rosicki, R. (2010). Ogólna charakterystyka międzynarodowego prawa Ochrony środowiska, *Środkowoeuropejskie Studia Polityczne* (3): 79–104.

Rusin, Andrzej, and Wojaczek, Adam. (2012). Application of Fault Tree Analysis in the Maintenance Intervals Planning for Power Unit Systems. *Archiwum Energetyki* 152(3–4): 95–106. https://yadda.icm.edu.pl/baztech/element/bwmeta1.element.baztech-4ca2cb31-5dc3-4835-9df4-5fbad27ad0c7/c/Rusin.pdf (accessed: 15.05. 2022).

S&P. (2021a). *Financial Institutions Rating Methodology*. New York: S&P Global Ratings. December 9.

S&P. (2021b). *S&P Global's Approach to ESG in Banks' Analysis*. New York: S&P Global Ratings. June 16.

S&P. (2021c). *ESG Credit Indicator Definitions and Application*. New York: S&P Global Ratings. October 13.

S&P. (2022). *How We Rate Financial Institutions*. New York: S&P Global Ratings. February 2.

Santos, Joost R., Yu, Krista Danielle S., Pagsuyoin, Sheree Ann T., and Tan, Raymond R. (2014). Time-Varying Disaster Recovery Model for Interdependent Economic Systems Using Hybrid Input–Output and Event Tree Analysis. *Economic Systems Research* 26(1): 60–80. https://dx.doi.org/10.1080/09535314.2013.872602

Schaltegger, S., Hansen, E. G., and Lüdeke-Freund, F. (2016). Business Models for Sustainability: Origins, Present Research, and Future Avenues. *Organization & Environment* 29(1): 3–10.

Schaltegger, S., Lüdeke-Freund, F., and Hansen, E. (2016). Business Models for Sustainability: A Co-Evolutionary Analysis of Sustainable Entrepreneurship, Innovation, and Transformation. *Organization & Environment* 29(3): 264–289.

Schaltegger, S., Viere, T., and Zvezdov, D. (2012). Tapping Environmental Accounting Potentials of Beerbrewing: Information Needs for Successful Cleaner Production. *Journal of Cleaner Production*, 29: 1–10.

Schmidheiny, S., and Zorraquin, Federico J. L. (1996). *Financing Change: The Financial Community, Eco-Efficiency and Sustainable Development*. Cambridge, MA: MIT Press.

Schoenmaker, D. (2021). A New Integrated-Value Assessment Method Forcorporate Investment. *Policy Contribution* 19/21: 1–8.

Schoenmaker, D., and Schramade, W. (2019). *Principles of Sustainable Finance*. Oxford: Oxford University Press. Available at SSRN: https://ssrn.com/abstract=3282699

Scholtens, B., and van't Klooster, S. (2019). Sustainability and Bank Risk. *Palgrave Communications*. https://doi.org/10.1057/s41599-019-0315-9

Schoormann, T., Behrens, D., Kolek, E., and Knackstedt, R. (2016). *Sustainability in Business Models—A Literature-Review-Based Design-Science-Oriented Research Agenda*. Proceedings of the European Conference on Information Systems (ECIS) 2016, Istanbul, Turkey, 12–15 June 2016.

Schutten, W. (2016). *Sustainable Banking Business Models*. https://essay.utwente.nl/70548/1/Schutten_MA_BMS.pdf (accessed: 20.05.2022).

Sebbag, N., and Denaye, D. (2017). *Banks' Business Models: Enhanced Monitoring by the ECB*. Avantage Reply, pp. 1–4, January. www.reply.com (accessed:18.09.2022).

Sheehan, J. (2006). Understanding Service Sector Innovation. *Communications of the ACM* 49(7): 42–47.

Shen, C. H., Wu, M. W., Chen, T. H., and Fang, H. (2016). To Engage or Not to Engage in Corporate Social Responsibility: Empirical Evidence from Global Banking Sector. *Economic Model* 55: 207–225.

Starik, M., and Kanashiro, P. (2013). Toward a Theory of Sustainability Management: Uncovering and Integrating the Nearly Obvious. *Organization & Environment* 26(1): 7–30. https://doi.org/10.1177/1086026612474958

Stankeviciene, J., and Nikonorova, M. (2014). Sustainable Value Creation in Commercial Banks During Financial Crisis, Contemporary Issues in Business, Management and Education 2013. *Procedia—Social and Behavioral Sciences* 110: 1197–1208.

Starnini, Michele, Boguñá, Marián, and Ángeles Serrano, M. (2019). The Interconnected Wealth of Nations: Shock Propagation on Global Trade-Investment Multiplex Networks. *Scientific Reports* 9: Article number: 13079.

Stec, T., and Zwolinski, P. (2018). Using Values Management for Shifting Companies to Circular Economy. *Procedia CIRP* 69: 805–809.

Stolbova, Veronika, Irene Monasterolo, and Stefano Battiston. (2018). A Financial Macro-Network Approach to Climate Policy Evaluation. *Ecological Economics* 149: 239–253.

Stroie, Elena Ramona. (2011). Advantages and Disadvantages of Quantitative and Qualitative Information Risk Approaches. *Chinese Business Review* 10(12): 1106–1110. www.davidpublisher.com/Public/uploads/Contribute/555d6fdde07cc.pdf (accessed: 15.05.2022).

Stubbs, W., and Cocklin, C. (2008). Conceptualizing a Sustainability Business Model. *Organization & Environment* 21(2): 103–127.

Tejaswi, D., and Samuel, C. (2017). Techniques for Environmental Risk Assessment: A Review. *Rasayan Journal of Chemistry* 10(2): 499–506. http://dx.doi.org/10.7324/RJC.2017.1021657

Trenca, Ioan. (2009). The Use in Banks of Value at Risk Method in Market Risk Management. *Analele Ştiinłifice Ale Universităłii "Alexandru Ioan Cuza"* 56: 186–196. http://anale.feaa.uaic.ro/anale/resurse/16_F12_Trenca.pdf (accessed: 18.05.2022).

UNEP. (2019). *Addressing Climate-Related Security Risks*. https://www.unep.org/resources/toolkits-manuals-and-guides/addressing-climate-related-security-risks (accessed: 18.09.2022).

UNEP FI. *Principles for Responsible Banking. Guidance Document*. www.unepfi.org/publications/principles-for-responsible-banking-guidance-document/.

UNEP FI. (2019). *Annual Overview 07/2018–06/2019*. www.unepfi.org/wordpress/wp-content/uploads/2019/09/UNEP-FI-Annual-Overview-2019-.pdf (accessed: 22.05.2022).

USACoE. (2018). *Risk Assessment—Quantitative Methods*. www.iwr.usace.army.mil/Portals/70/docs/risk/Risk_Assessment_Quantitative_Methods_dft.pdf?ver=2018-07-03-134519-250 (accessed: 10.05.2022).

USGCRP. (2017). *Climate Science Special Report: Fourth National Climate Assessment*, Vol. I [D. J. Wuebbles, D. W. Fahey, K. A. Hibbard, D. J. Dokken, B. C. Stewart, and T. K. Maycock (eds.)]. Washington, DC, USA: U.S. Global Change Research Program, 470 pp.

Ustawa z dnia 16 kwietnia 2004 roku o ochronie przyrody. Dz. U. 2004 Nr 92. poz. 880. https://eli.gov.pl/api/acts/DU/2004/880/text/U/D20040880Lj.pdf (accessed: 20.09.2022).

Ustawa z dnia 27 kwietnia 2001 r. Prawo ochrony środowiska. Dz. U. 2001 Nr 62. poz. 627. https://eli.gov.pl/api/acts/DU/2001/627/text/U/D20010627Lj.pdf (accessed: 20.09.2022).

Varcholová, Tatiana, and Rimarčík, Marián. (2003). Value-at-Risk Methods and Models and Their Application. *BIATEC* 11: 32–34. www.nbs.sk/_img/documents/biatec/bia10_03/32_34.pdf (accessed: 18.05.2022).

Vermeer, A. (2014). *A New Guide to Managing Environmental Risk*. Duke Corporate Education. www.dukece.com/insights/new-guide-managing-environmental-risk/ (accessed: 26.06.2022).

Vermeulen, R., Schets, E., Lohuis, M., Kölbl, B., Jansen, D. J., and Heeringa, W. (2018). An Energy Transition Risk Stress Test for the Financial System of the Netherlands. *Occasional Studies*, 16–17, October.

Vladimirova, D. (2019). Building Sustainable Value Propositions for Multiple Stakeholders: A Practical Tool. *Journal of Business Models* 7(1): 1–8.

Wang, Dehong, Song, Jianbo, and Lin, Yongzhao. (2017). Does the VaR Measurement Using Monte-Carlo Simulation Work in China?—Evidence from Chinese Listed Banks. *Journal of Financial Risk Management* 6(1): 66–78. https://dx.doi.org/10.4236/jfrm.2017.61006

Watson, R. T., Boudreau, M.-C., and Chen, A. J. (2010). Information Systems and Environmentally Sustainable Development: Energy Informatics and New Directions for the IS Community. *Management Information Systems (MIS) Quarterly* 34(1): 4.

Weber, O. (2012). *Sustainable Banking—History and Current Developments*. Pozyskano z. https://ssrn.com/abstract=2159947.

Weber, O., Hoque, A., and Islam, M. A. (2015). Incorporating Environmental Criteria into Credit Risk Management in Bangladeshi Banks. *Journal of Sustainable Finance & Investment* 5(1–2): 1–15.

Weill, P., Malone, T. W., D'Urso, V. T., Herman, G., and Woerner, S. (2005). *Do Some Business Models Perform Better than Others? A Study of the 1000 Largest US Firms*. Working Paper No. 226. MIT Sloan School of Management.

Wild-River, S., and Cunningham, R. (1997). *Brisbane City Council Environmental Benchmarking Study: A Report into Environmental and Related Outcomes from Brisbane City Council's* 1995–97 Implementation of the Environmental Protection Act 1994.

Wong, Tak-Chuen, Fong, Tom, Li, Ka-Fai, and Choi, Henry. (2011). Loan-to-Value Ratio as a Macroprudential Tool—Hong Kong's Experience and Cross-Country Evidence. *Systemic Risk, Basel III, Financial Stability and Regulation*. http://dx.doi.org/10.2139/ssrn.1768546

Wright, C., and Rwabizambuga, A. (2006). Institutional Pressures, Corporate Reputation, and Voluntary Codes of Conduct: An Examination of the Equator Principles. *Business and Society Review* 111(1): 89–117.

Wu, Desheng Dash, and Olson, David L. (2013). Computational Simulation and Risk Analysis: An Introduction of State of the Art Research. *Mathematical and Computer Modelling* 58(9–13): 1581–1587. https://doi.org/10.1016/j.mcm.2013.07.004

Yanenkova, Iryna, Nehoda, Yuliia, Drobyazko, Svetlana, Zavhorodnii, Andrii, and Berezovska, Lyudmyla. (2021). Modelling of Bank Credit Risk Management Using the Cost Risk Model. *Journal of Risk and Financial Management* 14: 211. https://doi.org/10.3390/jrfm14050211

Yang, M. (2015). *Sustainable Value Creation for Product-Service Systems (PSS)*. Cambridge, UK: University of Cambridge.

Yang, M., Evans, S., Vladimirova, D., and Rana, P. (2016). Value Uncaptured Perspective for Sustainable Business Model Innovation. *Journal of Cleaner Production* 140(3): 1794–1804. https://dx.doi.org/10.1016/j.jclepro.2016.07.102

Yang, M., Rana, P., and Evans, S. (2013). *Product Service System (PSS) Life Cycle Value Analysis for Sustainability*. Proceedings of the 6th Conference on Design and Manufacture for Sustainable Development (ISBN: 978-1-84919-709-0). Hangzhou, China.

Ye, Nan. (2019). *The Credit Risk Identification of Commercial Banks in China*. Proceedings of the 2nd International Symposium on Social Science (ISSS 2016), Xi'an City, China, 29–30 November. https://doi.org/10.2991/isss-16.2016.10

Yip, A. W. H., and Bocken, N. M. P. (2018). Sustainable Business Model Archetypes for the Banking Industry. *Journal of Cleaner Production* 174: 150–169.

Zamanifar, M., and Hartmann, T. (2021). A Prescriptive Framework for Recommending Decision Attributes of Infrastructure Disaster Recovery Problems. *Environment Systems and Decisions* 41: 633–650. https://doi.org/10.1007/s10669-021-09824-0

Zhelyazkova, V. and Kitanov, Y. (2015). Green Banking – Definition, Scope and Proposed Business Model. *Ecology & Safety, Journal of International Scientific Publications* 9: 309–315.

Zioło, M. (2017). Instytucjonalny i prawny wymiar zrównoważonego rozwoju oraz finansów zrównoważonych. In *Strefa finansowa wobec wyzwań zrównoważonego rozwoju*, W. K. Raczkowski and M. Zioło (red.). Warszawa: CeDeWu.

Zioło, M., Filipiak, B. Z., Bąk, I., and Cheba, K. (2019). How to Design More Sustainable Financial Systems: The Roles of Environmental, Social, and Governance Factors in the Decision-Making Process. *Sustainability* 11(20): 5604.

Ziolo, M., Filipiak, B. Z., and Tundys, B. (2021). *Sustainability in Bank and Corporate Business Models. The Link Between ESG Risk Assessment and Corporate Sustainability*. Palgrave, Macmillan. https://doi.org/10.1007/978-3-030-72098-8

Zioło, M., Spoz, A., and Kulińska-Sadłocha, E. (2021). *Zrównoważone rynki finansowe. Perspektywa krajowa i międzynarodowa*. Warszawa: PWE.

Zucman, Gabriel. (2013). The Missing Wealth of Nations: Are Europe and the U.S. Net Debtors or Net Creditors? *The Quarterly Journal of Economics* 128(3): 1321–1364. August. https://doi.org/10.1093/qje/qjt012

INDEX